JAPAN AS A 'NORMAL COUNTRY'?
A NATION IN SEARCH OF ITS PLACE IN THE WORLD

For decades, Japan's foreign policy has been seen by both internal and external observers as abnormal in relation to its size and level of sophistication. *Japan as a 'Normal Country'?* is a thematic and geographically comparative discussion of the unique limitations of Japanese foreign and defence policy. The contributors reappraise the definition of normality and ask whether Japan is indeed abnormal, what it would mean to become normal, and whether the country can – or should – become so.

Identifying constraints such as an inflexible constitution, inherent antimilitarism, and the nation's position as a U.S. security client, *Japan as a 'Normal Country'?* goes on to analyse factors that could make Japan a more effective regional and global player. Taken together, the essays in this volume ultimately consider how Japan could leverage its considerable human, cultural, technological, and financial capital to the benefit of both its citizens and the world.

(Japan and Global Society)

YOSHIHIDE SOEYA is a professor in the Faculty of Law at Keio University.

MASAYUKI TADOKORO is a professor in the Faculty of Law at Keio University.

DAVID A. WELCH is a professor in the Balsillie School of International Affairs at the University of Waterloo.

Japan and Global Society

Editors: AKIRA IRIYE, Harvard University; MASATO KIMURA, Shibusawa Eiichi Memorial Foundation; DAVID A. WELCH, Balsillie School of International Affairs, University of Waterloo

How has Japan shaped, and been shaped by, globalization – politically, economically, socially, and culturally? How has its identity, and how have its objectives, changed? *Japan and Global Society* explores Japan's past, present, and future interactions with the Asia Pacific and the world from a wide variety of disciplinary and interdisciplinary perspectives and through diverse paradigmatic lenses. Titles in this series are intended to showcase international scholarship on Japan and its regional neighbours that will appeal to scholars in disciplines in both the humanities and the social sciences.

Japan and Global Society is supported by generous grants from the Shibusawa Eiichi Memorial Foundation and the University of Missouri–St Louis.

EDITED BY YOSHIHIDE SOEYA,
MASAYUKI TADOKORO, AND
DAVID A. WELCH

Japan as a 'Normal Country'?

A Nation in Search of Its Place in the World

UNIVERSITY OF TORONTO PRESS
Toronto Buffalo London

Toronto Buffalo London
www.utppublishing.com
Printed in Canada

ISBN 978-1-4426-4253-9 (cloth)
ISBN 978-1-4426-1140-5 (paper)

Printed on acid-free, 100% post-consumer recycled paper with vegetable-based inks.

Library and Archives Canada Cataloguing in Publication

Japan as a 'normal country'? : a nation in search of its place in the world / edited by Yoshihide Soeya, Masayuki Tadokoro, and David A. Welch.

(Japan and global society)
Includes bibliographical references.
ISBN 978-1-4426-4253-9 (bound). – ISBN 978-1-4426-1140-5 (pbk.)

1. Japan – Foreign relations – 1945–. 2. Japan – Military policy. 3. Japan – Politics and government – 1945–. I. Soeya, Yoshihide, 1955– II. Tadokoro, Masayuki, 1956– III. Welch, David A. IV. Series: Japan and global society series

JZ1745.J37 2011 327.5209'045 C2011-902098-X

University of Toronto Press acknowledges the financial assistance to its publishing program of the Canada Council for the Arts and the Ontario Arts Council.

Canada Council for the Arts
Conseil des Arts du Canada

ONTARIO ARTS COUNCIL
CONSEIL DES ARTS DE L'ONTARIO

University of Toronto Press acknowledges the financial support of the Government of Canada through the Canada Book Fund for its publishing activities.

Contents

Preface

University of Toronto Press, in cooperation with the University of Missouri–St Louis and the Shibusawa Eiichi Memorial Foundation of Tokyo, is launching an ambitious new series, 'Japan and Global Society.' The volumes in the series will explore how Japan has defined its identity and objectives in the larger region of Asia and the Pacific and, at the same time, how the global community has been shaped by Japan and its interactions with other countries.

The dual focus on Japan and on global society reflects the series editors' and publishers' commitment to globalizing national studies. Scholars and readers have become increasingly aware that it makes little sense to treat a country in isolation. All countries are interdependent and shaped by cross-national forces so that mono-national studies, those that examine a country's past and present in isolation, are never satisfactory. Such awareness has grown during the past few decades when global, transnational phenomena and forces have gained prominence. In the age of globalization, no country retains complete autonomy or freedom of action. Yet nations continue to act in pursuit of their respective national interests, which frequently results in international tensions. Financial, social, and educational policies continue to be defined domestically, with national communities as units. But transnational economic, environmental, and cultural forces always infringe upon national entities, transforming them in subtle and sometimes even violent ways. Global society, consisting of billions of individuals and their organizations, evolves and shapes national communities even as the latter contribute to defining the overall human community.

Japan provides a particularly pertinent instance of such interaction, but this series is not limited to studies of that country alone. Indeed, the books published in the series will show that there is little unique about Japan, whose history has been shaped by interactions with China, Korea, the United States, and many other countries. For this reason, forthcoming volumes will deal with countries in the Asia-Pacific region and compare their respective developments and shared destinies. At the same time, some studies in the series will transcend national frameworks and discuss more transnational themes, such as humanitarianism, migration, and diseases, documenting how these phenomena affect Japan and other countries and how, at the same time, they contribute to the making of a more interdependent global society.

Lastly, we hope these studies will help to promote an understanding of non-national entities, such as regions, religions, and civilizations. Modern history continues to be examined in terms of nations as the key units of analysis, and yet these other entities have their own vibrant histories, which do not necessarily coincide with nation-centred narratives. To look at Japan, or for that matter any other country, and to examine its past and present in these alternative frameworks will enrich our understanding of modern world history and of the contemporary global civilization.

Akira Iriye

JAPAN AS A 'NORMAL COUNTRY'?
A NATION IN SEARCH OF ITS PLACE IN THE WORLD

Introduction: What Is a 'Normal Country'?

YOSHIHIDE SOEYA, MASAYUKI TADOKORO,
AND DAVID A. WELCH

In recent years there has been a vibrant debate in Japan about whether Japan can or should become a 'normal country,' a term first popularized by Ichirō Ozawa in his influential 1993 book, *Blueprint for a New Japan*.[1] But while Ozawa gave voice to the impression that Japan was not a normal country, he was not the first to feel it. In fact, for decades the received wisdom has been that Japan – at least in its international presence – lacked something vitally necessary for it to be taken seriously and treated with the respect befitting a country of its size and sophistication.

Despite the general sense that Japan was not a 'normal country,' neither the Japanese people nor their leaders and officials have been able to agree on the nature of the problem or the appropriate solution. For that matter, it has been a matter of some debate whether there is even a problem to fix. In what sense, if at all, is Japan an 'abnormal' country? What would it mean for it to become normal? Can it? Should it?

These are the questions animating the present volume. In this book we bring together scholars from a wide variety of countries and academic approaches to try to help shed light on them. We open with a brief discussion of the concept of 'normalcy,' then turn over the discussion to individual contributors. In Chapter 1, David Welch examines the mainsprings of Japanese foreign and defence policy, arguing that the debate over Japanese normalcy is an essential element of a fundamental debate about national strategy. In Chapter 2, Masayuki Tadokoro examines Japanese beliefs and values for evidence of a coherent understanding of a 'normal' Japan's role in the world. In Chapter 3, Yoshihide Soeya argues that a 'normal' Japan is tantamount to a 'normal' middle power, and that Japanese foreign policy discourse has not yet caught up with the reality. In Chapter 4, Cheol Hee Park compares the views of three prominent Japanese conservatives who have particular visions of what a 'normal' Japan would do in the world. In Chapter 5, Jianwei Wang examines the Chinese discourse on Japanese normalcy, arguing that pragmatic acceptance of the notion of a 'normal' Japan increasingly characterizes Chinese policy. In Chapter 6, John Swenson-Wright explores the constraints on Japanese normalcy evident in Japanese-South Korean relations. Finally, in Chapter 7, Peng Er Lam examines Japan's relations with Southeast Asian countries, arguing that Japan is already considered a normal country in the region.

Collectively, these essays demonstrate just how difficult it is to nail down a single understanding of 'normalcy' that would help focus and guide both the academic and policy debates. The problem has two dimensions. First, whether Japan is, or can become, a 'normal country' raises the question of whether there is some international standard of normalcy for Japan to meet. If every country is unique, then there is no 'normal' for Japan to conform to, and the entire discussion is moot. Second, if there is such a standard and Japan does not meet it, the problem could lie in what Japan *is*, in what Japan *does*, or both. Put another way, a country can be normal either in its status or in its behaviour. Our authors do not agree on which is more important.

The fact that our contributors do not agree is perhaps not surprising: Ozawa's seminal discussion is ambiguous on this very point. In Ozawa's view, Japan ought to become a 'normal country' by stepping up and shouldering its rightful international responsibilities and by cooperating with other states to build prosperous societies around the globe. The obstacles it faces, however, include an inability to make political decisions, and a military constrained in its capability and roles. Japan's 'abnormalcy,' in other words, lies in its *failure* to do certain things (behaviour; role) as a result of constitutional, institutional, and political constraints (status). We might surmise that these constraints include, but perhaps are not limited to, a number of internal and external factors.

Internal Constraints

Among internal constraints that limit Japan's emergence as a 'normal country' are its Constitution; the Japanese people's internalization, since World War Two, of antimilitarism as a norm; governmental and bureaucratic constraints; and the difficulty of making constitutional amendments.

The Constitution. Japan is unique in the world in having a constitution that specifically forbids it to exercise the sovereign right of war, or to maintain standing military forces, as a means of settling international disputes. Article 9 reads: 'Aspiring sincerely to an international peace based on justice and order, the Japanese people forever renounce war as a sovereign right of the nation and the threat or use of force as means of settling international disputes. In order to accomplish the aim of the preceding paragraph, land, sea, and air forces, as well as other war potential, will never be maintained. The right of belligerency of the state will not be recognized.'[2] Notwithstanding this proscription, Japan does maintain a formidable military. The apparent inconsistency arose early when the United States sought to enlist Japan's aid in the Far Eastern Cold War by encouraging it to develop military capabilities of its own. In the decades since, the attempt to paper over the contradiction between the Constitution and reality – by maintaining that Japan's 'Self–Defense Forces' (SDF) are not 'armed forces' – has warn increasingly thin.

Antimilitarism. As a reaction to the misery and humiliation brought upon the country by an overzealous military in the 1930s and early 1940s, the Japanese people have internalized, to a very significant degree, antimilitarist norms.[3] The SDF have never been very popular, and for that reason have been remarkably invisible – only recently, for example, have Japanese military officers worn uniforms in public. The Japanese people are keen to maintain tight civilian control of the military as well.[4] Most countries do not have such deeply ingrained antimilitarist norms, and in this respect Japan can be said to be 'abnormal' – but in many countries, and arguably around the globe as a whole, norms governing the use of force are tightening, and the purposes for which military force legitimately can be employed are changing. War-fighting for territory, honour, or prestige has gone out of fashion and favour;[5] humanitarian uses of force are increasingly permissible, though still viewed with great caution. In this respect the rest of the world is catching up to Japanese antimilitarism, and Japan is anything but 'abnormal.' Having said this, however, we would argue that the extent to which this culture of antimilitarism has immobilized domestic politics and the decision-making process with respect to defence and security policies has been unique.

Governmental and bureaucratic constraints. Japan's political system is a recipe for inertia. Politics both within and between major parties and the overlapping and interpenetration of highly bureaucratic ministries and agencies give aspiring veto players ample opportunity to try to frustrate significant foreign policy change. To some extent Japan has been stuck with 'abnormal' foreign and defence policies simply because they are so difficult to alter. Japan is not alone in experiencing a high degree of policy inertia as a result of such causes, and whether or not Japan is 'abnormal' in this respect is certainly debatable. Nonetheless the extent to which the culture of antimilitarism adds to bureaucratic inertia, out of fear that provoking it would lead to political deadlock, might be unique to postwar Japan.

Cumbersome processes of constitutional amendment. Should Japan wish to revise or scrap Article 9 of the Constitution, two-thirds of the members of both the lower and upper houses of the legislature (the National Diet) would have to agree, as would a majority of voters in a subsequent national referendum.[6] Given the nature of Japanese party politics and the polarization of the electorate on hot-button issues, constitutional amendment, as a practical matter, is all but impossible. In fact, there have been no amendments to the Constitution since its adoption in 1947. Many other countries have onerous amendment provisions, and Japan is not unique in this regard – though it does represent something of a limiting case.

External Constraints

External constraints on Japan's becoming a 'normal country' are posed by neighbours' suspicions of renascent Japanese militarism, the domestic political usefulness in China and South Korea of not letting Japan forget its militaristic past, fears that a 'normal' Japan might disrupt the regional balance of power, and the security guarantee that the United States provides.

Suspicions of renascent Japanese militarism. Many people in East Asia fear that, if Japan were to revise or eliminate Article 9 of the Constitution or to expand its military capabilities or missions, Japan would seek to impose its rule on others, as it did in the early twentieth century. In our view this fear is groundless – none of the contributors to this volume credits it – but historical memory still haunts many in neighbouring countries. Over time this fear might dissipate, but until it does any

Japanese government that sought an expanded, more muscular international role would face a barrage of criticism and resistance. Many countries have suspicious neighbours, but none has neighbours that are suspicious for exactly the same reasons as Japan's – so, again, whether or not this constraint is 'normal' is a matter of interpretation.

The domestic political value in China and South Korea of not letting Japan off probation. Related to the prior point is the fact that, while neither the Chinese nor the South Korean government has an interest in overtly hostile relations with Japan, both have found it useful from time to time to remind their people and the world that they have suffered at the hands of Japanese militarism. This has had the effects of distracting their people from issues that might generate dissatisfaction with the regime and of buttressing their cases in territorial disputes – in particular, over the Liancourt Rocks, known as Dokdo in South Korea and Takeshima in Japan, and over the Pinnacle Islands, called the Senkaku Islands in Japan and the Diaoyu Islands in China. While not especially common, it is certainly not unheard of for governments to externalize dissatisfaction, and as a lightning rod of this sort Japan is far from abnormal. Arguably, however, the extent to which the 'authoritative' interpretation of the memories of the past has become an indispensable and integral element of the legitimacy of the ruling regimes and/or the national identities of China and South Korea might be unique.

Potential disruption of the regional balance of power. While East Asia is not currently experiencing an aggressive arms race, and in fact has not seen one for many decades, it remains a region in which policy-makers pay attention to military balances and are sensitive to perturbations. Any significant enhancement of Japan's military capabilities or a Japanese embrace of certain military roles – those not obviously humanitarian in nature, for example – could well trigger balancing behaviour, generating a dangerous and counterproductive regional dynamic.[7] Japanese leaders are highly sensitive to this danger, a fact that helps explain Japan's caution. Is this concern 'normal'? Again, this is a matter of interpretation.

The U.S. security guarantee. Japan is a U.S. security client, and the Japanese military is tightly integrated operationally with the U.S. military. This is particularly true of the Maritime Self-Defense Forces, which boast Japan's most impressive power-projection capabilities. Unless

Japan were to abrogate the United States-Japan Security Treaty, any expansion of its roles and missions would have to pass muster in Washington. In recent decades, of course, this has not been much of an obstacle: most U.S. administrations have actively promoted the idea of a more muscular Japanese defence policy. In principle, however, U.S. preferences could represent a constraint on Japanese choices. Relatively few countries experience this kind of constraint to such a degree, but it is not 'abnormal' in the sense of 'utterly unprecedented.'

As a consequence of these various constraints, Japan punches far below its weight when it comes to contributing to regional and global security. Not being able to participate militarily in the liberation of Kuwait in 1991 – instead writing a cheque to cover much of the costs incurred by the U.S.-led international coalition – at a time when Japan was by far the largest developed-country importer of Persian Gulf oil, was an embarrassment that inspired Ozawa to write his seminal book in the first place. In the years since, the Japanese military has become a more active participant in UN peacekeeping operations and in relief and reconstruction efforts. Japanese naval vessels have participated in refuelling operations in the Indian Ocean and in anti-piracy patrols off the coast of Somalia. But in view of Japan's size, wealth, and actual military capability, it shoulders a disproportionately light share of the regional and global security burden.

How, then, is Japan 'abnormal'? In our view, Japan is abnormal in two crucial respects. First, it is unprecedented for a sovereign state not to have the right to wage war or maintain armed forces: no other country has a constitutional provision remotely similar to Article 9. Arguably, these constraints are self-imposed and, therefore, within the sovereign right of Japan to articulate and live by if it so chooses – just as Japan has the sovereign right to revise or eliminate these restrictions. But the reality is that Japan was forced to accept its U.S.-written Constitution and the very existence of the SDF is *prima facie* unconstitutional. If Japan were to become a fully 'normal country,' in our view this anomaly would have to be resolved.

Second, it is clearly abnormal for Japan to punch so far below its weight in the provision of regional and global security. While many countries free ride to some extent on the security provided by more powerful allies, Japan is unique, as a global economic powerhouse, in the small degree to which it contributes to the heavy lifting. A 'normal' Japan would not be so constrained, relative to other advanced economies, in the use of its many enviable assets for the purpose of contributing to international peace and security. Whether it chose to do so regionally or globally, bilaterally or multilaterally, or in the style of a Great or Middle Power, are matters that would be fully within the realm of 'normal' foreign policy choice.

Of these two anomalies, at the end of the day it is the second that is probably the most important. Japan has managed to live with the contradiction of Article 9 for more than fifty years and could probably do so for another fifty if necessary; this dimension of 'abnormalcy' might be something that cannot be addressed quickly. The second dimension, however, has material consequences for Japan and others; in the short run it is probably more important for Japan to carry more of the regional and global security burden than to try to iron out a symbolic constitutional anomaly.

Our suspicion is that a behaviourally 'normal' Japan would, over time, soothe rather than unnerve both Japan and its neighbours. It would make apparent the stark difference between the current postmodern liberal democratic Japan and the militaristic imperial Japan of the 1930s. Behavioural normalcy would be a winning formula both for Japan and for the world; Japan then could fully leverage its considerable human, cultural, technological, and financial capital for the welfare of all. Perhaps at that point, Japan could begin the process of liberating itself from dated artificial constitutional constraints.

An Orientation to the Volume

Anyone who has edited a book with multiple contributors knows that the greatest challenge is to ensure that the authors speak not only to each other but to a single, overarching question or theme. When the topic under discussion falls broadly within the category of current events, timeliness is important as well.

With respect to the first challenge, our international cast posed particular difficulties. Coming as they do from a wide variety of national and disciplinary perspectives, our contributors bring to bear very particular understandings of Japanese foreign and defence policy and of Japan's international role. Indeed, it was our view, when we initially proposed this book, that its multiperspectival approach would represent a significant fraction of its added value. We are gratified that our authors shared this belief, and we are pleased by their spirit of collaboration and their willingness to learn from each other (as we have certainly learned from them). Nevertheless, at the end of the day it proved impossible for the contributors to reach closure on the nature of the 'problem' (or, indeed, even whether there is one), on the nature of the 'solution' (again, if there is one), or on the regional or global role that a fully 'normal' Japan would play. The lack of closure in no way reflects lack of effort but a simple and important reality – namely, that these issues are fundamentally contested. We believe that this is a vitally important fact, and that the multiperspectival treatment we offer here succeeds in bringing it into sharp relief. The practical implication of this is that any attempt to 'normalize' Japanese foreign and defence policy – or to change constitutional, legislative, or administrative provisions so as to make it easier to do so – is likely to trigger both domestic and international controversy. This is because any such attempt is likely to appear to some a constructive and positive step in the direction of normalcy and to others a step in the unfortunate, and possibly even dangerous, direction of revisionism.

The patience and energy with which our contributors have pursued our collective objective mean that we have come dangerously close to jeopardizing the book's timeliness on more than one occasion. We first conceived the project nearly a decade ago. It began in earnest six years ago. We have held meetings and conferences at various places in three countries (Japan, Canada, and the United Kingdom) as the project unfolded. Our authors have patiently put up with three rounds of revisions to their chapters prompted both by feedback from their co-contributors, their co-editors, and our two anonymous reviewers, and by the exigencies of updating in the light of important political developments. To put all of this in perspective, one need only note that, since the project began, Japan has had five different prime ministers. To some extent this book has been tracking a moving target.

As we went to press, Japan's prime minister was Yukio Hatoyama of the Democratic Party of Japan (DPJ) – the first non-Liberal Democratic Party prime minister since Tomiichi Murayama of the Japan Socialist Party briefly formed a government in 1994 and 1995. Hatoyama's electoral victory in August 2009 was not entirely unexpected, as both the national mood and intra-party dynamics indicated a general thirst for change; but the scale of his victory was surprising, and the DPJ found itself somewhat caught off guard. Years of being in opposition had cultivated an oppositional temperament, and Hatoyama found himself holding the reins of government without having had much opportunity to prepare for the role.

As is often the case when the leader of a long-standing opposition party forms a government, Hatoyama discovered that domestic and international pressures constrained his room for manoeuvre. So, while Hatoyama campaigned against Japan's heavy reliance upon the United States for security and promised to 'rebalance' its foreign policy – giving greater weight and importance to Japan's immediate neighbours and to regional affairs – he quickly discovered that this was easier said than done. To some extent, Hatoyama's campaign rhetoric simply reflected the historic left-leaning pacifistic elements of his heterogeneous party.[8] But more important, it was more boilerplate than the result of careful strategic deliberation. Indeed the Hatoyama government only belatedly began the process of attempting to formulate and articulate a genuine national strategy of the kind discussed in Chapter 1. While seeking to find its bearings, it managed to alienate both its most important ally and a significant number of Japanese voters, for whom the popularity of the United States-Japan Security Treaty is at an all-time high.

There is no predicting who will be prime minister – let alone which party will form the government – when this book is published in mid-2011. We are comfortable predicting, however, that, barring some dramatic geopolitical shock, the fundamentals of Japan's foreign and defence policy will not have changed significantly between now and then. The alliance with the United States likely will remain the cornerstone of Japan's security for some time. Tokyo and Washington will find some way to manage the discord and frayed nerves triggered by Hatoyama's insistence on revisiting the 2006 agreement on the relocation of Okinawa's Futenma Air Base.[9] Japan might find ways of improving relations with its neighbours in such a way as to make it appear that Japan is giving greater emphasis to the region, but it is unlikely to jeopardize the key pillar of its postwar prosperity. 'Over the half-century of the alliance,' writes Yoichi Funabashi, 'there have been crises and drift,' but, in the grand scheme of things, '[t]he fact that two nations with different languages and cultures have been able to deepen the relationship of trust to the extent that they have can only be considered a miracle of modern history.'[10]

The signal importance of the United States to Japan is likely to raise in the minds of readers the question of why we do not have a dedicated chapter on the U.S. view of Japan's 'normalization.' In fact, it had been our original intention to include such a chapter, but we came to believe it was unnecessary, for two reasons. First, there is no shortage of U.S. commentary on Japanese foreign and defence policy; a dedicated U.S.

chapter would not represent much in the way of news. Second, U.S. views on the subject evince remarkable consistency over the course of the postwar period. For the purposes of the volume, we believe the essential points can simply be stated here.

How might one best characterize the U.S. view of a 'normalizing' Japan? Quite simply, Washington has long been in favour of Japan's shouldering a greater proportion of regional and global security provision, consistent with its considerable resources, provided it does so in the context of the United States-Japan Security Treaty, and provided Japan continues to acknowledge and accept its supporting role. Notwithstanding the provisions of Article 9 – essentially dictated to Japan by the United States during the postwar occupation – Washington saw value in Japan's building up its defence capabilities relatively early in the Cold War. Very quickly the United States realized that it would be immensely useful to have local forces help patrol the airspace and waterways around Japan and contribute to deterrence of the Soviet Union. The quiet but impressive development of the SDF and their effective cooperation with U.S. forces amply demonstrate the wisdom of this view.

What made Japan a reliable and desirable ally during the Cold War – its military professionalism and sophistication, coupled with its willingness to play a secondary, supporting role – also have made it a reliable and important ally since. As a result the United States has had no difficulty embracing and encouraging Japanese efforts to contribute more to its own defence and to various multilateral efforts to promote peace and security regionally and globally. Yet at the same time, the United States has been sensitive to both domestic political and regional international unease. Japan's 'go-slow' attitude toward normalization has met with Washington's full understanding and support. During the period of Japan's economic bubble in the late 1980s, some Americans evinced concern – perhaps paranoia is the better term – that Japan might threaten core U.S. interests and come to pose a geopolitical challenge to the United States itself.[11] But these voices were few and the fears short lived. It is increasingly difficult to find evidence of them anywhere, which leads U.S. commentators to believe that the passage of time – through the mechanisms of socialization, generational change, and globalization – has done an excellent job of reifying Funabashi's 'modern miracle of history.'

The United States, in short, is best seen as an understanding supporter of a more 'normal' Japan. It is so understanding that Americans are happy to defer to the Japanese on the very terms and tempo of the debate. Indeed, the debate itself has morphed in recent years: it is conducted less and less on a rhetorical level and more and more on a pragmatic one. Because of its origins, the term 'normal country' has come to be associated primarily with conservative thinking in Japan, as Cheol Hee Park discusses in Chapter 4. As a result, the phrase itself has largely dropped out of the domestic foreign policy debate. Instead the debate takes the form of arguments for and against specific practical measures identified by earlier thinkers as consistent with Japan's being a normal country: most notably, greater visibility for the SDF at home and abroad, and a wider range of regional and global roles.

In our view, the general tendency is clearly toward a pragmatic embrace of normalcy. The SDF are indeed more visible at home and more active abroad. Since the 2007 elevation of the Japan Defense Agency to a genuine Ministry of Defense, its senior official has enjoyed cabinet-level status for the first time, giving the SDF a clearer and stronger voice in policy deliberations. Japan's military capabilities continue slowly to improve.[12] For the time being, however, constitutional revision is on the back burner – a fact that is entirely congenial not only to Japan's neighbours, but to the United States as well.

Some Words of Thanks and a Note on the Text

A multi-year international effort of this kind requires considerable aid, and we would like to take this opportunity to express our gratitude to our benefactors and supporters. First and foremost among these are the Shibusawa Eiichi Memorial Foundation and the University of Missouri–St Louis (UMSL), without whose generous financial and logistical support this project never would have gotten off the ground. We would particularly like to thank Masahide Shibusawa and Masato Kimura, president and research director, respectively, of the Shibusawa Eiichi Memorial foundation, and Joel Glassman, director of the UMSL's Center for International Studies. The project has also benefited enormously from the generosity of the Social Sciences and Humanities Research Council of Canada through its Standard Research Grants program (supporting the work of the Canadian co-editor), and of the Japan Foundation Toronto, which supported a pivotal 2005 seminar. Keio University in Tokyo and Cambridge University in the United Kingdom were excellent hosts for additional meetings and seminars. Stephen Kotowych and Daniel Quinlan were patient and supportive editors at the University of Toronto Press, giving generously of their wisdom and expertise.

Many people have read the manuscript in whole or in part, offering helpful comments and suggestions. At the risk of inadvertently omitting due acknowledgment, we would like to thank (in strictly alphabetical order) Amy Catalinac, Michael Donnelly, Peter Feaver, Takako Hikotani, Jacques Hymans, Makoto Iokibe, Akira Iriye, John Kirton, Fumiaki Kubo, Norihito Kubota, Gil Latz, Seung Hyok Lee, Tosh Minohara, Shaun Narine, Amiko Nobori, Joseph Nye, Tomoko Okagaki, Yasuyo Sakata, Nisha Shah, and Noboru Yamaguchi.

Using international sources requires adopting a few standard conventions, and for purposes of this English-language edition we have chosen to stick with Romanized transliterations for non-Western names, words, phrases, and titles, rather than use Japanese, Chinese, or Korean characters. We have also adopted the standard practice of putting family names last, except in the case of well-known public figures – such as Deng Xiaoping, Hu Jintao, and Kim Jong Il – who regularly appear in the Western press with family names first. With Koreans in particular, it is generally acceptable either to hyphenate personal names (Roh Moo-hyun) or to capitalize them (Roh Moo Hyun), and we have simply chosen to follow the latter practice. Authors who work with Asian-language sources cite original titles in transliteration, and provide English-language translations in square brackets.

Finally, we would like to offer the obligatory disclaimer that the opinions expressed in this volume, and any errors that appear, are the responsibility of the authors alone, not those of the organizations or individuals who have supported our work. As editors, however, we would be happy to learn of any errors so that they may be corrected in future editions or later reprintings.

NOTES

1 The English translation appeared the following year; Ichirō Ozawa, *Blueprint for a New Japan: The Rethinking of a Nation*, trans. Louisa Rubenfien (Tokyo: Kodansha International, 1994).

2 Constitution of Japan; available online at http://www.jicl.jp/kenpou_all/kenpou_english.html, accessed 13 April 2010.

3 Thomas U. Berger, *Cultures of Antimilitarism: National Security in Germany and Japan* (Baltimore: Johns Hopkins University Press, 1998).

4 Takako Hikotani, 'Japan's Changing Civil-Military Relations: From Containment to Re-Engagement?,' *Global Asia* 4 (1, 2009): 22–6.

5 The seminal work is John Mueller, *Retreat from Doomsday: The Obsolescence of Major War* (New York: Basic Books, 1989).

6 Article 96; available online at http://www.jicl.jp/kenpou_all/kenpou_english.html, accessed 13 April 2010.

7 Humanitarian operations have the potential, at least in principle, of improving Japan's relations with its neighbours. See, for example, Tomohide Murai, 'SDF Peace Missions for Stable Japan-China Relations,' *AJISS-Commentary* 25 (2008); available online at http://www.jiia.or.jp/en_commentary/pdf/AJISS-Commentary25.pdf, accessed 3 June 2009.

8 The DPJ (*Minshutō*) was officially launched in 1996, prior to the lower house elections in October. Winning 57 seats, it became the second-largest opposition party (after the New Frontier Party, *Shinshintō*). The presence in the DPJ of many former members of the Japan Socialist Party (*Nihon Shakaitō*) – which changed its name to the Social Democratic Party (*Shakai Minshutō*) in January 1996 – initially gave it a predominantly left-leaning cast. In 1998 the DPJ expanded, absorbing a number of smaller opposition parties in an effort to create a credible united front alternative to the Liberal Democratic Party, and in 2003 it merged with Ichirō Ozawa's centre-right Liberal Party (*Jiyūtō*). As a result the DPJ today has both strong progressive and strong conservative elements. For a detailed history, see online at http://www.dpj.or.jp/english/about_us/brief.html.

9 The agreement called for the relocation of the base to a less crowded location within Okinawa Prefecture (Nago). During the 2009 campaign, seeking to leverage local dissatisfaction with the heavy U.S. military presence, Hatoyama pledged to seek an alternative that would see the Marine Corps air station removed from Okinawa entirely. Thus far the lack of viable alternatives, combined with Washington's reluctance to renegotiate the agreement and fears of the potentially devastating economic consequences among Okinawa's political and business elites, led to an awkward stalemate.

10 Yoichi Funabashi, 'A 21st century vision for the alliance,' PacNet #7 (18 February 2010), p. 2; available online at http://csis.org/files/publication/pac1007.pdf, accessed 13 April 2010.

11 See, for example, George Friedman and Meredith LeBard, *The Coming War with Japan* (New York: St Martin's Press, 1991); and John H. Maurer, 'The United States and Japan: Collision Course?' *Strategic Review* 21 (2, 1993): 41–51.

12 See also Christopher W. Hughes, *Japan's Remilitarisation*, Adelphi Paper 403 (London: International Institute for Strategic Studies, 2009).

1 Embracing Normalcy: Toward a Japanese 'National Strategy'

DAVID A. WELCH[1]

In 2006 the newspaper *Asahi Shimbun* asked forty Japanese academics and officials whether Japan had a 'national strategy.' The overwhelming answer was no, as least far as the post–Cold War era was concerned. Opinion was divided as to whether Japan had a national strategy prior to that. Hiroshi Nakanishi, professor of international politics at Kyoto University, believed that the Yoshida Doctrine (1951–72) could be described as 'a national strategy of sorts.' Others were less sure. An anonymous high-level foreign ministry official felt that, during the Cold War, the Japanese foreign policy establishment 'lacked the proper mindset' for a national strategy, in part because 'we didn't have to think about' it. With the end of the Cold War, the sense that Japanese foreign policy was somehow adrift caused a good deal of angst.[2]

What exactly is a national strategy, and how do we know one when we see one? The *Oxford English Dictionary* defines a strategy as 'a plan for successful action based on the rationality and interdependence of the moves of the opposing participants.' A great deal is packed into this definition. First, a strategy is a *plan* – a road map, a blueprint, or some intelligible account of how one expects to get from A to B. Second, a strategy is a plan for *action*. It is not a plan for inaction, or for reaction; it presupposes a willingness and an intention to devote time, energy, and resources to the pursuit of one's goals. Third, a strategy is a plan for *successful* action, which logically requires an ability to articulate one's goals in a way that would enable one to know whether or not they have been achieved. Fourth, a strategy takes into account the fact that other actors will have goals of their own and can be expected to do their best to achieve them, too. Fifth, and finally (this is not an explicit element of the *OED* definition, but as a practical matter it is clearly implied in it), a strategy includes a vision of the *means* by which one rationally proposes to accomplish one's goals. What tools must one have? How will one wield them? What roles will one play, regionally or globally? What niches will one attempt to carve out? How will one conduct oneself, as a matter of style? With whom will one make common cause, and whom will one oppose?

At any given point in the history of Japanese foreign and defence policy, it is possible draw up a catalogue of goals, tools, roles, niches, styles, partners, and adversaries. One could do so today. The real question, however, is whether these things all hang together. Do they reflect a coherent vision? Can we detect a common thread linking them all to some underlying understanding of how world politics works? Are they the result of *planning?*

Most students of international relations assume that national strategies arise almost naturally, as it were, from context. One venerable view holds that national interests are given and immutable, and include, for example, the pursuit of security, autonomy, power, and wealth. This view also holds that, since policy-makers are 'rational,' the matching of means to ends happens more or less as a matter of course. This view is commonly associated with the 'realist' school of thought.[3] Realism is potentially very useful as a lens through which to see the world, for if it were true that states can reliably be expected to pursue a limited number of specific goals, it would also be possible to generate powerful and efficient theories of state behaviour that would enable us to explain and anticipate what states do. An example of such a realist theory is balance-of-power theory, which not only has a long intellectual pedigree, but also occasionally has been embraced by leaders as a guide to policy.[4]

Yet two difficulties have always plagued realist attempts to grapple with the fundamental forces of international political behaviour. First, even if it were true (for example) that states always seek to promote security, this general claim does not translate easily into specific policies, actions, and conceptions by national governments of what their security *is* and how best to promote it.[5] Isolationists and internationalists in U.S. foreign policy, for instance, have always argued that they have a superior understanding of what serves U.S. security, and yet the policies they advocate have always been diametrically opposed and mutually exclusive.[6]

Second, it is difficult to deny that states occasionally radically change their minds about what serves their national interests. Some states, such as Germany and France, used to insist that their national interest required independent foreign policies, high levels of armament, and physical possession of overseas colonies. Now they embrace supranationalism, integration, and the principle of self-determination of peoples.[7] Realism, in short, has strong views about the meaning of 'the national interest' as an abstract *concept*, but has difficulty making sense of the specific *conceptions* of national interest that states embrace at any given time.

The second view – or, more accurately, collection of views – holds that conceptions of national interests can, and do, change over time. Despite their various differences in other respects, classical liberalism, utopianism, utilitarianism, functionalism, and constructivism all fall into this category.[8] But non-realist approaches have not generated theories of state behaviour to compete with realist theories. They are most effective as critiques of realism. Moreover, while they quite correctly draw to our attention the fact that states often radically reconceive their understanding of the national interest, they imply radically different mechanisms by which this can happen.

Japanese foreign policy elites certainly have changed their minds over the years about Japan's long-term interests, at least with respect to the concrete (not abstract) goals Japan should pursue.[9] Japanese leaders have always sought 'security,' but specific conceptions of security have changed over time and are very much in flux today. We see this clearly in the ongoing debate about whether Japan is, or should become, a 'normal country,' and if so, what that would entail. This debate is fundamentally about national strategy; it concerns the ends Japanese foreign and defence policy should serve, and how best to achieve them.

What do I mean by 'conceptions' of security? Specifically, I mean (1) understandings of the 'referent object' of foreign and defence policy ('that which is to be secured'); (2) understandings of threats worth 'securitizing' (defined as *security threats* rather than as mere *problems* – elevated to the top of the political agenda, treated with particular urgency, and given scarce resources);[10] and (3) prevailing beliefs about the most appropriate ways of addressing security needs. Japan's recent sense of directionlessness in foreign and defence policy suggests both a hunger and an opportunity for the emergence of a new national strategy.

Japanese Conceptions of Security

The early history of Japanese foreign and defence policy no doubt will be broadly familiar to readers, and will need no rehearsing here. In a nutshell, Japan fairly successfully inoculated itself against foreign interference from the sixteenth to the nineteenth centuries. With the Industrial Revolution in Europe and the subsequent scramble for colonies and influence in East Asia, Japanese leaders perceived a choice between emulating the West and being dominated by it. Accordingly, they embarked upon a far-reaching program of modernization, industrialization, and state-building. Hugely successful reforms led to a demographic and economic boom that put enormous pressure on Japan's limited resource base. This, coupled with the desire to cultivate international prestige and respect as a great power, led to imperialistic adventures on the mainland and, ultimately, to conflict with, and defeat at the hands of, the United States and its allies in World War Two.[11] Throughout this period it is relatively easy to identify a series of coherent, if not uniformly successful, national strategies.

When we turn to the postwar period, we discover that foreigners are much more willing to ascribe consistency and coherence to Japanese foreign and defence policy than are Japanese themselves. For example, Eric Heginbotham and Richard Samuels insist that Japan has had a consistent postwar national strategy appropriately labelled 'mercantile realism' – a deliberate, conscious promotion of Japanese power through the accumulation of wealth rather than military capability.[12] Jennifer Lind argues that Japan's national strategy can be characterized accurately as 'realist buck-passing.' Thomas Berger calls Japanese policy 'remarkably consistent,' attributing the consistency to Japan's postwar political-military culture,[13] while Kent Calder attributes it to unique features of what he calls 'the San Francisco System': (1) a dense network of bilateral alliances; (2) an absence of multilateral security structures; (3) strong asymmetry in alliance relations, in both the security and economic domains; (4) precedence for Japan; and (5) liberal access to the U.S. market, coupled with limited development assistance.[14] Of the three most significant works on Japanese foreign and defence policy by prominent Western scholars in recent years, two attempt to make the case that Japan already has a coherent national strategy.[15]

Those who are inclined to interpret postwar Japanese policy as largely or fundamentally strategic sometimes perceive variation. Takashi Inoguchi and Paul Bacon, for instance, argue that Japanese policy has gone through five distinct phases since 1945, each lasting approximately fifteen years. The first phase (1945–60) was a period of instability and disagreement about national strategy, dominated by an internal battle between pro-alliance and anti-alliance elements in Japanese society. The second – a period of stability – saw the triumph of the Yoshida doctrine (1960–75). In the third, Japan emerged as 'a systemic supporter of the United States' (1975–90). In the fourth (1990–2005), Japan attempted play the role of 'global civilian power.' The fifth, now under way, will see, they contend, 'a gradual consolidation of Japan's emerging role as a global ordinary power' on the UK model.[16]

Despite disagreements about how best to characterize Japanese foreign policy, there is no disagreement about the overarching principle behind it. As Christian Hougen puts it, 'Japan's prosperity is its purpose.'[17] One can safely assert that this has always been the case. Prosperity is a very general concept, however, and it would be incorrect to unpack it in simple material terms, as political scientists are inclined to do. Throughout the history of Japanese foreign policy, we see nonmaterial values frequently trumping material ones. Foremost among these, I would submit, are identity, self-respect, and international prestige. We see evidence of the importance of these when Japan surprises the rest of the world by its uncharacteristic assertiveness and unwillingness to compromise over specific issues that hardly seem worth the international trouble and for which one could easily imagine face-saving compromises – for example, territorial disputes, whaling practices, and prime ministerial visits to Yasukuni Shrine.[18]

Leaders of states typically pursue a variety of specific goals that represent different facets of abstract concepts such as 'security' or 'prosperity,' and the notion that identity issues are particularly powerful in Japanese policy does not mean that material goals – physical security, economic wealth, a high standard of living – never inform policy. Clearly they do. And not all issues on the foreign policy agenda engage all goals simultaneously. What a national strategy does is to prioritize specific goals, identify appropriate means to pursue them, and generate practical policy guidelines to promote them. No specific element of the set of means at the Japanese government's disposal logically implies that any particular strategy is in place. Japan's dramatic and important recent foray into the international peacekeeping role, for example, could be evidence of a coherent 'global civilian power' national strategy at work, or it could be a mere reaction to transient pressures and incentives.[19]

The Sources of National Strategies

One way to tackle the question of where specific conceptions of security come from is to make use of the time-honoured 'levels of analysis' device.[20] We might look for the mainsprings of foreign policy at the level of the international system as a whole (that is, in the interactions of states), in domestic politics, in the specific structures of government or bureaucracy, or in the judgments, perceptions, desires, world views, or other personality characteristics of specific foreign policy-makers.

When we employ this device to make sense of postwar Japanese foreign and defence policy, we discover that, at best, each level of analysis can contribute but a piece of the puzzle. If we look, for example, to the international system as a whole, we might search for evidence that policy is a function of capability, a response to regional threats and opportunities, a response to global threats and opportunities, or something imposed (for example, by a hegemon or other dominant power). Estimating capability – or, as realists would say, 'measuring power' – is notoriously difficult, and any particular methodology would be controversial.[21] But most people would agree that we can do it at least roughly, and that demographic, economic, and military factors are all relevant. Let us see how Japan compares with other regional actors on these dimensions.

As Figure 1.1 indicates, Japan's population has been growing slowly compared with that of other regional great powers, with the exception of Russia, which has experienced a net decline even since the breakup of the Soviet Union. The Japanese population has also been aging, which will have significant long-run economic implications.[22] Figures 1.2 and 1.3 demonstrate Japan's considerable relative economic might: while the Japanese economy is no longer the world's second largest, having been surpassed by China in the 1990s (in purchasing power parity terms), China has a long way to go before it catches up to Japan's level of economic development. Figures 1.4 and 1.5 demonstrate Japan's relatively small armed forces and remarkably stable military spending, though it should be noted that the quality of the Japanese military is second only to that of the United States.[23]

Taken as a whole, these trends suggest that, if Japanese policy were a simple function of relative capability, Japan's national strategy would resemble that of other similarly situated great powers, at least since the 1970s. Japan would not be *aspiring* to resemble the United Kingdom, but would have done so for almost forty years. Clearly Japan's economic weight has enabled it to behave as a great power in international trade and finance, but Japan has soft-pedalled its military capability – for reasons that are entirely understandable but that are not simple functions of relative capability.[24] If regional or global threats and opportunities

Figure 1.1: Population, Selected Countries, 1950–2008

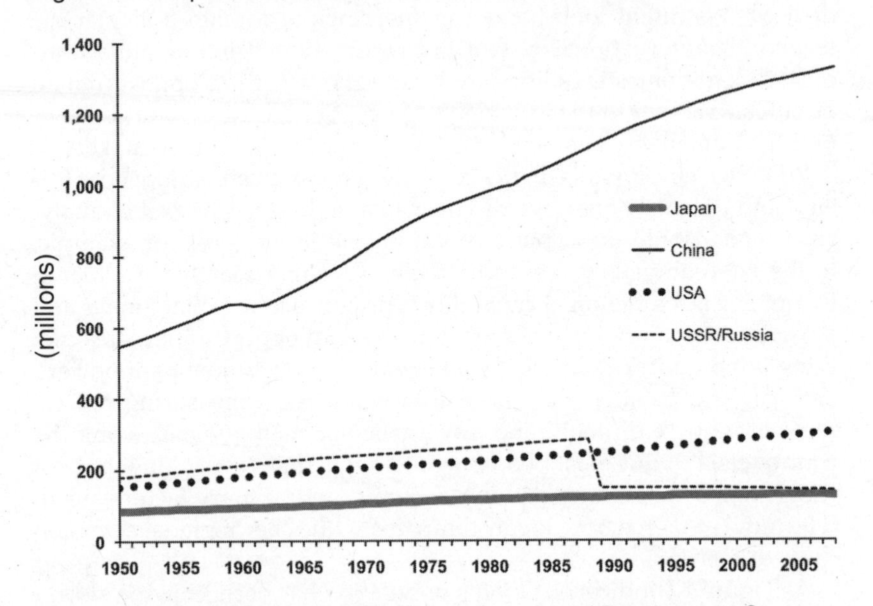

Source: Conference Board and Groningen Growth and Development Centre; available online at http://www.conference-board.org/economics/database.cfm, accessed 3 June 2009.

were definitive, then we should have witnessed a fairly dramatic series of adjustments to reflect the declining significance of the Soviet threat, the increasing North Korean challenge, the Chinese 'threat,' and the importance of cultivating close relationships with other states wary of Pyongyang and Beijing (the United States, South Korea, and Taiwan). We do see adjustments in Japanese policy that clearly indicate the salience of these considerations. Japanese defence white papers identify and track regional threats closely.[25] When he was foreign minister, Tarō Asō publicly identified China as a threat,[26] and Japan and the United States have moved closer, completing an important base realignment to improve the interoperability of the two countries' armed forces.[27] Yet Japan's responses have been almost exclusively diplomatic; it is virtually impossible to discern any adjustments in military strategy, force structure, doctrine, deployment, or procurement save for an accelerated ballistic missile defence program intended as a hedge again North

Figure 1.2: Total Gross Domestic Product, Selected Countries, 1950–2008

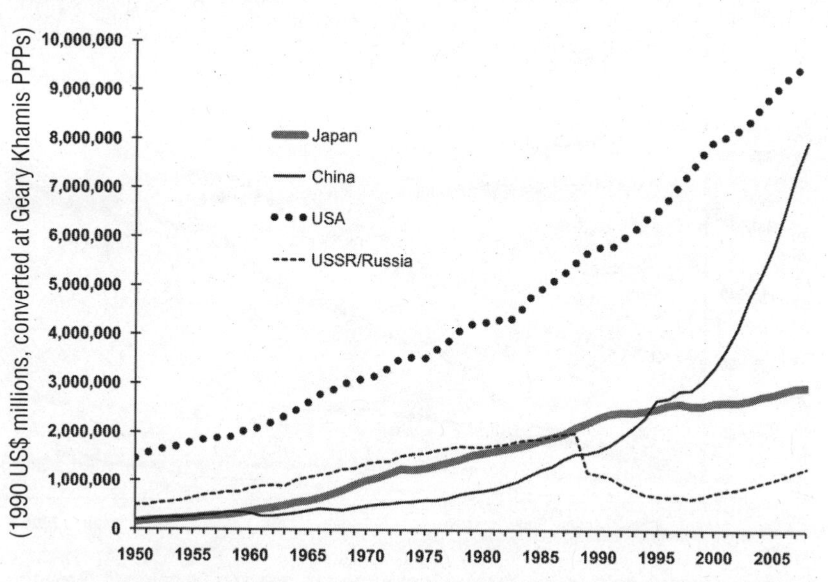

Source: Conference Board and Groningen Growth and Development Centre; available online at http://www.conference-board.org/economics/database.cfm, accessed 3 June 2009.

Korean missile capability.[28] And inexplicably, from a systemic perspective, Japan has allowed the abductee issue to dominate its North Korea policy;[29] it has allowed the Liancourt Rocks/Takeshima/Dokdo territorial dispute to poison its relationship with Seoul;[30] and it has equivocated on its support for Taiwan.[31]

The United States' 'War on Terror' has had a profound effect on many countries' foreign policies, and Japan's is no exception. As prime minister, Junichirō Koizumi positioned Japan as a front-line supporter of U.S. president George W. Bush's response to the 9/11 attacks on the World Trade Center and the Pentagon. Commentators generally remarked that this represented a watershed and resulted in an increased global role for Japan.[32] But was this a rational adjustment to systemic imperatives? One possible interpretation is that it reflected Japan's fundamentally subordinate position vis-à-vis the U.S. hegemon. But there are those who argue that it reflected in part – perhaps even in large part

Figure 1.3: GDP per capita, Selected Countries, 1950–2008

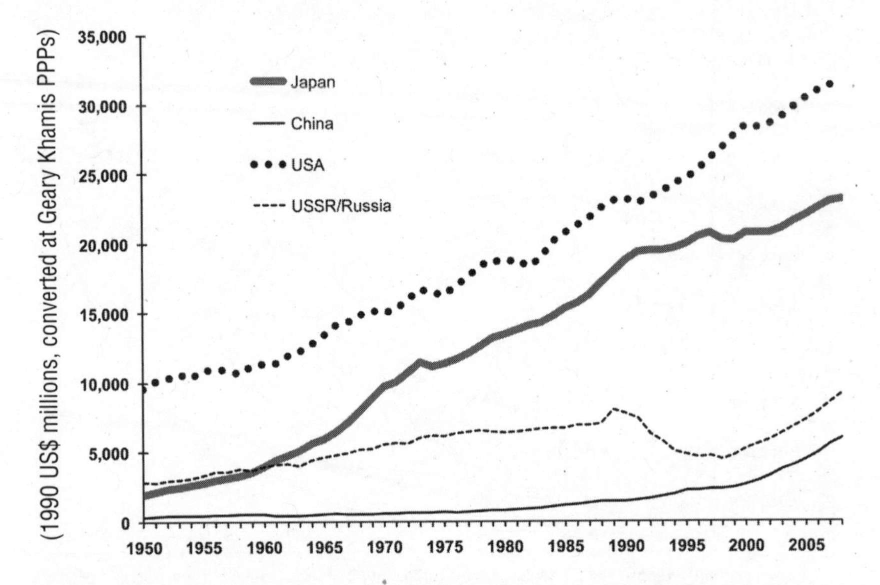

Source: Author's calculations, from Conference Board and Groningen Growth and Development Centre; available online at http://www.conference-board.org/economics/database.cfm, accessed 3 June 2009.

– the personal rapport between Koizumi and Bush, which is hardly a systemic imperative.[33]

Systemic considerations, in short, appear to have an influence on Japanese policy, but not a determinative one.[34] What about domestic politics? One might be tempted to suggest that it mops up the 'residual variance' left over from structural explanations. For example, the domestic popularity of irredentist claims, whaling practices, and prime ministerial visits to Yasukuni Shrine undoubtedly go some way toward explaining what would appear to be anomalies from a systemic perspective. The fact that the Japanese have internalized antimilitarist norms since World War Two undoubtedly has also constrained the development or use of military instruments in Japan's foreign policy.[35] Yet these very same norms ultimately did *not* prevent Japan (at first tentatively, and then fairly energetically) from embracing peacekeeping operations and deploying forces overseas in support of nation-building and the 'War on Terror.' Nor have they prevented a gradual but ine-

Figure 1.4: Armed Forces Personnel, Selected Countries, 1985–2003

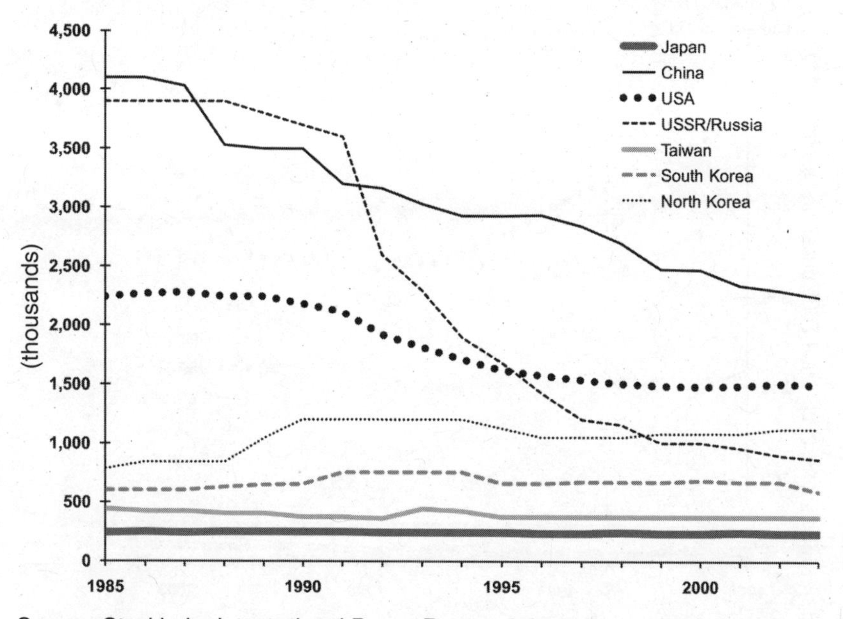

Source: Stockholm International Peace Research Institute; available online at http://www.sipri.org, accessed 3 June 2009.

luctable trend toward the normalization of social attitudes toward the Self-Defense Forces (SDF) and important changes in civil-military relations.[36] One might even say that changes in Japanese policy have helped drive changes in domestic norms and attitudes, raising the question of exactly what is cause and what is effect. Finally, Jennifer Lind argues that, '[a]lthough antimilitarist norms are widespread in Japan, they have not constrained Japanese security policy. They have not prevented it from building one of the most powerful military forces in the world, with potent offensive and defensive capabilities. And, as Japan's leaders have said repeatedly, if Japan felt threatened, these norms would not even prevent Japan from building nuclear weapons.'[37]

Domestic politics provides a tempting explanation for the consistency we see in Japanese foreign policy quite simply in view of the fact that a single party – the Liberal Democratic Party (LDP, *Jimintō*) – has dominated national politics since 1955. Ostensibly a conservative party, the LDP is in fact relatively non-ideological and pragmatic, with factions

Figure 1.5: Total Military Expenditures, Selected Countries, 1988–2007

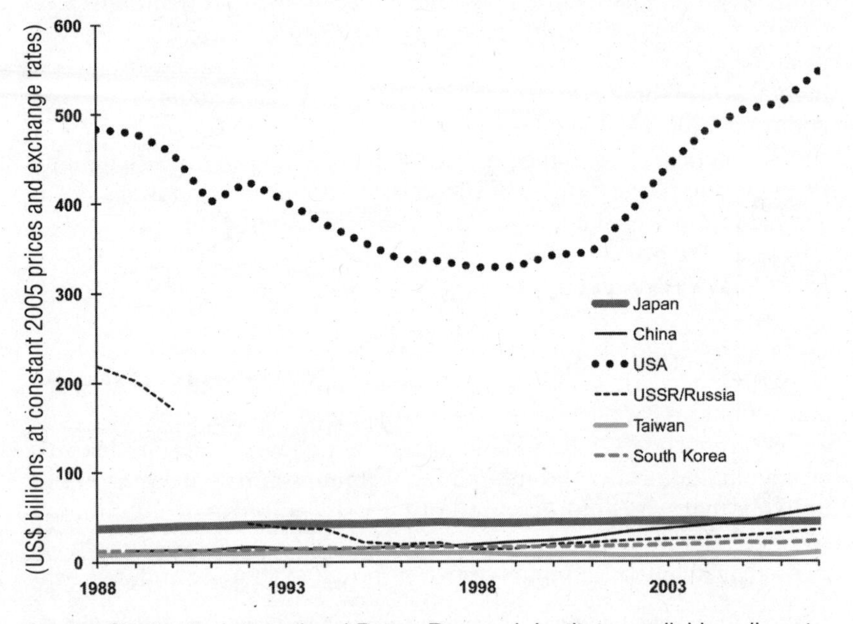

Source: Stockholm International Peace Research Institute; available online at http://www.sipri.org, accessed 3 June 2009.

and tendencies that stretch tepidly both to the left and right of centre. The same may be said of the Democratic Party of Japan (DPJ, *Minshutō*), the governing party as I write. Only the Japan Socialist Party (*Nihon Shakaitō*, until 1986) and the Japan Communist Party (*Nihon Kyūsantō*) could be described as doctrinaire, and neither has had a significant influence on Japanese foreign or defence policy.[38] But while this may help explain the inertia of Japanese policy, it is hard to find Japanese political parties playing a significant role in the formulation or articulation of national strategies. They do not, in short, provide satisfying answers to the question of the sources of national strategies.

Japan is often seen as a highly bureaucratic state, and it might be tempting to look to the inner workings of the Japanese government to find the mainsprings of strategic thought.[39] Such an attempt would be disappointing. No one agency or ministry has a lock on foreign policy-making, and interministry coordination is notoriously difficult – a fact that has repeatedly led to policy failure.[40] Nor is there a single foreign policy decision-making process: 'routine' situations do not attract high-level attention and evince the pulling and hauling typical of bureaucratic politics. In 'political' situations, matters are taken out of the hands of bureaucrats, and both party factions and extragovernmental actors come into play. In 'critical' situations, leaders take charge and work outside of regular channels.[41] Bureaucratic considerations, in short, may help explain the stability of national strategy once a national strategy is in place, but are highly unlikely to play an important role in any satisfactory explanation of the origins of national strategy.[42]

Ideational Entrepreneurship

What of individual sources? There is a sense in which the individual level of analysis is an intuitive place to look. All strategies, policies, and actions are, at the end of the day, the products of specific individuals' choices. The relevant players make their choices in a complex governmental, domestic, and international context, and so it seems highly unlikely that we could ever describe those choices as wholly unconstrained. But unless it were also true that *any* Japanese leader at any particular time would reliably pursue the same strategy and make the same choices, then clearly individuals matter.

Individual decision-makers can, and do, draw inspiration and take their cues from various levels of analysis. Some leaders are notoriously sensitive to domestic politics; others are keen practitioners of balance-of-power politics; still others listen to their own instincts and voices when they seek to promote the national interest as they understand it.[43] Tsuyoshi Kawasaki's fascinating study of the origins of the 1976 National Defense Program Outline provides a case in point. Kawasaki's reading of the evidence suggests that the policy preferences of two key civilian policy-makers, Michio Sakata and Takuya Kubo, more powerfully reflect balance-of-power than cultural considerations and that neither felt much constrained by domestic politics.[44] Whether *any* such similarly situated decision-makers would have evinced the same preferences and patterns is, of course, the relevant question when attempting to gauge the significance of personality.[45]

At the beginning of any particular identifiable strategic period, where there is a dominant conception of security and a dominant understanding of how to promote it, we find specific ideational entrepreneurs at work, either individually or in like-minded groups. The Emperor Meiji and a relatively small group of reform-minded officials and industrialists were behind Japan's early emulation of the West and its rapid modernization. Yukichi Fukuzawa provided a good deal of the intellectual justification, and Aritomo Yamagata and Taro Katsura provided the statecraft, for Japan's move into Asia.[46] Shigeru Yoshida had a vital hand in articulating and promoting his eponymous doctrine. Yoichi Funabashi made the case for Japan's becoming a global civilian power.[47] At any given time, there might well be – and there certainly has been in the past – a variety of intellectual entrepreneurs promoting different, sometimes incompatible visions of Japanese national strategy. Some win, some lose. We can think of intellectual entrepreneurs as a necessary but insufficient condition for any particular changing conception of security. Thus the individual level of analysis plays an important role in any explanation of Japanese national strategy.

What makes for a successful intellectual entrepreneur, as opposed to an unsuccessful one? There might or might not be a general answer to this question: what works in one time and place might not work in another. Ideational entrepreneurship might be much easier in a strong state with a powerful executive, as long as the entrepreneur is the executive, or close to the executive, as in France.[48] In other states, capturing parties and key policy-making positions might suffice, given an appropriate window of opportunity.[49]

Without for the moment assuming generality, we might suppose that the following questions are all relevant: the more affirmative answers, the more likely it is that an ideational entrepreneur's particular conception of security will take root:

- *Reach*: Does the entrepreneur have the ear of policy-makers and other members of the foreign policy elite? Does the entrepreneur have access to the broader public, through print publication or the broadcast media?
- *Goals*: Is the entrepreneur able to articulate a set of foreign policy goals that resonate with prevailing notions of 'prosperity,' taking both material and non-material considerations into account?
- *Roles and niches*: Is the entrepreneur able to articulate a set of specific functions the country ought to serve regionally and globally that are appropriate given national resources and relative capability, and that are consistent with self-respect and international prestige?
- *Means*: Does the entrepreneur have a clear and appealing vision of the means required to pursue the strategy? Are those means affordable and efficacious?

- *Style*: Does the entrepreneur have an appealing account of the manner in which the strategy should be pursued – that is, should the country speak softly or loudly, be assertive or accommodating, embrace unilateralism, bilateralism, or multilateralism?
- *Partners and foes*: Does the entrepreneur envision partnering with or opposing countries the audience will be inclined to approve?
- *Persuasiveness*: If there is an apparent disjuncture between the entrepreneur's vision and broadly accepted views, is he or she able to find appropriate rhetorical strategies and leverage appropriate discourse to minimize them and win over sceptics?

This list of questions points not only to the possible relevance of the *content* of a strategic vision, but also to the entrepreneur's *ability to publicize it* and *skill in making the case for it*. All other things being equal, the more effective case will prevail on all battlefields simultaneously: the entrepreneur will be able to argue effectively that his or her goals are widely shared in society (indeed, preferably, that they are unassailable); that his or her vision is broadly consistent with the country's material needs and self-respect; that it is a rational response to systemic pressures and incentives; that it satisfies key domestic political constituencies; and that it is both doable and affordable.

Conclusion: 'Normalcy' in Japan's Emerging National Strategy

A remarkable example of an overt attempt at ideational entrepreneurship is Ichirō Ozawa's *Blueprint for a New Japan*.[50] A former secretary-general of the LDP and founder of the Japan Renewal Party, Ozawa played a crucial role in 1993 in putting together Japan's first non-LDP coalition government in nearly fifty years, and later served as president of the DPJ. A prominent statesman as well as a widely read commentator, Ozawa is generally credited with beginning the debate about Japan's becoming a 'normal country,' an idea that began as iconoclastic and has now moved into the mainstream (see Chapter 4, in this volume). In his book, Ozawa lays out a detailed national strategy, many elements of which Japan has already embraced. While debate remains about some elements of Ozawa's vision, it is likely that something similar to it – and something definitely inspired by it – will define the next phase of Japanese policy that warrants the label *genuinely strategic*.

Ozawa provides an answer to every question on the checklist. Many of his answers are strongly affirmative; some are not. Arguably, this explains why Ozawa's ideas have had traction, but have not been fully embraced in detail. Not all of Ozawa's ideas strike the reader as practical even if they are desirable – for example, UN control of nuclear weapons, and a standing UN reserve force.[51] Nevertheless, the argument is extremely carefully constructed and amply displays Ozawa's remarkable rhetorical gifts.

Ozawa's blueprint is not the only vision competing in the current marketplace of ideas. Also in play, though apparently fading, is Shintaro Ishihara's *The Japan That Can Say No* – an unapologetically realist and nationalist manifesto.[52] More recently, Yoshihide Soeya has made the argument that Japan most appropriately fits the Middle Power mould[53] – an argument he elaborates elsewhere in this volume. Attitudinal trends in Japan might make possible some as-yet-unarticulated national strategy befitting an emerging postmodern, postmaterialist polity. We shall see. In the hands of an appropriately gifted ideational entrepreneur, many things are possible. But one thing seems fairly clear at the moment: Japan is losing patience with its lack of direction in the world and is increasingly eager to shoulder regional and global responsibilities that would be 'normal' for a country of its consequence.

NOTES

1 I would like to thank Adele Cassola, Seung Hyok Lee, and Aziza Mohammed for invaluable research assistance.

2 'Talk of Japan's 'National Strategy' has often been avoided in this country since the end of World War II, largely because of Japan's infamous past mistakes,' *Asahi Shimbun*, 4 May 2006. On the Yoshida Doctrine, see Bert Edström, *Japan's Evolving Foreign Policy Doctrine: From Yoshida to Miyazawa* (New York: St Martin's Press, 1999). Siew Mun Tang calls the Yoshida Doctrine 'an enduring and highly successful grand strategy'; Siew Mun Tang, 'A Nation in Search of Itself: Japanese Grand Strategy from Meiji to Heisei (1968–Present)' (PhD dissertation, Arizona State University, 2004), p. 160. The Yoshida Doctrine – concentrating on Japan's economic recovery and development while deferring to and relying upon the United States for security – was to some extent an attempt to make a virtue out of necessity, since the devaluation of military roles and capabilities was overdetermined by the domestic backlash against militarism and constraints imposed externally during the Occupation; see John W. Dower, *Empire and*

Aftermath: Yoshida Shigeru and the Japanese Experience, 1878–1954 (Cambridge, MA: Harvard University Press, 1979).

3 See, for example, Stephen Krasner, *Defending the National Interest: Raw Materials Investments and U.S. Foreign Policy* (Princeton, NJ: Princeton University Press, 1978); Hans J. Morgenthau, *In Defense of the National Interest: A Critical Examination of American Foreign Policy* (Lanham, MD: University Press of America, 1982); Robert G. Gilpin, 'The Richness of the Tradition of Political Realism,' in *Neorealism and Its Critics*, edited by Robert O. Keohane (New York: Columbia University Press, 1986); and Benjamin Frankel, ed., *Roots of Realism* (London: Frank Cass, 1996).

4 Most notably, during the nineteenth century in Europe; see Edward Vose Gulick, *Europe's Classical Balance of Power* (New York: Norton, 1967).

5 See, for example, Barry Buzan, Ole Wæver, and Jaap de Wilde, *Security: A New Framework for Analysis* (Boulder, CO: Lynne Rienner, 1998); and Kjell Goldmann, 'The Concept of 'Realism' as a Source of Confusion,' *Cooperation and Conflict* 23 (1, 1988): 2–14.

6 See Henry A. Kissinger, *American Foreign Policy* (New York: Norton, 1977); H.W. Brands, *What America Owes the World: The Struggle for the Soul of Foreign Policy* (Cambridge, UK: Cambridge University Press, 1998); Jeffrey W. Legro, 'Whence American Internationalism,' *International Organization* 54 (2, 2000): 253–89.

7 More pointedly, they used to wage war on each other. Today, that prospect seems well-nigh impossible, in part because, remarkably, France and Germany identify with each other to a considerable extent. See, generally, Emanuel Adler and Michael Barnett, eds, *Security Communities* (Cambridge, UK: Cambridge University Press, 1998).

8 Michael Doyle, 'Liberalism and World Politics,' *American Political Science Review* 80 (4, 1986): 1151–69; David A. Baldwin, ed., *Neorealism and Neoliberalism: The Contemporary Debate* (New York: Columbia University Press, 1993); Ann Florini, 'The Evolution of International Norms,' *International Studies Quarterly* 40 (3, 1996): 363–89; Torbjørn L. Knutsen, *A History of International Relations Theory*, 2nd ed. (Manchester, UK: Manchester University Press, 1997); Andrew Moravcsik, 'Taking Preferences Seriously: A Liberal Theory of International Politics,' *International Organization* 51 (4, 1997): 513–53; and Vendulk Kubálková, Nicholas Onuf, and Paul Kowert, eds, *International Relations in a Constructed World* (Armonk, NY: M.E. Sharpe, 1998).

9 Foreign policy elites include political leaders, senior bureaucrats, prominent academics, and knowledgeable commentators. The prevailing beliefs of these elites matter because they powerfully affect what states do in

international affairs. They prime decision-making groups to approach and manage problems in particular ways, and they delegitimize competing views. See, for example, Gregory G. Brunk, Donald Secrest, and Howard Tamashiro, *Understanding Attitudes about War: Modeling Moral Judgments* (Pittsburgh: University of Pittsburgh Press, 1996); Fawaz A. Gerges, *America and Political Islam: Clash of Cultures or Clash of Interests?* (Cambridge, UK: Cambridge University Press, 1999); and William Zimmerman, *The Russian People and Foreign Policy: Russian Elite and Mass Perspectives, 1993–2000* (Princeton, NJ: Princeton University Press, 2002).

10 Buzan, Wæver, and de Wilde, *Security*.

11 The relevant literature is enormous, but see especially J.W. Ballantine, 'Mukden to Pearl Harbor: The Foreign Policies of Japan,' *Foreign Affairs* 27 (July 1949): 651–64; Joyce Lebra-Chapman, ed., *Japan's Greater East Asia Co-Prosperity Sphere in World War II: Selected Readings and Documents* (Oxford: Oxford University Press, 1975); Akira Iriye, *The Origins of the Second World War in Asia and the Pacific* (London: Longman, 1987); Sydney Giffard, *Japan among the Powers, 1890–1990* (New Haven, CT: Yale University Press, 1994); John Benson and Takao Matsumura, *Japan, 1868–1945: From Isolation to Occupation* (London: Longman, 2001); Tomoko Okagaki, 'The Sovereign State and Its Conformists: Japan's Entrance into International Society' (PhD dissertation, University of Michigan, 2005); and John W. Steinberg et al., eds, *The Russo-Japanese War in Global Perspective: World War Zero* (Leiden, Netherlands: Brill, 2005).

12 Eric Heginbotham and Richard J. Samuels, 'Mercantile Realism and Japanese Foreign Policy,' *International Security* 22 (4, 1998): 171–203. During Japan's economic boom of the late 1980s and early 1990s, fear of Japanese neomercantilism prompted a good deal of unseemly hysteria, most of which has been displaced toward China in recent years. See, for example, George Friedman and Meredith LeBard, *The Coming War with Japan* (New York: St Martin's Press, 1991); Joseph S. Nye, Jr, 'Coping with Japan,' *Foreign Policy* (Winter 1992): 96–115; and John H. Maurer, 'The United States and Japan: Collision Course?' *Strategic Review* 21 (2, 1993): 41–51. It also prompted some attempts at paternalistic interference in Japanese domestic affairs; see, for example, Michael Mastanduno, 'Framing the Japan Problem: The Bush Administration and the Structural Impediments Initiative,' in *Choosing to Co-Operate: How States Avoid Loss*, edited by Janice Gross Stein and Louis Pauly (Baltimore: Johns Hopkins University Press, 1993).

13 Thomas U. Berger, 'Norms, Identity, and National Security in Germany and Japan,' in *The Culture of National Security*, edited by Peter J. Katzenstein (New York: Columbia University Press, 1996).

14 Kent E. Calder, 'Securing Security through Prosperity: The San Francisco System in Comparative Perspective,' *The Pacific Review* 17 (1, 2004): 135–57. In contrast to Heginbotham and Samuels, and also to Lind, Calder sees Japanese policy as consistent, but not necessarily strategic, since he considers it essentially reactive; Kent E. Calder, 'Asia's Shifting Strategic Landscape. Japan as a Post-Reactive State?' *Orbis* 47 (4, 2003): 605–16. See also, for example, Jonathan Rynhold, 'Japan's Cautious New Activism in the Middle East: A Qualitative Change or More of the Same?' *International Relations of the Asia-Pacific* 2 (2, 2002): 245–63.

15 See Kenneth B. Pyle, *Japan Rising: The Resurgence of Japanese Power and Purpose* (New York: PublicAffairs, 2007); and Richard J. Samuels, *Securing Japan: Tokyo's Grand Strategy and the Future of East Asia* (Ithaca, NY: Cornell University Press, 2007). The third is more cautious: Peter J. Katzenstein, *Rethinking Japanese Security: Internal and External Dimensions* (New York: Routledge, 2008).

16 Takashi Inoguchi and Paul Bacon, 'Japan's Emerging Role as a "Global Ordinary Power,"' *International Relations of the Asia-Pacific* 6 (1, 2006): 2. It is interesting that Inoguchi and Bacon project a 2020 horizon for this particular new phase. Offhand it is difficult for me to understand what might limit it if an emerging national strategy were to prove advantageous. It seems that they draw heavily upon Henry Kissinger's observation that it takes Japan fifteen years to respond to major international events; Henry Kissinger, *Does America Need a Foreign Policy? Towards a Diplomacy for the 21st Century* (New York: Simon & Schuster, 2001), p. 123. If Peter Drucker is correct that '[t]wice during the last 40 years, Japan has overcome major and apparently insoluble social problems not by "solving" them but by delaying until, in the end, the problems evaporated,' then perhaps these lags reflect wisdom rather than incapacity; see Peter F. Drucker, 'In Defense of Japanese Bureaucracy,' *Foreign Affairs* 77 (5, 1998): 68–80, referring to agricultural reform and retail distribution. Elsewhere I have argued that significant foreign policy change is rare; that foreign policy can best be understood as a punctuated equilibrium; and that the inertia of foreign policy can be explained in both organizational and psychological terms; David A. Welch, *Painful Choices: A Theory of Foreign Policy Change* (Princeton, NJ: Princeton University Press, 2005).

17 Christian Hougen, 'The Problems and Promises of Japan's Economic-Growth-Led Foreign Policy in Perspective,' *Fletcher Forum of World Affairs* 21 (2, 1997): 133.

18 See Masato Kimura and David A. Welch, 'Specifying "Interests": Japan's Claim to the Northern Territories and Its Implications for International

Relations Theory,' *International Studies Quarterly* 42 (2, 1998): 213–44; S. Javed Maswood, 'Japanese Foreign Policy: Leadership and Style,' *Policy and Society* 23 (1, 2004): 38–57; Daiki Shibuichi, 'The Yasukuni Shrine Dispute and the Politics of Identity in Japan: Why All the Fuss?' *Asian Survey* 45 (2, 2005): 197–215; Allona Sund, 'Exceptional States: National Esteem and Nonconformity in International Relations' (PhD dissertation, University of Toronto, 2007); and Amy L. Catalinac, 'How Identities Become Securitized: Japan's Whaling Policy Explained' (unpublished paper, Department of Government, Harvard University, 23 June 2009).

19 Katsumi Ishizuka, 'Japan's Policy towards UN Peacekeeping Operations,' *International Peacekeeping* 12 (1, 2005): 56–72. Masaru Tamamoto argues, for example, that the increasing importance of Japanese soft power 'has come about not because of some grand design cooked up by bureaucrats in Tokyo, but because of the individual choices of Japanese businesspeople and of Asian nations that have warmly welcomed their example and their capital'; 'Japan's Uncertain Role,' *World Policy Journal* 8 (4, 1991): 596–7. This soft power nevertheless might be a tool available to Japanese foreign policy-makers. On foreign aid as another important tool of Japanese foreign policy, see Saori N. Katada, 'Why Did Japan Suspend Foreign Aid to China? Japan's Foreign Aid Decision-Making and Sources of Aid Sanction,' *Social Science Japan Journal* 4 (1, 2001): 39–58.

20 See Kenneth N. Waltz, *Man, the State and War* (New York: Columbia University Press, 1959); and J. David Singer, 'The Levels of Analysis Problem in International Relations,' in *International Politics and Foreign Policy*, edited by James N. Rosenau (New York: Free Press, 1969).

21 Among the most intriguing and most provocative attempts of which I am aware are Ray S. Cline, *World Power Assessment: A Calculus of Strategic Drift* (Washington, DC: Center for Strategic and International Studies, Georgetown University, 1975); idem, *World Power Assessment 1977: A Calculus of Strategic Drift* (Boulder, CO: Westview Press, 1977); and idem, *World Power Trends and U.S. Foreign Policy for the 1980s* (Boulder, CO: Westview Press, 1980).

22 See Hamid Faruqee and Martin Mühleisen, 'Population Aging in Japan: Demographic Shock and Fiscal Sustainability,' *Japan and the World Economy* 15 (2, April 2003): 185–210.

23 Japan's maritime capabilities are particularly impressive; its aerial capabilities are excellent as well. Japan's only weak link is land warfare capability. See Jennifer M. Lind, 'Pacifism or Passing the Buck? Testing Theories of Japanese Security Policy,' *International Security* 29 (1, 2004): 92–121.

24 Tsuyoshi Kawasaki argues that, according to Waltzian neo-realist logic,

systemic forces would have punished Japan by now for its failure to behave as a traditional great power; 'Why Is Japan Not Punished by International Anarchy?' (paper presented to the International Studies Association Annual Meeting, New Orleans, LA, 17 February 2010); available online at http://www.allacademic.com/meta/p_mla_apa_research_citation/4/1/5/9/4/pages415942/p415942-1.php, accessed 15 April 2010.

25 A list of such publications is available online at http://www.mod.go.jp/e/publ/w_paper/index.html, accessed 3 June 2009.

26 'Foreign minister Aso calls China "considerable threat,"' *Kyodo News*, 22 December 2005.

27 Thomas U. Berger, 'Focus on a Changing Japan' (statement before the House International Relations Subcommittee on Asia and the Pacific, Washington, DC, 20 April 2005); Bennett Richardson, 'Japan to step up its Asia security role,' *Christian Science Monitor*, 1 May 2006; Janice Tang, 'Japan, U.S. enter new stage with troop realignment by 2014,' *Kyodo News*, 1 May 2006.

28 Japan, Ministry of Defense, 'Japan's BMD' (Tokyo, February 2009); available online at http://www.mod.go.jp/e/d_policy/bmd/bmd2009.pdf, accessed 1 June 2009.

29 See Sebastian Moffett, 'Koizumi's Korea Gambit ' *Far Eastern Economic Review*, 27 May 2004, pp. 22–3; but see also Gilbert Rozman, 'Japan's North Korea Initiative and U.S.-Japanese Relations,' *Orbis* 47 (3, 2003): 527–39.

30 See Jim Frederick, 'Rocky Relations: A Feud over Some Barren Islands Reignites Old Tensions between South Korea and Japan,' *Time International*, 8 May 2006, p. 22.

31 See Gregory W. Noble, 'What Can Taiwan (and the United States) Expect from Japan?,' *Journal of East Asian Studies* 5 (1, 2005): 1–34.

32 See, for example, Robert Uriu, 'Japan in 2003: Muddling Ahead?' *Asian Survey* 44 (1, 2004): 168–81; and Akio Watanabe, 'A Continuum of Change,' *Washington Quarterly* 27 (4, 2004): 137–46.

33 Richardson, 'Japan to step up its Asia security role.'

34 See also Berger, 'Norms, Identity, and National Security in Germany and Japan,' pp. 319–25. Even analysts who are inclined to interpret Japanese policy as responsive to systemic pressures and constraints note the vital importance of non-systemic considerations, such as ideational or historical factors. See, for example, Yoshihide Soeya, 'The Evolution of Japanese Thinking and Policies on Cooperative Security in the 1980s and 1990s,' *Australian Journal of International Affairs* 48 (1, 1994): 87–95.

35 Berger, 'Norms, Identity, and National Security in Germany and Japan.'

36 See Peter D. Feaver, Takako Hikotani, and Shaun Narine, 'Civilian Control

and Civil-Military Gaps in the United States, Japan, and China,' *Asian Perspective* 29 (1, 2005): 233–71.

37 Lind, 'Pacifism or Passing the Buck?' 120.

38 See Bradley M. Richardson, *Japanese Democracy: Power, Coordination, and Performance* (New Haven, CT: Yale University Press, 1997); and Steven R. Reed, *Japanese Electoral Politics: Creating a New Party System* (London: RoutledgeCurzon, 2003).

39 For background, see David A. Welch, 'A Positive Science of Bureaucratic Politics?' *Mershon International Studies Review* 42 (2, 1998): 210–16.

40 See C.S. Ahn, 'Interministry Coordination in Japan's Foreign Policy Making,' *Pacific Affairs* 71 (1, 1998): 41–60.

41 See Michael Minor, 'Decision Models and Japanese Foreign Policy Decision Making,' *Asian Survey* 25 (12, 1985): 1229–41.

42 It is in any case difficult to find much evidence, even when one looks for it, of specifically 'bureaucratic' interests shaping national ones. See, for example, David A. Welch, 'The Organizational Process and Bureaucratic Politics Paradigms: Retrospect and Prospect,' *International Security* 17 (2, 1992): 112–46; and Edward Rhodes, 'Do Bureaucratic Politics Matter? Some Disconfirming Findings from the Case of the U.S. Navy,' *World Politics* 47 (1, 1994): 1–41.

43 Welch, *Painful Choices*, pp. 18–23.

44 Tsuyoshi Kawasaki, 'Japan and Two Theories of Military Doctrine Formation: Civilian Policymakers, Policy Preference, and the 1976 National Defense Program Outline,' *International Relations of the Asia-Pacific* 1 (1, 2001): 67–93.

45 Decision-makers are, of course, agents operating in thick social and political structures. From a structurationist perspective, we ought to think of them as only 'partially free' agents. See Anthony Giddens, *The Constitution of Society: Outline of the Theory of Structuration* (Cambridge, UK: Polity Press, 1984); Alexander Wendt, 'The Agent-Structure Problem in International Relations Theory,' *International Organization* 41 (3, 1987): 3350–70; and David Dessler, 'What's at Stake in the Agent-Structure Debate?' *International Organization* 43 (3, 1989): 441–74.

46 Giffard, *Japan among the Powers 1890–1990*, pp. x, 1–23.

47 Yoichi Funabashi, 'Japan and the New World Order,' *Foreign Affairs* 70 (5, 1991/92): 58–74.

48 See Sten Rynning, 'In Search of Security: Statesmanship and Strategy in France, 1974–1999' (PhD dissertation, University of South Carolina, 1999).

49 See, for example, Richard A. Clarke, *Against All Enemies: Inside America's War on Terror* (New York: Free Press, 2004); Gary J. Dorrien, *Imperial*

Designs: Neoconservatism and the New Pax Americana (New York: Routledge, 2004); and James Mann, *Rise of the Vulcans: The History of Bush's War Cabinet* (New York: Viking, 2004).

50 Ichirō Ozawa, *Nihon Kaizo Keikaku* (Tokyo: Kodansha, 1993); published in English as *Blueprint for a New Japan: The Rethinking of a Nation*, translated by Louisa Rubenfien (Tokyo: Kodansha International, 1994).

51 Ibid., pp. 116–21.

52 Shintaro Ishihara, *The Japan That Can Say No*, translated by Frank Baldwin (New York: Simon & Schuster, 1991).

53 Yoshihide Soeya, *Nihon No 'Middle Power' Gaikoo: Sengo Nihon No Sentaku to Koosoo [Japan's 'Middle Power' Diplomacy]* (Tokyo: Chikuma Shobo, 2005). Compare Max Otte and Jürgen Greve, *A Rising Middle Power? German Foreign Policy in Transformation, 1989–1999* (New York: St Martin's Press, 2000). The seminal work is Annette Baker Fox, *The Politics of Attraction: Four Middle Powers and the United States* (New York: Columbia University Press, 1977).

2 Change and Continuity in Japan's 'Abnormalcy': An Emerging External Attitude of the Japanese Public

MASAYUKI TADOKORO

Japan's perceived 'abnormalcy' is symbolized in its postwar Constitution, in particular Article 9, or the 'peace clause.' Written by the United States during the postwar occupation of Japan, it was originally intended to prevent Japan from re-emerging as a military threat. Japan's 'abnormalcy' is thus an institutionalized device to keep Japan on probation, despite its having regained formal sovereignty in the San Francisco Peace Treaty.

For some Article 9 is a shameful relic of the war, a badge of disgrace that Japan is forced to wear. It is therefore not difficult to understand why traditional Japanese nationalists argue that the postwar Constitution is a source of national humiliation imposed by the war's victors. From this nationalist perspective, Article 9 is designed to hobble Japan's international status permanently. In order to recover Japan's full sovereignty and international prestige, they argue, the Constitution must be rewritten.

Article 9, however, is not merely symbolic. It also imposes upon Japan a range of practical difficulties. Specifically, despite Japan's large economic capacity and increased demands by the United States for more active military support, Article 9 severely limits the scope of Japan's security policy. Although the Japanese government has met its security needs by stretching interpretations of various sections of the Constitution when necessary, Article 9 has always stood in the way of Japanese foreign policy, effectively handicapping Japan's involvement in international affairs.

Beyond these practical difficulties, Article 9 has generated a distinctive discourse and approach to security policy in Japan. As there is no explicit constitutional foundation for a Japanese military, debates about security policy usually are limited to discussions about the constitutionality of specific decisions or actions, rather than whether they make sense from the perspective of promoting Japanese interests within Japan's broader politico-strategic context. The Constitution, therefore, places peculiar limits on Japanese attitudes as well as on Japan's actual external behaviour, which has led to the perception that Japan is an economic giant concerned solely with making money but a political midget with no strategic vision.

It is, however, puzzling that this 'abnormalcy' has persisted for so long after the occupation, and especially in light of the enormous changes that Japan has undergone since the end of the World War Two. Despite its associated difficulties, the majority of Japanese have supported the postwar Constitution; without this support, Japan's 'abnormalcy' would not have survived for the sixty years since the Constitution came into force, a period of time longer than the lifespan of Japan's prewar constitution.

Since the 1990s, however, 'abnormalcy' has been giving way steadily to 'normalcy.' Within the limitations imposed by Article 9, Japan's defence policy has clearly become more active. Amendments to the Constitution are openly discussed in lively fashion among the public. Domestic discourse on security policy is shifting away from earlier, almost theological debate about the constitutionality of maintaining armed forces to the practical desirability of specific policies. Many commentators, both within and outside Japan, have called this trend 'the rightward drift' (*Ukeika*).

In this chapter, I examine Japanese attitudes toward the country's postwar 'abnormalcy,' and analyse Japanese foreign policy by investigating how the Japanese population accepted the special limitations imposed by the postwar Constitution and how attitudes have been changing since the 1990s. It is true that public attitudes alone do not explain actual foreign policies; political leadership, political institutions, and the international environment are all relevant factors. However, in a democracy, it is neither a small number of political leaders, nor media elites, but ultimately the general public that determines the direction and destiny of a country. Thus, rather than focusing on developments within the Japanese political arena, I explore changes in Japanese postwar social consciousness.

I first discuss a variety of conditions that have enabled the continued 'abnormalcy' of postwar Japan. I then move on to explain what has prompted the growing normalization of Japan in light of the changed conditions surrounding the country since the 1990s. This discussion addresses the political significance of economic growth as an important component of Japanese 'abnormalcy' but counters the argument that the economic stagnation since the 1990s has led to a 'rightward drift' and a subsequent desire to expand Japan's security policy. Rather, by using a variety of public opinion surveys, I argue that 'normalization' represents an outgrowth of postwar values and institutions.

Postwar Abnormalcy as a Delicate Equilibrium

Soon after Japan regained its sovereignty by signing the San Francisco Peace Treaty in 1951, Japanese society was divided over the status of its new Constitution. Given the U.S. influence on the Constitution, revisionists questioned its legitimacy, arguing that Japanese sovereignty required an indigenous document. A central element of the revisionist position was that Japanese independence required a constitution that not only was formulated by the Japanese people themselves but that also ensured Japan's right to protect itself from acts of aggression.[1]

Supporters of the postwar Constitution argued that disarmament and neutrality would ensure Japan's security. Although this group included a small number of Soviet supporters, the majority came from a progressive element in Japanese society that vigorously advocated the ideal of unarmed neutrality as a realistic means of ensuring security in the nuclear age. Supporters therefore called for strict adherence to the letter of Article 9 and promoted a position of non-alignment rather than an alliance with the United States.[2]

The foundation of Japan's basic postwar policy was laid by Prime Minister Shigeru Yoshida, who, while maintaining the Constitution and its peace clause, decided to rely upon the United States for Japan's security. Taking a minimalist attitude toward security, Yoshida prioritized economic growth and international trade for rebuilding Japan. At first, both right- and left-wing groups criticized his posture for its dependence on the United States. By the 1960s, however, when the 'Yoshida Doctrine' became the prevailing consensus in Japanese society, constitutional debates had subsided.

The essence of Yoshida's policy was to accept *both* the postwar Constitution and the alliance with the United States. The former, a product of Japan's defeat, was premised on a vision of a stable world order maintained by cooperating with the victors; the latter, a product of the Cold War, placed Japan clearly on the side of the 'Free World' and committed it to the defence of the West. Not surprisingly, with these two pillars based upon two completely different world views – one involving global cooperation and the other ideological conflict and military rivalry – inconsistencies often emerged in Japanese foreign policy. The postwar Japanese foreign policy regime, in fact, became a bizarre halfway house: despite the peace clause, and on the basis of its alignment with the United States, the Self-Defense Forces (SDF) were created and gradually expanded. But Japan attempted to evade U.S. demands for further rearmament as a Cold War ally by pointing to Article 9. Although Yoshida and successive Liberal Democratic Party (LDP) governments paid significant political costs to maintain the alliance with the United States, Japan was never willing to expand military capacity beyond what it required strictly for territorial self-defence.

Effectively, then, Japan's postwar Constitution remained intact, despite the obvious inconsistencies with the security policy dictated by its alliance with the United States. This proved to be a source of irritation for both Americans and the Japanese right wing, as the limitations stemming from the peace clause prevented Japan from playing a sufficient military role either independently or in alliance with the United States. It also dissatisfied Japanese left-wing and pacifist progressives, since the SDF, by cooperating with the United States, severely stretched, if not fully contradicted, the peace clause.

Despite the tensions within the Yoshida Doctrine, Japan's 'abnormal' status persisted. In light of those tensions, why did Japan not try to normalize its basic policy, either by modifying the Constitution to make it more consistent with Japan's actual foreign policy – in particular, the alliance with the United States and the creation of the SDF – or by modifying its foreign policy in a way that was more clearly consistent with the Constitution?

The most likely explanation is that, during the Cold War, political divisions between different factions in Japanese society were so deep that reaching a consensus on basic policy, let alone on the Constitution, was a practical impossibility. On the one hand, the right wing, which had been close to the prewar ruling elite, favoured a constitution that revived Japan as a full-fledged independent power. On the other hand, pro-Soviet communists, socialists, and, most important, progressives who exerted significant influence in academic circles and the mass media called for unarmed neutrality.

In principle there was no way to reconcile these two sharply contradicting positions. This was tantamount to an ideological and political

'Berlin Wall' within Japanese society. Similar to the divided Germany, the two camps could not find a middle ground, though they coexisted at least in a fragile peace without resorting to organized violence. Yoshida's ambiguous policy line was thus a tolerable *modus vivendi* for both camps.

In the postwar years a very strong antimilitary sentiment has been widely shared among the Japanese. The popular perception that the prewar military regime had brutally and recklessly dragged Japan into a war that resulted in more than three million casualties, including many civilians killed during the United States' atomic bomb attacks, inclined many Japanese to distrust any discussion that smacked of militarism.

The hatred of militarism, however, did not translate into support for unarmed neutrality. The Soviet violation of the neutrality treaty in August 1945, the subsequent internment of many Japanese in Siberia, and the occupation of the Kurile Islands – generally perceived as Japanese territory – bred widespread suspicion of the Soviets in Japanese society. Garnering support for the pacifist position only became harder after the Korean War, as unarmed neutrality did not appear to protect the hard-won peace. Japanese society was thus caught in the paradoxical position of wanting to avoid any kind of military conflict but feeling that unarmed neutrality was not a realistic policy option with communist China and the Soviet Union as neighbours. Yoshida's policy line was responsive to the paradoxical desires held by the Japanese of the day.

On the other hand, although Japanese society was divided in its opinion about the nation's basic security posture, there was a clear consensus that its primary goals were economic reconstruction and growth. Not only would this strategy meet concerns about basic survival needs in the immediate postwar era, but it appeared to be a more attractive and less costly way to regain international stature without having to resort to an extensive military buildup. This approach bore fruit as the remarkable economic growth of the 1960s not only improved the living standards of many Japanese but also transformed Japan's image from that of a humiliated loser in World War Two into that of a dynamic Western democracy.

Postwar 'abnormalcy,' therefore, represented a delicate equilibrium that permitted divided elements in Japanese society to coexist peacefully. It also seemed to give the Japanese almost everything they wanted: Japan could avoid excessive entanglement in power politics while defending itself from the threat of the Soviet Union by forming an alliance with the United States that entailed only minimal involvement in its Cold War strategy. In other words, Japan's 'abnormalcy' minimized its military role and allowed it to concentrate on economic growth under the aegis of the United States. Effectively, 'abnormalcy' avoided domestic political disruption and military commitments, while facilitating economic prosperity and Japan's improved international status.

To bè sure, many Japanese were frustrated by the constant presence of U.S. military bases, which gave the impression that Japan was still under occupation. The Vietnam War was a particularly unsettling irritant. Large segments of Japanese society were disturbed by Japan's indirect contribution to the U.S. war effort, both because it seemed to contravene Japan's commitment to its pacifist philosophy and because the legitimacy of the war itself was highly questionable. In light of the Constitution's peace clause, U.S. actions in Vietnam led to a growing unease in Japanese society about the SDF, which appeared to be steadily expanding and cooperating with U.S. forces.

Despite these irritants, disputes over the Constitution subsided after the 1960s, stabilized by a consensus that resulted from Yoshida's *modus vivendi*, under which the Constitution was maintained while the SDF's size was limited to the very 'minimum' required for Japan's territorial defence. In this way the Constitution effectively institutionalized Japan's 'abnormalcy': what was once seen as a badge of disgrace gradually became a proud symbol of Japan's commitment to peace. Shelving basic constitutional uncertainty about its military role, Japan was able to concentrate upon and further its successful program of economic growth.[3] In this political context, Japanese public opinion largely supported the Constitution, a limited defence capability, and the alliance with the United States.

Despite the initial feelings of humiliation associated with it and the inconsistent policies to which it gave rise, the postwar Constitution had the effect of reassuring many Japanese that there would not be a resurgence of the militarism that had marked the prewar period. Although adopting unarmed neutrality was neither realistic nor attractive, 'normalizing' Japan by revising the Constitution appeared unnecessary. Japan was able to enjoy peace, prosperity and an improved international status, so why change? 'Abnormalcy,' therefore, became deeply embedded in Japanese society, remaining virtually unchallenged until the 1990s.

Changed Conditions since the 1990s

This delicate equilibrium was not without its problems. As the economy grew, the gap between Japan's economic weight and its limited security role became a source of growing frustration for both Japanese and Americans. On the one hand, U.S. demands grew as Japan became richer. By the early 1980s, voices in the U.S. Congress criticizing Japan for free-riding on the security provided by the United States became too loud to ignore. A major Western publication even mockingly called the Japanese 'Kamikaze Pacifists.'[4] Endless trade disputes with the United States also made it apparent that Americans, especially those in Congress and within the rather narrow Washington media and political circles, were becoming increasingly ambivalent about the apparent economic challenge from a junior ally whose security the United States was underwriting.

At the same time, Japan was becoming irritated by its inability to behave as a 'normal,' independent country. Given its increased economic contributions to the hosting of U.S. forces, its increasingly heavy spending on official development assistance, and its growing financial contributions to international organizations such as the United Nations and the International Monetary Fund, among others, many Japanese felt that Japan's growing affluence was not matched by an increase in its international status and that its alliance with the United States was unduly constraining and was serving as a symbol of Japan's subordination to the United States.[5]

It was not until the experience of the first Gulf War in 1991, however, that the limits of prioritizing the economy in the postwar period became evident. Article 9 prevented Japan from contributing to the UN-authorized military operation, yet Japan's professed UN-centred internationalism dictated sharing the burden of this kind of international effort. Rather than fostering a more respectful international status, Japan's contribution of US$13 billion to the multilateral forces in lieu of military support was viewed with contempt, as others grew resentful of Japan's economic prosperity.

When it came to participating in UN missions, 'unarmed neutrality' revealed its inherent hypocrisy. During the Cold War, with the UN relatively paralyzed by the United States-Soviet rivalry, the inconsistencies in Japan's pacifist position were not evident. Once the UN began assuming more active collective security functions in the early 1990s, however, Japan's pacifism began to look like an isolationist policy motivated by a selfish desire to steer clear of any international conflicts and uncertainties.

It became increasingly clear in the eyes of Japanese that their country, if it continued to abstain from actively promoting international security, would be treated like a broken cash dispenser, viewed merely as an uncritical provider of financial resources. Such a role – bankrolling initiatives over which it had little, if any, influence – was inherently humiliating. Consequently, Japan's postwar 'abnormalcy' started to be recognized as a major obstacle to its legitimate and honourable international status rather than a proud, lofty symbol of the nation's pacifist ideals.

This humiliating and confusing experience prompted serious soul-searching on the part of Japanese leaders about Japan's international role. Immediately after the first Gulf War, Japan sent its Maritime Self-Defense Force to Iraq to sweep for mines. Then in 1992, it commissioned the SDF for a UN peacekeeping mission in Cambodia. Given Japan's imperial history, however, some Asian leaders viewed such moves, although modest, with great unease. Lee Kwan-Yew, then prime minister of Singapore, expressed his concern by stating that letting 'an armed Japan participate in [peacekeeping operations] is like giving a chocolate filled with whisky to an alcoholic.'[6]

Progressives within Japan echoed this hostile response, likening peacekeeping to 'a small hole made by ants,' a small but critical first step that ultimately would erode the bulwark of pacifism that had prevented the resurgence of militarism during the postwar era. The decision to participate even in very limited humanitarian missions abroad, therefore, sparked heated debates in Japan. A government bill authorizing the despatch of the peacekeeping mission to Cambodia encountered intensive filibustering by socialists and communists. Even following the passage of the legislation, public support for Japan's involvement was far from solid, and the mission turned out to be riskier than had been initially expected. Tokyo faced a difficult political challenge as it became increasingly apparent in autumn 1992 that the Khmer Rouge were reneging on the agreed peace process by refusing to cooperate with UN peacekeepers, making the prospect of a successful national election in Cambodia increasingly uncertain. When a Japanese civilian police official and a UN volunteer were killed the following year, even some within the ruling party called vociferously for a unilateral withdrawal of the SDF.

By sending peacekeeping forces to Cambodia, however, Tokyo was able to demonstrate, at not inconsiderable risk – given the Japanese public's acute sensitivity to exposing the SDF to hostile situations – its capability and willingness to play a serious security role in the region.

This trend has continued into the twenty-first century as successive Japanese administrations have maintained Japan's participation in a variety of UN missions – for example, in the Golan Heights, Bosnia-Herzegovina, and East Timor. In the aftermath of the terrorist attacks of 11 September 2001, Japan stepped up its participation in peacekeeping missions by sending maritime forces to the Indian Ocean to support U.S.-led efforts in the Afghan War, and even sent troops to Iraq when traditional U.S. allies such as France refused to do so.

Not only did a more active military presence appear necessary for a more respected international role, it seemed useful for maintaining regional peace. The North Korean nuclear crisis in 1993–94 brought the United States very close to taking military action for which Japan was utterly unprepared. The discovery of North Korean spy boat activities and abductions of Japanese citizens made it appear that Japan actually had been under attack. This was a severe blow to advocates of unarmed neutrality who thought that, in the absence of Japanese aggression, Japan would face no external threats. In addition, the missile exercise China conducted off the coast of Taiwan to intimidate voters during the 1996 Taiwanese presidential election left the impression that Japan's repentance of its war crimes and its massive official development assistance to the Chinese government were not enough to address the challenge of a growing China.

Thus, despite the end of the Cold War and the dissolution of the Soviet Union, regional military conflicts appeared to threaten Japan's vital interests. The Japanese began to feel a variety of limitations imposed by the country's postwar constitutional system; it increasingly appeared to be hampering Japan's capability to be an effective ally of the United States, whose military presence looked more important than ever as the ultimate guarantor of regional stability.

In light of this situation, Japanese authorities took steps to reaffirm and even tighten the alliance with the United States. After the collapse of the Soviet Union, the United States-Japan alliance had drifted for some time and economic frictions between the two countries had dominated bilateral relations. But in 1997 the New Defense Guideline reconfirmed and redefined the security alliance, focusing more on achieving regional stability than on countering a direct attack on Japan. The Japanese population accepted this reaffirmation of bilateral defence cooperation without significant protest.

The change in Japan's military roles and commitments from its initial postwar position is, at first sight, impressive. Despite this modest change, however, Japanese military activities remain very cautious: although they have been deployed for various international security endeavours, the SDF are strictly limited to non-combat missions. And regardless of Japan's alliance with the United States, it is highly unlikely that the SDF will be deployed overseas for any actions that are not endorsed by the UN.

Japan's regional security roles are even more limited by the Constitution, the current official interpretation of which prohibits Japan from exercising the right of collective self-defence. Effectively, this renders even minor logistical assistance to U.S. forces in possible campaigns for contingencies on the Korean peninsula or in the Taiwan Strait unconstitutional.

Changing Constitutional Discourse

While the postwar Constitution sharply divided Japanese society in the 1950s and early 1960s, when Japan began its period of economic growth in the 1960s, the delicate and odd balance struck by the *modus vivendi* created by the Yoshida Doctrine resulted in widespread acceptance of the Constitution. Public attitudes began to shift, however, in the 1990s, as clearly reflected in public opinion polls in two major newspapers, *Asahi Shimbun* and *Yomiuri Shimbun* (see Figures 2.1 and 2.2).[7] Both polls display the same trend: in the 1950s, soon after Japan recovered its sovereignty as a result of the San Francisco Peace Treaty, the proportion of Japanese in favour of revising the Constitution was more or less equal to, or slightly larger than, that against amending it; then, from the 1960s onward, the majority supported the Constitution, with those in favour of amending it limited to a small group of traditional nationalists and extreme right-wingers.

Beginning in the late 1990s, however, the majority has favoured revising the Constitution. A 2004 poll of members of Japan's legislature, the Diet, revealed even stronger support for amendment among this group, with even a majority of the Democratic Party of Japan (DPJ), which was regarded as more progressive and even counted former Socialists among its members, embracing constitutional revision (see Figure 2.3).[8] In 2007, the government of Shinzo Abe, which openly put the issue on its agenda, managed to pass a law stipulating detailed procedures for a national referendum that would be necessary to revise the Constitution.

This sea change in once hesitant Japanese public opinion about constitutional revision had obvious consequences for Japan's security

Figure 2.1: Japanese Public Opinion on Amending the Constitution, 1952–2002, as Reported by *Yomiuri Shimbun*

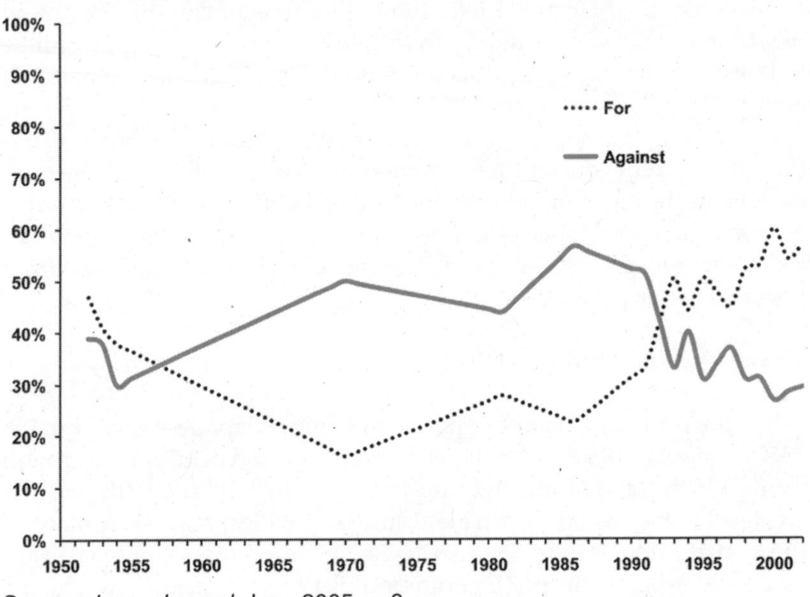

Source: *Japan Journal*, June 2005, p. 8.

agenda in the 1990s. Alongside the new public attitude toward the Constitution, the prevailing view became one that peace missions had to be undertaken and a U.S. presence facilitated in order to foster regional stability. It also led to the fall of the Socialist Party, whose platform of neutrality appeared to become irrelevant after the collapse of the Soviet Union and the shift by a still-authoritarian China to develop itself into a capitalist market economy.[9] Further, the Socialists erred in categorically objecting to Japan's participation in UN peacekeeping operations and by becoming a coalition partner of the LDP in 1994, despite the clear inconsistency in the basic principles of the two political parties. North Korean dictator Kim Jong Il's surprising admission in 2002 of the abduction of a number of Japanese citizens was a further crippling, if not fatal, blow for the Socialists, who traditionally had taken a pro–North Korean position and blindly accepted Pyongyang's denials of involvement in such illicit activities.

The Socialists were for a long time the largest opposition party, representing the most important component of the 'progressive' camp in the

Figure 2.2: Japanese Public Opinion on Amending the Constitution, 1955–2005, as Reported by *Asahi Shimbun*

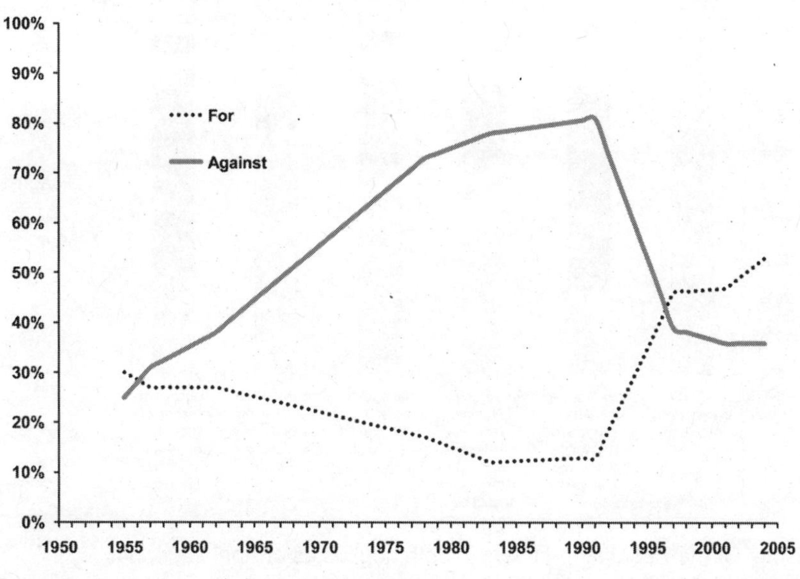

Source: *Japan Journal*, June 2005, p. 8.

postwar constitutional system. As late as 1990, they had won as many as 136 seats out of 512 in the lower house election under the party leadership of Takako Doi, an iconic figure seen by some as the guardian of the postwar Constitution. A decade later, the strength of the party was much reduced: the Social Democratic Party of Japan (SDPJ), which had succeeded the Socialist Party in 1996, managed to win only six seats in the 2003 general election and even Ms. Doi herself lost her seat. The Socialists became nothing more than a marginalized group, leaving no core organized political opposition to constitutional revision. The earlier invisible 'Berlin Wall' that had divided Japan had, it seemed, quietly but unmistakably collapsed.

It is important to note that increased support for revising the Constitution and the subsequent decline of support for the unarmed neutrality platform advocated by the Socialist Party were not the result of a sudden 'rightward drift' in Japanese politics. As Figure 2.4 shows, supporters of revision cited the increased need to contribute to international security, such as peacekeeping operations, rather than growing

Figure 2.3: Opinions of Diet Members on Article 9 of the Constitution, 2004 Survey

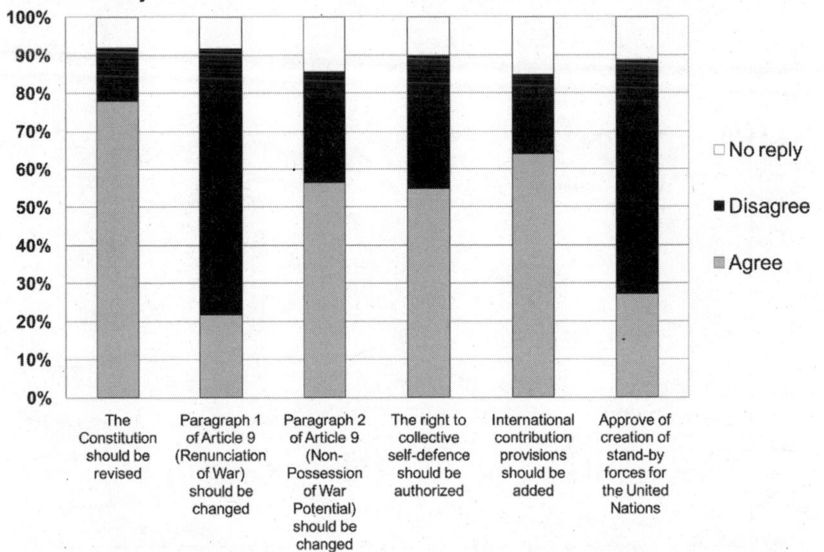

Note: Of the 722 Diet members in both houses as of April 2004, 545 responded to the questionnaire.
Source: *Mainichi Shimbun*, 3 May 2004 (edited by *The Japan Journal*).

doubts about the legitimacy of liberal values, as the primary reason for constitutional change; for many, constitutional change was considered a means by which to maintain postwar values and institutions. This shift in attitudes toward constitutional reform, therefore, should not be interpreted as a denial of the Constitution, and even less a desire to return to Japan's prewar regime.

Following the change in public opinion in the 1990s, constitutional revision became openly and widely discussed. The LDP presented a new draft constitution to the public in 2004, and other political parties issued reports on constitutional amendments. Private think tanks and business associations actively discussed constitutional reforms, with some drafting new constitutions. Yet despite general agreement that constitutional reform was required, little agreement existed on the exact nature of revision – although, as Table 2.1 shows, there was wide agreement on the general direction of the necessary amendments. All the proposals supported the basic principles of the existing Constitution,

Figure 2.4: Reasons Cited for Amending the Constitution, 2005

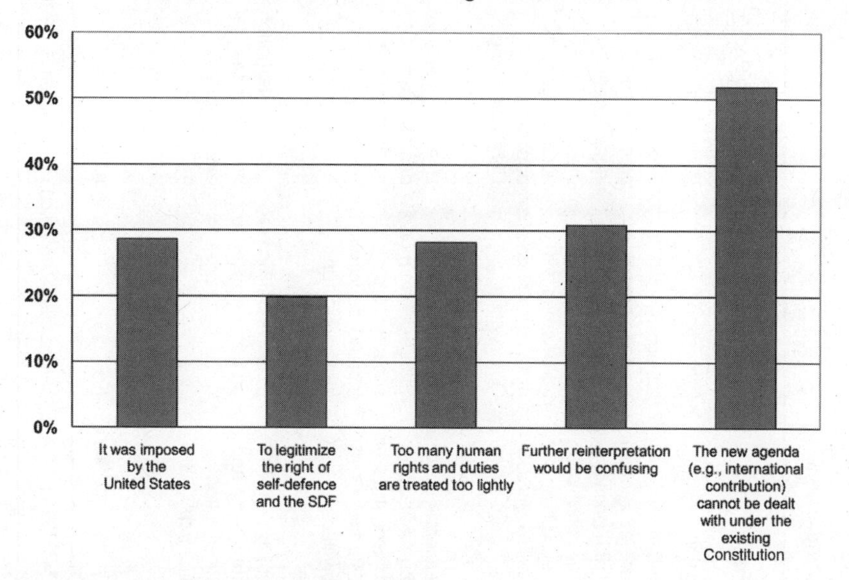

Source: *Yomiuri Shimbun*, 8 April 2005.

which include democracy, the recognition of the Emperor as a national symbol, respect for human rights, and pacifism. Article 9 remained the focal point of discussions, but even here almost all groups agreed that the SDF and the right of self-defence must be legitimized explicitly through constitutional reform. The most contentious issue was with respect to the right of collective self-defence and the role that Japan should play in UN missions. Despite arguing in favour of individual self-defence and the SDF, most Japanese argued that the Constitution also should place limits on Japan's military role beyond its own territory. Particularly when it came to combat missions abroad, most Japanese were troubled, perhaps even frightened, by the idea.

The proposed revisions of the Constitution, then, while substantial, represented no radical departure from Japan's basic postwar institutions and values. They were also fairly modest and, from the perspective of Washington, still fell well short of what one would expect of an ally such as the United Kingdom, France, or Germany, all of which were involved in combat operations in the first Gulf War and in Afghanistan. But, after all, Article 96 of the Constitution specifies that a two-thirds

Table 2.1: Stances of Major Japanese Political Parties on Constitutional Amendment

Issue	Liberal Democratic Party	Democratic Party of Japan	Komeito	Japanese Communist Party	Social Democratic Party
Attitude	Revision	(Re)formulation	Addition	Protection	Protection
Security and military force for defence	Use SDF to defend Japan and contribute to international peace and security	Restrict right of self-defence as prescribed in UN Charter; defence-only policy	Maintain renunciation of war and non-possession of war potential; make explicit provision for SDF	Object to amendment; promote peaceful diplomacy in accordance with philosophy of pacifist Constitution	Object to amendment; independent diplomacy in accordance with principles of UN Charter and Constitution
Right to collective self-defence	Exercise without stipulation; it is included in concept of right to self-defence	Participate mainly in UN operations and creation of Asian collective security organization	Unacceptable: focus on humanitarian and reconstruction assistance, mainly by civilians	Cancel United States-Japan mutual security treaty; instead, conclude amity treaty on equal terms	Use SDF solely for defence; reduce to minimal necessary scale
International contribution	Make international contribution; approve overseas use of military force	Make minimal overseas use of military force	Focus on humanitarian and reconstruction assistance	Dissolve SDF based on public consensus	Limit to international humanitarian relief aid
Number of seats in the House of Representatives	296 (116)	113 (306)	31 (21)	9 (9)	7 (6)

Source: *Japanese Journal*, June 2005, p. 9; the numbers of seats were modified by the author to reflect the election of September 2005; numbers in parentheses indicate representation as of December 2010.

majority in both houses of the Diet must approve any constitutional amendment, so that, as long as the Japanese public remained happy with its basic postwar values and institutions, no revision that contradicted them could ever occur.

First, the perceived main need for revision – to allow Japan to participate more actively in UN peacekeeping operations – has lost some of its urgency: the government has managed to send troops on UN missions under the current Constitution despite awkward constraints on the activities of the troops dispatched. In addition, there was some disillusionment with recent operations in Iraq and Afghanistan, which not only turned out to be riskier than Japanese were prepared to accept, but also seemed less legitimate because they were less clearly multilateral in nature. Under such circumstances, Article 9 could be regarded as a convenient way to avoid excessive entanglement with the United States' thinly disguised global strategy. But if Article 9 is perceived to be an obstacle to genuinely multilateral operations – such as anti-piracy operations off the coast of Somalia, authorized by a UN resolution in December 2008 – more Japanese prefer constitutional revision. As Figure 2.5 shows, the major difference of current opinion among the Japanese public is not an ideological one, pitting 'pacifists' who wish to stick to the letter of Article 9 against those who wish to transform Japan into a fully fledged independent military power, but a pragmatic one between those who prefer to muddle through with the existing Constitution and those who would rather clarify it so as to permit an expanded but still limited military role for Japan.

Second, while the multilateralist rationale for revision has become less pressing, many Japanese have been spooked by increasingly vociferous hawkish nationalist intellectuals – stimulated by the revelation of the abduction of Japanese citizens by Kim Jong Il in 2002 and anti-Japan riots in China in 2005 – who deny postwar values and institutions. While North Korea is seen as a pariah by the Japanese public and while the general public image of China has deteriorated further (see Figure 2.6), these have not translated into stronger support for revision of the Constitution to allow Japan to deal with either of these issues by lifting its self-imposed restrictions on its security policy. The Japanese public on the whole seems to be more troubled by hawkish discourse at home than by anti-Japanese sentiments or actions abroad.

While a great majority of Japanese regard violent anti-Japan riots as unacceptable, it should not be forgotten that Koizumi's Yasukuni Shrine visits, which triggered the riots, were controversial among Japanese

Figure 2.5: Japanese Public Opinion on Article 9 of the Constitution, 2009, as Reported by *Yomiuri Shimbun*

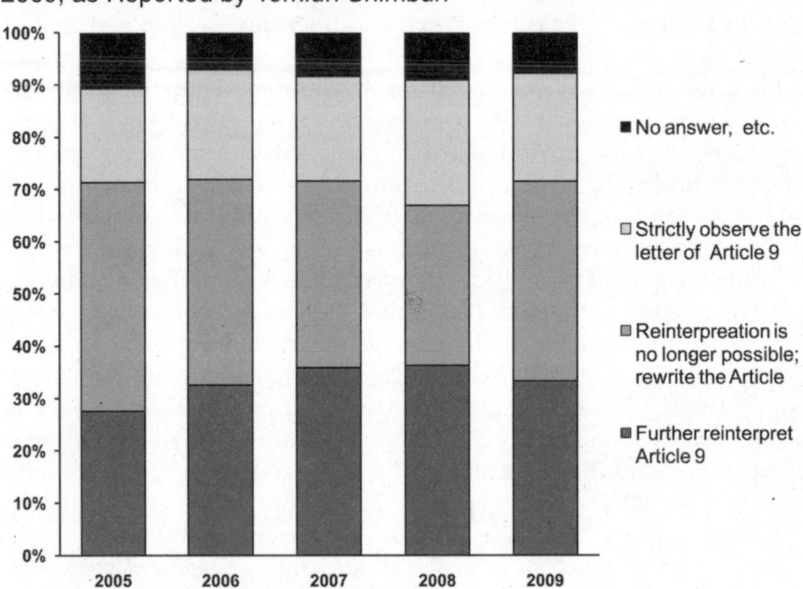

Source: *Yomiuri Shimbun*, 8 May 2009.

themselves. As well, the ideological attitude of the Abe government, which succeeded Koizumi's in 2006, did not help cultivate a broad consensus required for the revision of the Constitution. Although the Abe government managed to pass a national referendum law before it left office in 2007, it failed to secure bipartisan support. Thus, the greater exposure of hawkish nationalist intellectuals in Japan's mass media – for the longest time largely dominated by utopian pacifists – ironically has made constitutional revision more, rather than less, difficult. The Japanese public has become more cautious about revision because they have come to understand the issue in a partisan rather than pragmatic frame.

The recent reversal of the trend toward favouring constitutional revision, however, does not mean a return to the 'abnormal' intellectual landscape that prevailed before the 1990s. Discussion about revision is no longer regarded as the purview of extremists: even those who oppose revision now take a more practical attitude toward the issue, and some are even prepared to accept de facto revision by accepting

Figure 2.6: Japanese Public Feelings of Friendship for China, 1978–2008

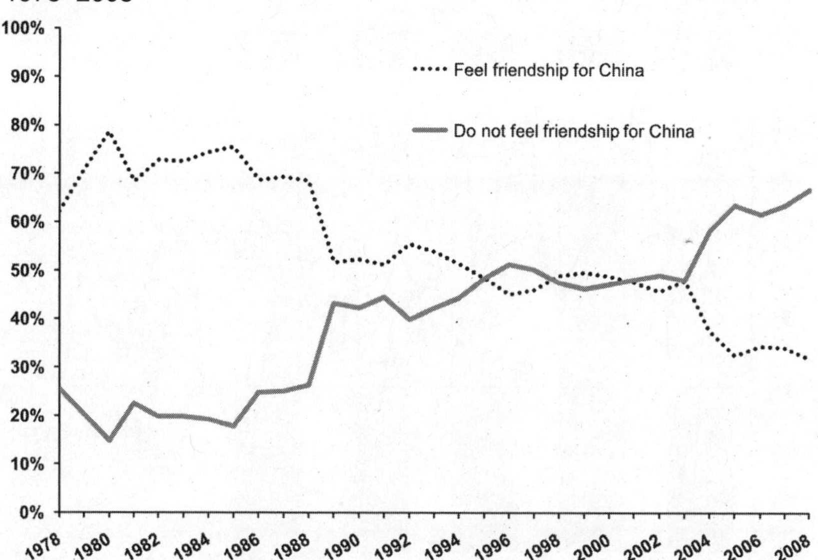

Source: Naikakuhu, Gaiko ni Kansuru Seronchosa, 2008; available online [in Japanese] at http://www8.cao.go.jp/survey/h20/h20-gaiko/ index.html, accessed 21January 2009.

constitutional reinterpretation to meet Japan's minimum but expanded security needs. Active discussion will continue, and revision will remain a realistic possibility, but it will occur only by retaining the basic values and institutions nurtured under the current Constitution, which the overwhelming majority of Japanese support.

The End of a 'Unique' Economy

While public opinion about the postwar constitutional system was undergoing significant change, the Japanese economy was fluctuating. In the late 1980s, it seemed invincible. Japan's economic performance was admired and even feared.[10] In the early 1990s, however, Japan entered a long period of economic stagnation; once admired, the Japanese economy soon became the subject of mockery, experiencing troughs in 1994 and again in 1998 (see Figure 2.7; see also Figure 2.8 for a comparison of Japan's growth rate in the 1990s with that of other

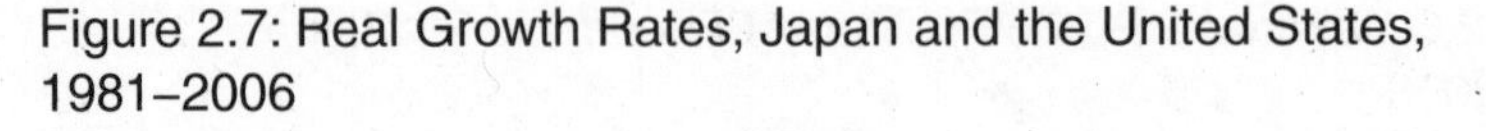

Figure 2.7: Real Growth Rates, Japan and the United States, 1981–2006

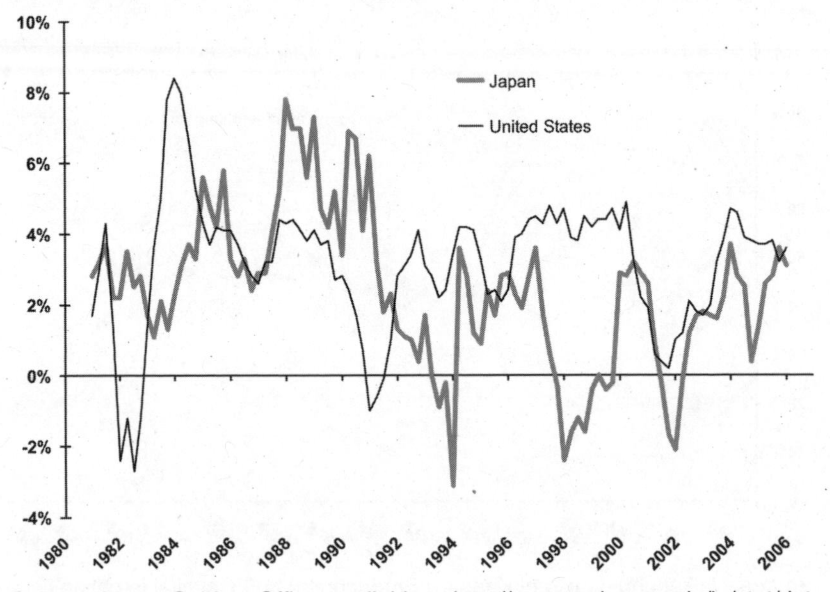

Source: Japan, Cabinet Office; available at http://www.esri.cao.go.jp/jp/stat/data, accessed 3 June 2009.

major economies). Both times, the Japanese government launched massive fiscal spending programs to stimulate demand, but the economy failed to reach its previous growth rates, and in 2002 the unemployment rate rose to as high as 5.4 per cent.[11] That year, *The Economist* summarized world opinion about Japan's economy in the following terms: 'The charitable consider Japan an irrelevance. The less charitable see it as a liability. The panicky see it as a danger. Most Japanese simply shrug their shoulders.'[12] But, just at the moment when Japan's economy began to look inconsequential, it took a turn for the better.

A lack of determination to settle bad loan problems is often blamed for prolonging Japan's economic stagnation. Although it would have been painful, an earlier decision to let insolvent banks go under would have led to a more rapid economic recovery. Major reforms to overhaul the very economic structure that created the financial bubble and perpetuated loan problems were often called for, but this was easier said than done. In fact, between 1996 and 1998, the government of Ryu-

Figure 2.8: Annual Economic Growth in the 1990s, Selected Countries

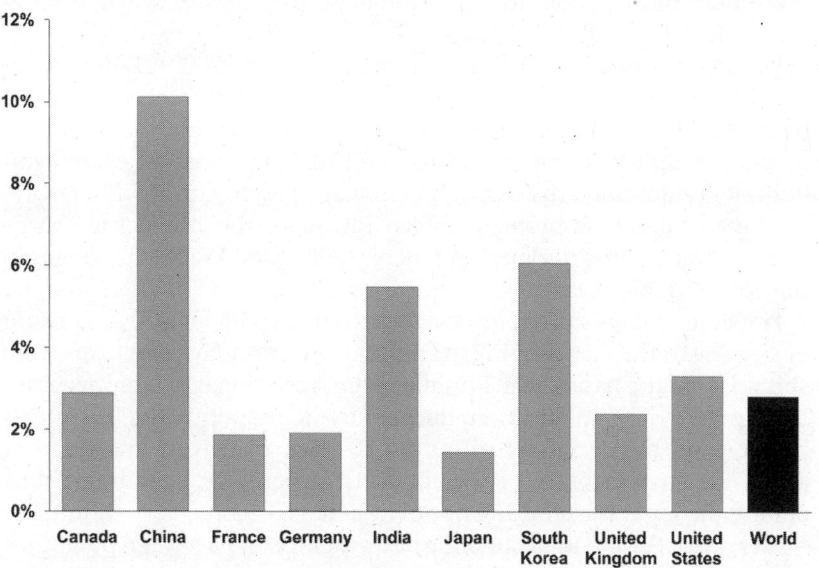

Source: World Bank, *World Development Index*; various issues.

taro Hashimoto launched a series of structural reforms with optimistic macroeconomic prospects, focusing on reforming central administration, economic regulations, the financial system, and fiscal and social security. The highly ambitious reform packages were largely in accordance with the prevailing neoclassical economic consensus and were blessed by a number of mainstream economists. When the mass media criticized Hashimoto's efforts, it was largely because they saw them as insufficient rather than as too drastic. The reforms were abandoned, however, as their deflationary impact coincided with the Asian financial crisis of 1997. Hashimoto was subsequently forced to resign, following the LDP's dismal performance in the Upper House election of 1998 in the face of severe criticism both within and outside Japan that called for reflation rather than a painful deflationary structural reform program.

Nonetheless, by 2004 Japan's self-sustained economic recovery had begun, and in 2005, despite its earlier pessimistic view, *The Economist* now claimed that 'The slow and steady really do win races, and ... Japan has been going through a long wave of incremental reforms, which together have changed politics, the economy and financial markets far more than most people realize, promising the country a bright long-term future.'[13]

Unlike the short-lived expansions of 1996–97 and 2000–01, this recovery was not the result of fiscal spending. The balance sheets of Japanese banks and businesses improved a great deal as a result of a decade of restructuring; the rescue in 2004 of the Daiei supermarket chain symbolically represented the end of the process of restructuring and resolving Japan's bad loan problem. Heizo Takenaka, the minister in charge of economic affairs, declared in January 2005 that 'We are no longer in the "post bubble" era.'[14]

However, Japan's economy still faces several challenges. As a result of large-scale deficit spending to stimulate the economy, bad loans were shifted from the banks to the public sector, resulting in a large accumulated public debt. In addition, the rapidly aging population is putting pressure on the social security system. With perceived uncertainties about the sustainability of social security spending, spending habits among the Japanese working population have become very cautious.

The impact of Japan's economic performance on its foreign policy has been variably interpreted. For some, Japan's growing economy translated into a desire to have greater political influence in world politics; for others, it was a threat that had to be contained. From this perspective, Japan's economic stagnation would maintain its 'abnormalcy' and diminish its aspirations for political influence as its relative economic power declined. By contrast, during the decade after the financial bubble, when economic stagnation was at its worst, many argued that Japan's economic setbacks had resulted in a 'rightward drift,' prompting the government leadership to attempt to alleviate social frustration through aggressive nationalist policies.

Neither explanation, however, is persuasive. First, even during the period of economic stagnation, economic life for most Japanese had not deteriorated as dramatically as some foreign commentators suggested. Although Japan's economic success was exaggerated in the late 1980s, its weaknesses, while real, were also overstated. Despite stagnation, most Japanese continued to enjoy affluent material lives. The total loss of capital when Japan's economic bubble burst is estimated to have been as high as ¥1,100 trillion, comparable to the 44 per cent drop in gross domestic product that the United States underwent during the Great Depression between 1929 and 1933, and yet Japan experienced nothing like the same degree of social dislocation and economic stress.

Figure 2.9: Unemployment Rate, Selected Countries, 1991–2003

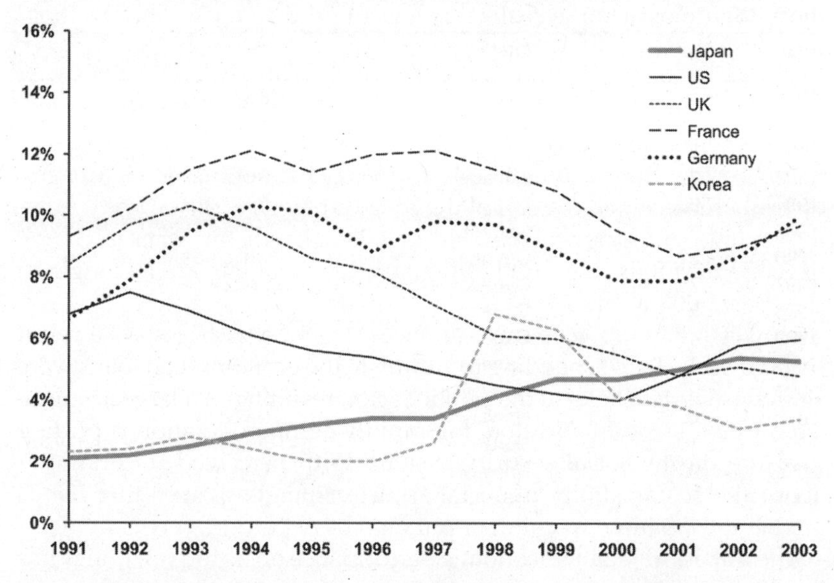

Source: International Labour Organization; available online at http://ilo.org/, accessed 3 June 2009.

Even during stagnation, Japan's economy managed to grow by more than 1 per cent per year – not an impressive figure, but far from disastrous. And, as Figure 2.9 shows, while Japan's unemployment rate rose substantially during this time, it was still relatively lower than that of the United States and many wealthy European countries. Even during the 'lost decade,' Japan ranked highly according to the Human Development Index used by the United Nations Development Program (see Table 2.2). Thus, although the Japanese economy clearly lacked vitality in the 1990s, the Japanese standard of living was maintained. Japanese economic life in the 1990s is thus best described as 'stagnation under affluence.'

Nonetheless, gradual but steady changes in Japanese economic life may have brought deeper changes than many expected. The cumulative effects of repetitive deregulation and privatization suggest that the Japanese economy, for better or worse, has become more liberal. The greatly increased foreign direct investment of the past few years could transform the economic landscape. Japan's downturn also shattered the authority of the economic bureaucracy, as was evident by the out-

Table 2.2: Human Development Index (HDI) Rankings, Japan and Top Countries, 1990–2007

Year	Japan's Rank	First	Second (Third)
1990	1	Japan	Sweden
1991	1	Japan	Canada
1992	2	Canada	Japan
1993	3	Canada	Switzerland
1994	3	Canada	Switzerland
1995	3	Canada	United States
1996	3	Canada	United States
1997	7	Canada	France
1998	8	Canada	France
1999	4	Canada	Norway
2000	9	Canada	Norway
2001	9	Norway	Australia
2002	9	Norway	Sweden
2003	10	Norway	Australia and Iceland (tied)
2004	9	Norway	Canada
2005	9 (tied with Switzerland and France)	Iceland and Norway (tied)	(Canada)
2006	8 (tied with Luxembourg)	Iceland and Norway (tied)	(Canada)
2007	10	Norway	Australia

Source: United Nations Development Programme, *Human Development Indices* (New York: UNDP, various years); available online at http://hdr.undp.org/en/, accessed 6 January 2011.

cry over Ministry of Finance scandals. But the stagnation was not devastating enough to make the Japanese desperate. As well, economic growth already had ceased to be the unquestionable top concern of the Japanese public long before the bubble burst. With per capita income nearly 30 times greater than in China, economic growth had long since lost its postwar urgency as a primary goal for the Japanese. Despite the pessimistic economic outlook, Japanese themselves were not alarmed. Able to enjoy basic stability and maintain an affluent quality of life despite the economic stagnation, their frustration was focused more on structural corruption resulting from the symbiotic relationship among politicians, interest groups, and bureaucrats.

In fact, over the decade following the burst of the financial bubble, it was not economic growth that dominated Japan's political agenda.

The priority of the Morihiro Hosokawa government, which came into power in 1993 as the first non-LDP cabinet in 38 years, with enormous popular support and high expectations, was not economic reflation but political reform. The Hashimoto administration, the next significant government after a brief interlude of two weak cabinets, also focused on politico-economic reforms rather than economic recovery. Hashimoto's successor, Keizo Obuchi, was preoccupied with reflating the Japanese economy after the financial crisis in 1997. Junichirō Koizumi came into office stressing structural reform, rather than simple reflation, as the route to long-term, sustainable economic recovery.

It is true that economic growth under the postwar Japanese constitutional system meant more than just material affluence; it was a means to improve Japan's international status while at the same time remaining committed to a policy that precluded heavy and direct involvement in the military politics of the day. The hard lesson of the 1980s bubble economy was that, rather than garnering international respect, Japan's prosperity and peacefulness prompted criticism and jealousy from abroad. In fact, economic growth, once effective in integrating an ideologically divided Japan, ceased to be a cohesive force once Japan had caught up economically in the 1980s. The converse was also true: as economic growth became less critical in the minds of Japanese, a stagnant economy did not produce notable social unrest.

The economic stagnation of the past decade in Japan was neither serious nor important enough to panic the Japanese or cause them to give up on the basic postwar values and institutions that had served their interests so remarkably well over the previous 60 years. The shift in Japanese external attitudes in the 1990s was not a product of economic stagnation; rather, it resulted from long-term changes in basic conditions that had previously sustained Japan's 'abnormalcy,' such as the end of ideological division within the country, the completion of economic catch-up, and the desire to respond to newly emerging post–Cold War security demands, including peacekeeping and the maintenance of regional stability.

What Would a 'Normal' Japan Want?

If its primary goal is no longer to further its material affluence, much less pursue military supremacy, what would Japan want by becoming 'normal'? In other words, what would a 'normal' Japan want to do? The most prominent answer suggests that a 'normal' Japan would be more

Figure 2.10: How Strongly Do Japanese Love Their Country?

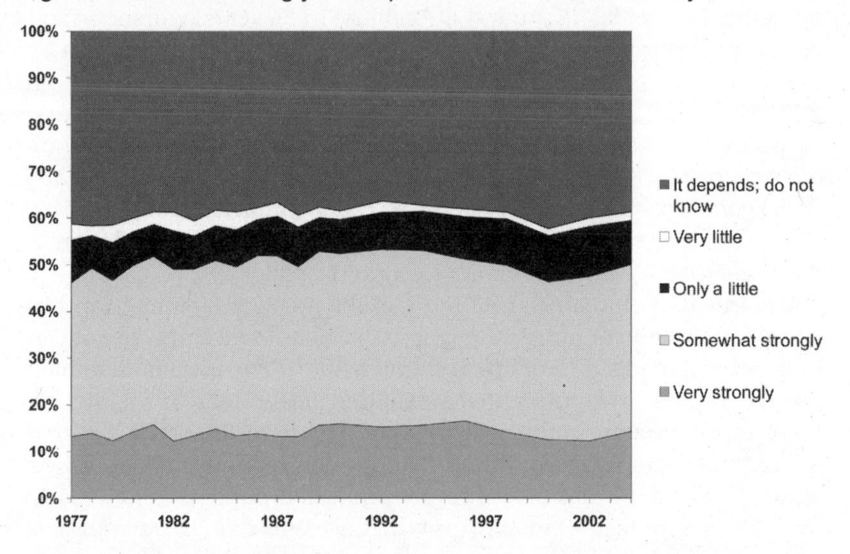

Source: Naikaku Daijinkanbo Seihukohoshitsu, Seikatsu Ishiki ni Kansuru Ishikichosa (interpolated); available online [in Japanese] at http://www.cao/go/survey/index-sha.html, accessed 1 November 2005.

nationalistic. Japan's 'rising nationalism' has been a recurrent theme in discussions of its normalization, beginning as early as the 1960s during its economic ascent. Debates about Japanese nationalism persisted well into the 1980s and early 1990s, when Japan's financial bubble led to exaggerated images of the country's economic might. Interestingly, even during the decade of economic stagnation, Japanese nationalism persisted as a focal point of discussion, albeit for completely different reasons. Yet opinion surveys conducted in the 1990s reveal remarkable stability in national attitudes: consistently, about half the population demonstrates positive attitudes toward their country, while only 10 per cent have a negative view (Figure 2.10).

Japanese also fail to demonstrate a strong nationalist sentiment when compared with attitudes in other countries. A 2000 World Values Survey showed that the Japanese are one of the least 'nationalistic' people in the world: of 74 countries ranked from highest to lowest in terms of nationalist sentiment, Japan came in seventy-first, a ranking similar to other high-income countries such as the Netherlands (fifty-seventh),

Figure 2.11: The Kind of Love Japanese Have for Their Country, 1973–2003

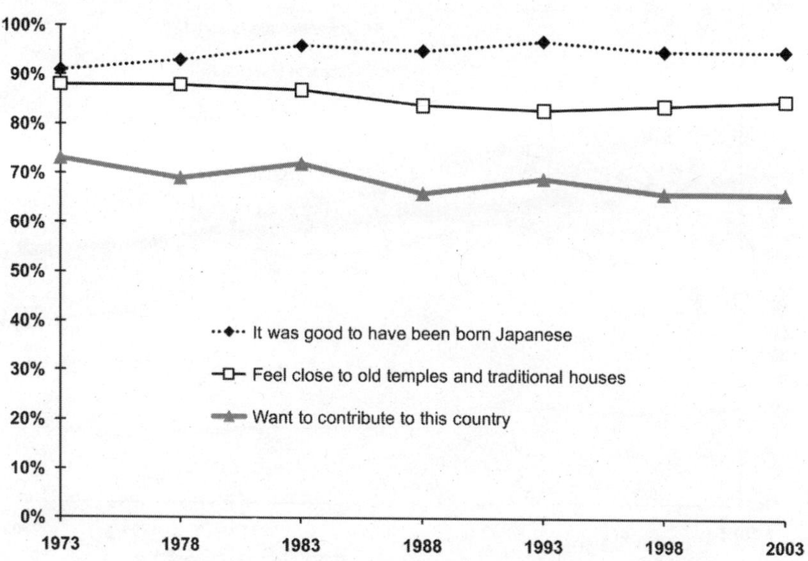

Source: Kono Kei and Kao Motonori, 'Nihonjin no Ishikichosa Ni Miru Sanjunen 1 - Teikasuru Jikokueno Jishin, 1,' *Hoso Kenkyu to Chosa*, February 2004, p. 28.

Belgium (sixty-seventh), and Germany (sixty-eighth). The highest-ranked countries, in contrast, were relatively Egypt (first), the Philippines (second), and Vietnam (third).[15] The percentage of those who answered 'yes' to the question of whether one was prepared to fight in a war was lowest among Japanese, a result similar to a study conducted in 1995.[16] In the same 2000 survey, China ranked fourth, South Korea twentieth, India twenty-first, and the United States thirty-sixth, Italy thirty-ninth, Canada fortieth, France forty-first, and Germany fifty-sixth. Thus, even among countries with low rankings, the level of aversion to war on the part of Japanese was conspicuous.

'Nationalism,' however, is a notoriously vague term, and these surveys should not be taken to mean that Japanese are overwhelmingly dissatisfied with being Japanese. An opinion survey conducted by NHK, the national broadcasting company, showed that a great many Japanese are happy to be Japanese (Figure 2.11), although their satisfaction seems to be related more to cultural identity than to particular political ideologies or a sense of material superiority to other countries.

Figure 2.12: Japanese Self-confidence, 1973–2003

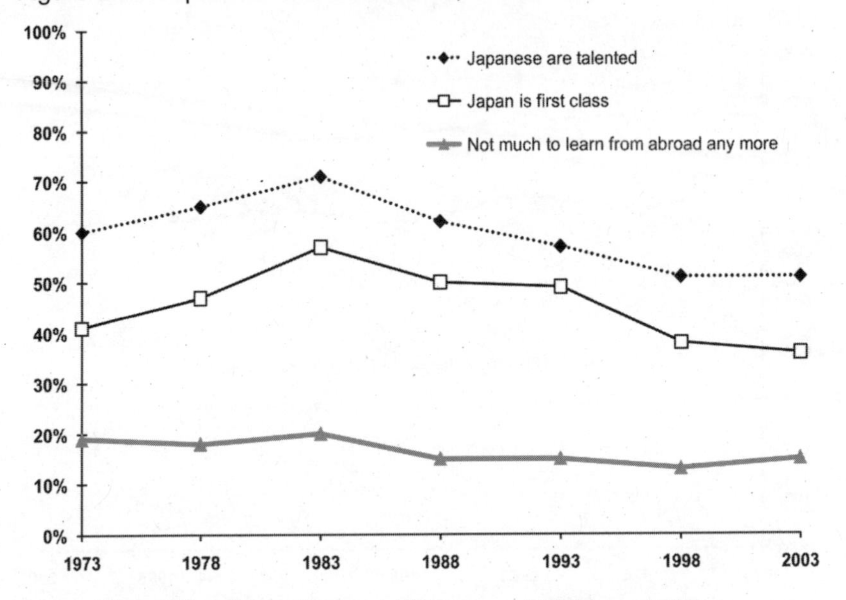

Source: Kono Kei and Kao Motonori, 'Nihonjin no Ishikichosa Ni Miru Sanjunen 1 - Teikasuru Jikokueno Jishin, 1,' *Hoso Kenkyu to Chosa*, February 2004, p. 27.

If 'nationalism' is not a major driving force of the Japanese mentality, what do Japanese value about their country? Over the past three decades, the government has conducted a series of surveys that ask: 'What aspects of Japan are you proud of?' NHK has also been asking questions concerning Japanese 'self-confidence' since 1973. Figures 2.12 and 2.13 summarize findings from two surveys that potentially contradict assumptions about Japan that are held abroad.

First, economic prosperity in itself has never been the most important part of Japanese self-esteem, a finding that is consistent with the fact that Japanese 'self-esteem' declined in the late 1980s during the peak of Japan's economic prosperity. Economic prosperity had already been comprehensively realized by then, generating its own distinctive set of problems. The financial bubble might have attracted the attention of those who were interested in Japanese money, but that was not matched by increased respect for the Japanese people and their way of life. Endless trade disputes with the United States, and negative reactions on the part of some Americans to Japan's eye-catching economic

Figure 2.13: Things that Make Japanese Proud, 1974–2005

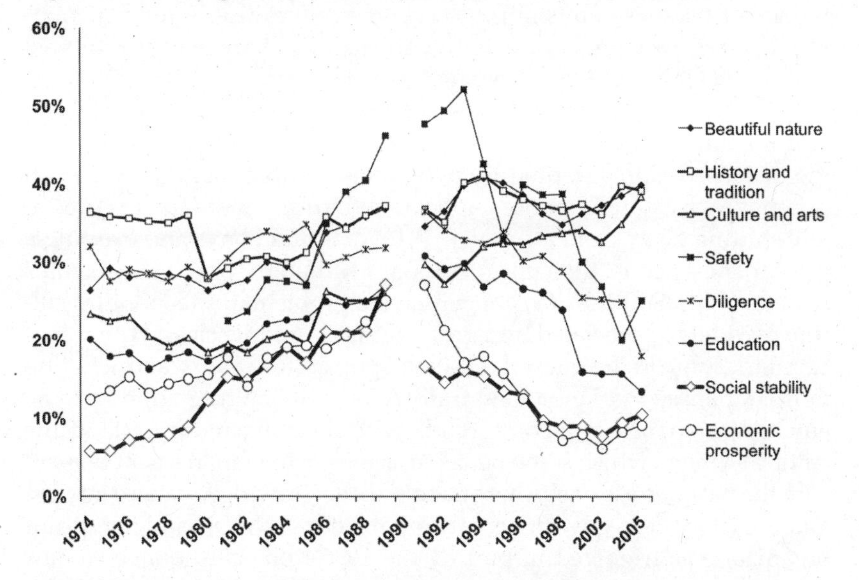

Source: Naikakuhu, Shakai Ishiki ni Kansuru Chosa; available online [in Japanese] at http://www8.cao.go.jp/survey/index-sha.html, accessed 5 June 2009.

performance during the bubble phase caused the Japanese people sadness and bitterness, not self-satisfaction. Second, over the past decade, Japanese have become less materialistic in their values. There has been both a clear decline of popular concern for economic prosperity and the work ethic and greater importance attached to culture, the arts, and environmental conservation. Third, while Japanese are generally happy with their standard of living and way of life, there is a growing sense of insecurity and lack of self-confidence about the future of their country.

From these observations, it is difficult to characterize the Japanese social consciousness as having undergone a 'rightward drift.' The current Japanese value orientation seems to be consistent with what Ronald Inglehart has called 'post-materialism.'[17] A cross-national opinion survey of Japanese society today supports this claim. Japanese are generally characterized as largely satisfied with the material aspects of their lives. They value tolerance and responsibility, but regard diligence as less important than was once the case; they are relatively indifferent to religion or to any kind of doctrinal value system; and their political identification with their country is weak. In this sense, the value orientations of Japanese are similar to citizens of wealthy European countries such as Sweden, France, Italy, and Spain, and are in sharp contrast to those of Chinese, South Koreans, or Americans.[18]

This characterization of Japanese values is also consistent with several notable sociological developments since the 1990s. For instance, the increased global popularity of 'manga,' animation films, and even pop novels by young authors appears to indicate that Japan is gradually shifting away from a country of Toyotas and Sonys and exerting a greater presence in the cultural arena.[19] Although, politically, Japan's relations with South Korea and China are problematic, its popular culture is widely appreciated by a growing Asian middle class. With a concomitant surge in the interest of Korean pop culture overseas, including in the Japanese market, a new trans-Asian civil culture appears to be emerging. Japanese are comfortable with their expanding role in the cultural sphere, which some perceive as increasing Japan's 'soft power.'

In the past decade or so, there has also been growing Japanese interest and activity in non-governmental organizations (NGOs) and non-profit organizations, triggered in part by the 1995 Kobe earthquake. Today, an increasing number of ambitious young Japanese, who traditionally would have joined the civil service or taken jobs in the corporate sector, now look for careers in the international public sector. Such a trend also indicates that young and talented Japanese are motivated by non-materialistic values or personally rewarding goals.

Conclusion

Japan's postwar 'abnormalcy,' which emerged as an equilibrium of a variety of contradictory elements in the country's domestic and international situation, is no longer consistent with its security needs or with the emotional needs of the Japanese people. Although Japan has been cautiously lifting its self-imposed restrictions on its security policy, the demise of its postwar utopian pacifism, coupled with economic slowdown, neither represents a rejection of postwar institutions and ideals nor heralds a return to the militarism of the 1930s. On the contrary, the shift in attitudes since the 1990s is motivated by the values and practices that the existing Constitution has nurtured. Given the existing value orientation of the Japanese people, it is unthinkable that a revision of the Constitution, if it were to take place at all, would change basic postwar values such as democracy, respect for human rights, and

Figure 2.14: Japanese Public Opinion on Amending the Constitution, 1993–2010, as Reported by *Yomiuri Shimbun*

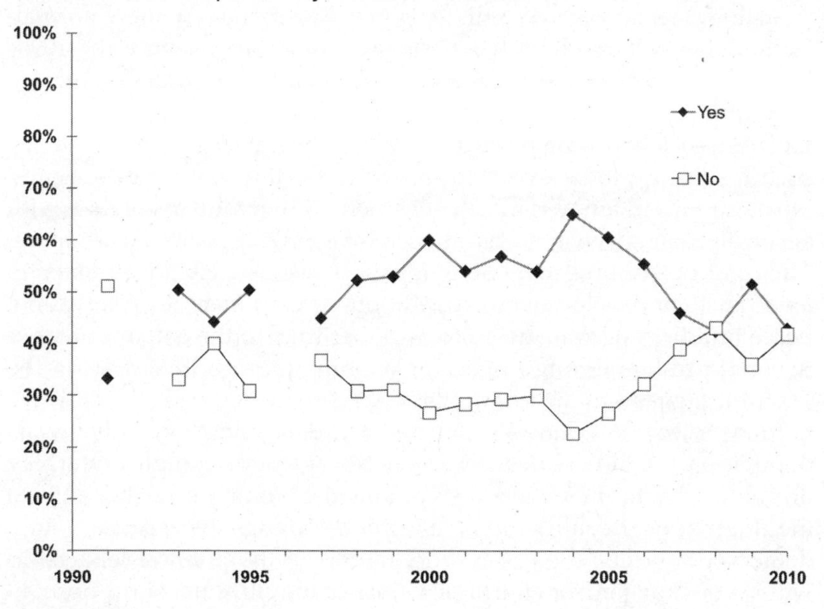

Source: *Yomiuri Shimbun*.

a renunciation of the search for military supremacy. Thus, to the chagrin of anachronistic nationalists such as General Toshio Tamogami,[20] the louder the voices denying postwar values and practices, the more likely the Japanese population will stick with postwar 'abnormalcy.'

The recent trend of opinion polls regarding revision of the Constitution may be indicative of the Japanese attitude. The surveys conducted by the *Yomiuri Shimbun* show a decline of support for revision (see Figure 2.14). Opinion favourable to revision peaked in 2004, but in spring 2008 a narrow majority opposed revision for the first time since 1993. The timing coincided with a rapid rise of hawkish traditionalist voices denying the postwar Japanese identity, which seems to have alarmed the Japanese public.

A stagnant economy coupled with an active security policy is often interpreted as a cause for 'rightward drift' in Japanese society. However, Japanese economic hardship since the 1990s tends to be exaggerated. More significantly, material values have become less important for the Japanese than many assume.

If a 'normal' Japan implies neither a return to militarism prompted by economic stagnation nor an economic animal trying to transform its material resources into military power, what does Japanese normalization signify? Trends in Japanese value orientations since the 1990s indicate that postmodern values are supplanting desires for material wealth. This outcome should not be surprising. Given changes in Japanese society during 60 years of relative peace and great prosperity, such results are to be expected. As with wealthy European societies, Japanese society today is more concerned with quality of life than with ensuring basic survival needs and achieving greater material affluence. Thus, it is no surprise that young Japanese increasingly are attracted to areas such as development cooperation, environmental preservation, peace building, or arts and culture, rather than to the enhancement of national prestige through riches or winning more gold medals in the Olympic games – much less military supremacy.

To be sure, no country's policies are determined directly by its population's value orientations. They result from a complex interplay of political institutions, leadership, and the country's relationship to the international community, among other things. Nevertheless, in a democratic society, the policy orientations of the political leadership will never stray far from the basic values of the citizenry. For a 'normal' Japan, the quest for traditional great power status comparable to that of the United States or China is an unattractive goal, even if it were possible. Rather, the value orientations of a normal Japan suggest an inclination toward multilateralism and the international rule of law, not the attainment of economic or strategic supremacy.

This benevolent future is certainly not inevitable: postmodern behaviour, after all, is possible only after modern values are sufficiently attained. A severe economic crisis or proximate military threats could drag Japan into games of strategic competition and economic survival. Given apprehension about the rapid rise of an assertive China and a unilateralist United States, it is conceivable that a serious sense of threat or national humiliation could change the dominant value orientation of Japanese. Moreover, unlike their European counterparts, whose security is generally guaranteed by a concerted effort on the part of the European Union and whose members largely share postmodern values, Japanese are still surrounded by modern or modernizing countries whose world views are still strongly conditioned by concerns about competition for territory and economic dominance.[21] In such a regional environment, Japan still could face difficulties pursuing postmodern values in its foreign policy. Thus, a 'normal' Japan must strive to create regional and international environments that allow it to pursue its postmodern goals.

NOTES

1 For this type of view, see, for example, Tsuneari Fukuda, *Nihon o Omou* [Thinking of Japan] (Tokyo: Bungeishunju, 1969). For a more recent argument on the same line, see Hidetsugu Yagi, *Nihonkoku Kenpou Towa Nanika* [What is the Japanese Constitution?] (Tokyo: PHP, 2003).

2 For an influential contemporary view on this position, see for example, Heiwamondai Kondaikai, 'Mitabi Heiwa ni Tsuite' [On peace, for the third time], *Sekai*, December 1950.

3 I have discussed the structure of the constitutional system and its establishment in the 1960s elsewhere: 'Keizaitaikoku no Gaiko no Genkei' [The prototype of diplomacy as an economic power], in *Sengo Nihon Gaikoshi* [Diplomatic history of postwar Japan], edited by Makoto Iokibe (Tokyo: Yushikaku, 1999).

4 'Kamikaze Pacifists,' *The Economist*, 18 December 1982, p. 11.

5 Naohiro Amaya, a former official of the Ministry of International Trade and Industry who represented Japan on many tough trade negotiations with the United States, called Japan a 'Choninkokka,' or tradesman (as opposed to Samurai) state. He had clearly noticed the limit of an economic giant without political power by the early 1980s. See his article, 'Choninkokka Nihon, Tedai no Kurigoto' [Tradesman nation Japan: The grumble of an assistant manager], *Bungeishunju*, March 1980.

6 Steven Erlanger, 'The world: the search for a new security umbrella,' *New York Times*, 12 May 1991; available online at http://www.nytimes.com/1991/05/12/weekinreview/the-world-the-search-for-a-new-security-umbrella.html?pagewanted=2.

7 Both newspapers have strong and differing attitudes toward constitutional revisions, with *Asahi* committed to protecting the Constitution and *Yomiuri* calling for revision. Questions are phrased differently and framed in different contexts. Some survey respondents, when aware of the identity of the newspaper conducting a given survey, declined to respond to the questionnaire, citing their opposition to the newspaper's political position. As a result, there is a limited but significant distortion in the two surveys, with respondents to each questionnaire tending to be somewhat sympathetic to the ideological position of the originating newspaper. Thus, the results of

the two set of surveys are shown separately. The two sets of surveys show precisely the same trend, although one tends to overstate and the other to understate this pattern.

8 Seiji Maehara and Ichirō Ozawa were successively elected leaders the DPJ in 2005 and 2006. Both were supporters of constitutional revision.

9 Regarding the Socialist Party, see, for example, Yoshihisa Hara, *Sengoshi no Naka no Nihonsyakaito* [The Socialist Party of Japan in postwar Japanese history] (Tokyo: Chuokoron-Shinsha, 2000); and Jiro Yamaguchi and Masumi Ishikawa, eds., *Nihonshakaito: Sengokakushin no Shiso to Kodo* [The Socialist Party of Japan: The thought and behaviour of postwar reformists] (Tokyo: Nihon Keizai Hyoronsha, 2003).

10 See, for example, James Fallows, 'Containing Japan,' *Atlantic Monthly,* May 1989.

11 Japan, Ministry of Internal Affairs and Communications, Statistics Bureau, Director-General for Policy Planning; available online at http://www.stat.go.jp/data/roudou/sokuhou/tsuki/index.htm, accessed 15 May 2005.

12 'The Sadness of Japan,' *The Economist*, 16 February 2002, p. 11.

13 'The Sun Also Rises,' *The Economist*, 8 October 2005, p. 11.

14 Minister Takenaka's economic address in the lower house on 21 January 2005 is available online at http://www.ioc.u-tokyo.ac.jp/~worlDPJn/, accessed 25 May 2005.

15 Takahashi Toru, *Nihonjin no Kachikan, Sekai Rankingu* [Value consciousness of the Japanese in global perspective] (Tokyo: Chuokoron-Shinsha, 2003), pp. 74–5.

16 Ibid., pp. 66–7.

17 See Ronald Inglehart, *Culture Shift in Advanced Industrial Society* (Princeton, NJ: Princeton University Press, 1990).

18 Takahashi, *Nihonjin no Kachikan, Sekai Rankingu*, pp. 17–32.

19 Douglas McGray, 'Japan's Gross National Cool,' *Foreign Policy,* June 2002; and 'Japan's Culture,' *Time*, 11 August 2003.

20 General Tamogami, then chief of staff of the Air Self-Defense Force, argued in a prize-winning submission to a 2008 APA Group essay competition that Japan is falsely accused of invading China and that Japan's Pearl Harbor attack was caused by U.S. conspiracy ('Nihon wa Shiryaku Kokka de Attaka' ['Was Japan an Aggressor Nation?'] reprinted in the January 2009 issue of *Seiron* and available in English translation at http://www.apa.co.jp/book_report/images/2008jyusyou_saiyuusyu_english.pdf). While his essay does not merit serious academic examination, it represents a typical right-wing frustration that Japan's past is unfairly treated by the victors of World War Two, and this imposed history still prevents Japan from

acting as a fully independent nation. General Tamogami was immediately sacked by the government. Later, in his parliamentary testimony, he repeated his view and called for revision of the Constitution.

21 Akihiko Tanaka, in dividing the world into the three spheres – postmodern, modern, and chaotic – argues that, between the postmodern and modern, the interplay resembles the one of modernity. See his *Atarashii Chusei* [A new middle age] (Tokyo: Nihon Keizai Shimbun Sha, 1996).

3 A 'Normal' Middle Power: Interpreting Changes in Japanese Security Policy in the 1990s and After

YOSHIHIDE SOEYA

The concept of 'Japan as a normal country' presupposes some 'abnormalcy' in postwar Japanese security policy. The context in which the concept initially was raised indicates that 'abnormalcy' had to do with Japan's inadequate adjustment to the end of the Cold War in general and its inability to respond to the crisis leading to the Gulf War in 1990 and 1991 in particular. The Gulf War was the first test case for the international community to manage a major crisis after the end of the Cold War. Japan's catastrophic failure to be part of multinational efforts to counter the invasion of Kuwait by Iraq, except for providing a gigantic financial contribution of US$13 billion, gave rise to an acute sense of crisis among policy-makers and opinion leaders in Japan regarding the relevance of Japanese security policy for the post–Cold War global order. Here, the basic assumption shared by the central opinion- and decision-makers was that the 'abnormalcy' in postwar Japanese security policy was rooted in Japan's inability to play an appropriate role in the management of international security.

During and after this crisis, therefore, how to get over dominant postwar constraints on Japanese participation in international security – most notably, United Nations peacekeeping operations – became an issue of central concern for the Japanese government. It was precisely in this context that Ichirō Ozawa raised the concept of 'Japan as a normal country.' His motivations were essentially internationalist rather than nationalistic, and the debate about a possible revision of the postwar peace Constitution began to gain some legitimacy in Japanese society precisely because of this internationalist bent.

Japan's post–Cold War awakening to the mission of international security laid the groundwork for a series of changes in its security policies in the 1990s and thereafter, in the overall context of responding to newly emerging challenges. They include the 'reaffirmation' of the United States-Japan alliance in the mid-1990s, a commitment to human security toward the end of the decade, and, more recently, the resurgence of a somewhat 'normal' agenda concerning national security. This sequence of evolution is important because this implies that the Japanese public would not have given due attention to a traditional security and defence agenda without changes in internationalist domains both triggering and preceding the process of 'normalization.'

A confusion in the discourse on Japan as a 'normal country' often arises from the conviction of sceptics – dominant in China and, to a lesser extent, in South Korea – who mistake this process for Japan's 'conspiring' to revert to traditional great power status in geopolitical terms. Realities in the 1990s proved, however, that the sceptics' concerns are entirely unfounded. Adding to the confusion in more recent years is the fact that somewhat nationalistic political actors and a somewhat nationalistic agenda gradually have gained influence in Japanese society. Explicating this phenomenon is extremely important, because even if its resurgence had happened only on the basis of Japan's move toward an internationally 'normal' direction, it is not entirely impossible for traditional nationalists to take advantage of the changes and hijack the process of 'normalization.' For many observers outside of Japan, this may appear to be the case, but I argue that this is simply a transitional and somewhat 'reactionary' phenomenon after the collapse of the '1955 regime,' characterized by the monopoly of power during the Cold War by the Liberal Democratic Party (LDP) over the Japan Socialist Party (JSP), the perennial opposition party.

This argument implies that a nationalist agenda, deriving essentially from historical revisionism and anti-Chinese sentiment, compounded by a hard-line stance against North Korea, has no place to go and eventually will be frustrated not only by the dominant international realities rooted in the postwar San Francisco peace regime, but also by Japan's still-robust 'postwar consensus,' also rooted in the peace constructed in 1951 in San Francisco.

The impact of the landslide victory of the Democratic Party of Japan (DPJ) in the lower house election on 30 August 2009 is still uncertain. The shattering defeat of the LDP was not a verdict on its relatively conservative foreign policy agenda, but there appears to be considerable support for the rather liberal tone of DPJ foreign policy discourse, which emphasizes the importance of global issues, a non-traditional security agenda, and neighbourly diplomacy, including a positive vision of an East Asian Community.

What is likely to remain, I would argue – and what will likely guide the future course of Japanese diplomacy – is Japan's de facto 'middle power' choice. Much of Japan's postwar security policy was the product of the country's de facto middle power diplomacy, and the changes associated with Japan's move toward becoming a 'normal country' are relevant as an attempt to fix the 'abnormalcy' of a postwar Japan that prevented it from playing a due international role as a full-fledged middle power.

I thus contend that the incremental changes in Japanese security policy since the end of the Cold War in the domains of international security and the United States-Japan alliance, in fact, have consolidated the foundation of Japan's de facto middle power security policy. I also argue that, while this consolidation is important in itself, preoccupation with it has never been central to Japan's overall post–Cold War security policy agenda. Middle power diplomacy will be unstable without a solid foundation of traditional security and defence policy, but the strength of such diplomacy is to be demonstrated in areas other than where traditional security issues are central. In this context, I examine the Japanese devotion to human security as the diplomatic agenda that is appropriate for middle power diplomacy.

Japan's 'Postwar Consensus' and Middle Power Diplomacy

Japan's security policy after the nation's defeat in World War Two was built on deep remorse over its aggression in China and other Asian countries. Many in the defeated country embraced the pacifist Constitution, enacted in 1946, as the cornerstone of its postwar identity. In 1947, however, the Cold War broke out in Europe and gradually encroached on the Asian theatre. The beginning of the Korean War in 1950 dealt a decisive blow to the concept of a postwar order embraced by the allied powers during and immediately after World War Two. With the United States and communist China fighting on the Korean peninsula, Washington scrapped the idea of a postwar Asia with China as the central stabilizing factor and instead saw Japan as the cornerstone of its Asian strategy to confront the Soviet Union and China.

Thus, only a few years after its imposition, the constitutional stipulation of unarmed neutrality became an unrealistic option for Japan, and the constitutional renunciation of military capability lost its international relevance. Even so, then-prime minister Shigeru Yoshida resisted Washington's pressure to rearm by effectively arguing that Japan's Asian neighbours would resist and that there was a latent danger of resurgent militarism. In this resistance he had the support of the Japanese public. It was clear by then, however, that Japan could not ensure its security without arms, and, in 1951, in the midst of the Korean War, a security treaty with the United States was born.

This was the start of the 'Yoshida line' of foreign policy, built on the twin pillars of the war-renouncing Constitution and the United States-Japan Security Treaty. In adopting this policy, Japan renounced any ambition of winning a place among the major powers through the exercise of force. The policy thus eloquently expressed Japan's 'postwar consensus,' built on remorse over the country's wartime aggression in Asia and a determination to step down from the stage of power politics among major powers and follow a de facto middle power strategy.[1] With the signing of the San Francisco Peace Treaty in 1951, Japan embarked on a fresh start. The postwar 'San Francisco regime' served as the foundation for the Yoshida line, and contributed to Japan's postwar peace and prosperity.

The experience of postwar Japanese diplomacy is thus unique. From the ashes of war, Japan became the world's second-largest economy, but did not re-emerge as a traditional great power. A critical fact to recognize in explicating this experience is that Japan became an economic power precisely *by* engaging in de facto middle power diplomacy in the domain of traditional security. This, however, did not evolve without cost. Arguably, Japanese security policy in the postwar years fell short of that of a middle power, since Japan could not engage in the domain of international security other than through its alliance with the United States.

Article 9 of Japan's postwar peace Constitution, prohibiting the use of force as a means of settling international disputes, confined the military dimension of Japanese defence policy to the domain of self-defence in the strict sense of the term, delegitimizing the right of collective self-defence in the United States-Japan security arrangement, as well as involvement in the collective security mechanism under the UN Charter. Traditional security needs in the vicinity of Japan, in turn, were taken care of by the U.S. military presence. In the meantime, not having to face traditional security needs squarely and independently, Japan's postwar pacifism, rooted in the peace Constitution, became firmly rooted in the country's postwar strategic culture, making even the discussion of a Japanese military role almost taboo.

Structurally, this was possible precisely because of the security presence of the United States through the treaty arrangements. Thus, the peace Constitution and the United States-Japan Security Treaty have strangely coexisted under the fabric of the Yoshida line. Under these circumstances, while the United States managed the regional security environment around Japan during the Cold War, Japanese domestic politics evolved into a unique system, called the '1955 regime,' characterized by the ideological confrontation between the ruling LDP and left-wing opposition parties – most notably, the JSP and the Japan Communist Party. While the former was busy defending the legality of the Self-Defense Forces (SDF) and the Security Treaty, the latter two denounced these basic premises of the Yoshida line as unconstitutional.

The substance of Japan's postwar security policy-making process during the Cold War, therefore, was in essence a legal and constitutional debate between opposing political camps that hardly addressed any elements of a rational security strategy. The Yoshida line turned out to be long lived, mostly because the alternative course advocated by the left-wing opposition was simply unrealistic and because the capable bureaucrats of the Japanese government successfully defended the constitutionality of the SDF and the Security Treaty through a series of constitutional reinterpretations tantamount to 'intellectual acrobatics.'[2]

Conspicuous changes since the end of Cold War have ended the lack of rational strategic thinking imbedded in the Yoshida line, the basic cause of Japanese inaction in international security as well as in the management of the United States-Japan security relationship. Japan's move toward becoming a 'normal country' is, in essence, an attempt to fill the vacuum in its postwar security thinking and policy. What was once described as an insular 'one-country pacifism' has now become an internationalist proactive pacifism, opening the way for Japan's involvement in multinational peacekeeping activities. Meanwhile, the long-overdue task of substantiating the alliance cooperation with the United States for the peace and stability of the Far East and the world has also been making steady progress. In short, Japan has finally begun to follow the path of what is no doubt a long-term process of realizing a fully fledged middle power role.

There is still a long way to go, however. The roles and missions of the Japanese SDF for multilateral security operation are still fundamentally constrained by Article 9, while the Japanese government still denies that the right of collective self-defence is lawful under the United States-Japan alliance. After the March 2003 Iraq War, for instance, the Japanese government swiftly passed laws allowing the dispatch of Japanese troops to Iraq, but they were forbidden to engage in activities involving the use of force; instead, they conducted humanitarian relief activities such as purifying water, building and repairing roads and schools, and providing medical care under the military shield provided by Dutch, British, and Australian troops.[3]

Explaining the Rise of 'Nationalism'

Despite the obvious internationalist inclinations evident in the changes in Japanese security policy after the Cold War, there remains a strong tendency to interpret them as indicating a shift toward a greater military role for Japan in the traditional sense. This is largely due to the phenomenon of the rise of traditional 'nationalism' in Japanese domestic politics, which is wrongly taken as the central driver of these changes. Yet, as I demonstrate below, the rise of traditional 'nationalism' is but a symptom of a peculiar structural problem of postwar Japanese diplomacy, and it is a gross mistake to interpret it as providing a solution to the lack of 'autonomy.' Changes in Japanese security policy since the Cold War have been possible only because they have been sustained by internationalist inspirations and aspirations. Traditional nationalists have attempted to take advantage of these changes to advance their own agenda, but without much success.

Recent changes in Japan's security policy can be categorized into two types. The first is attempts to remedy exceedingly minimalist policies in the domain of international security, often labelled as 'one-country pacifism,' the context in which the concept of Japan as a 'normal country' was raised. This line of change constitutes the central aspect of the transformation of Japanese security policy in the 1990s and since. The same applies to the debate about Article 9. Previously, simply to say that revision should be 'debated' sounded hawkish, but today various opinion-makers and politicians have begun to debate alternative ideas. On balance, this is a sign of progress in the Japanese security debate. Public opinion in support of constitutional revision has steadily risen in this process, indicating that such revision is far from being an issue of nationalism for the majority of the Japanese public.

Having said this, however, the second set of changes entails a more complex set of elements that have been manifest – particularly since the demise of the '1955 regime' caused by the collapse of the Socialist Party – in the vocal protests by Japanese traditional nationalists against the postwar state of Japanese security policy and its premises. In fact, some conservatives in Japan have begun making arguments, even if unconsciously, that appear to advocate a 'revolutionary' course of action that would contravene the 'postwar consensus' and the peace formulated in San Francisco in 1951. Strong self-assertive views held by Japanese conservatives on the 'history problem' – such as the Tokyo war tribunal, the Yasukuni Shrine, and 'comfort women' – are cases in point. It is no secret that Shinzo Abe, who was prime minister between September 2006 and September 2007 was a strong believer in these somewhat revisionist views, which he categorically placed under the general slogan of 'departure from the postwar regime.'

Closely associated with these conservative urges is the call for 'assertive diplomacy,' which places a premium on universal values such as democracy and human rights. Abe's central agenda was the democratic alliance among Japan, the United States, Australia, and India,[4] and then-foreign minister Tarō Asō (prime minister from September 2008 to September 2009) advanced the concept of the 'arch of freedom and prosperity.'[5]

Hypothetically, this combination of historical revisionism and value-oriented 'assertive diplomacy' is a product of some trauma rooted in Japan's defeat in war and the subsequent experience of occupation, which many believe resulted in postwar Japan's lack of true 'independence.' Abe, for instance, explicitly argued that the ultimate purpose of the revision of the postwar Constitution, which was not written by the Japanese, was to 'regain independence.'[6]

In the perception of these conservative politicians, the biggest external obstacle to their agenda is China. They strongly believe that China uses the 'history card' to keep Japan down and to check Japan's move toward 'independence.' Thus, anti-China sentiments, historical revisionism, and the call for 'assertive diplomacy' have become inseparable in the post-traumatic psychology of many traditional nationalists in Japan.

If this hypothesis is correct, the good news is that their agenda could never develop into a workable strategy for Japan, because such a strategy would be tantamount to a 'revolution' not only in postwar Japanese diplomacy, but, more important, against the existing international regime, which is still essentially rooted in the San Francisco peace of which the United States is the ultimate guarantor. Apparently, these nationalistic assertions are nothing more than the sporadic venting of build-up frustrations, emanating from the trauma about the 'postwar consensus,' and are not part of an explicit strategy to turn back the clock.[7] The bad news, however, is that Chinese (and South Korean) obsession with and vocal opposition to the nationalist tone of these assertions only provides fuel for these nationalistic views and political forces in Japanese domestic politics. Such frustrations, therefore, increasingly are being vented haphazardly out of resentment toward attacks from China and South Korea.

Against this background, paradoxically enough, these isolated expressions by traditional nationalists have gained a degree of public support precisely because of a lack of a strategy on their part. Were a desire to revive Japan's prewar aspirations actually articulated clearly as a strategy, the Japanese public would be the first to reject it. This is why and how Abe's policy to mend relations with China and South Korea soon after his inauguration as prime minister in the fall of 2006, despite his deep-seated beliefs and ideology, were reasonably popular among the Japanese public. By breaking the vicious circle of emotionally charged criticism and countercriticism, the vast majority of the Japanese public undoubtedly would identify strongly with the 'postwar consensus,' which is still the basis of Japanese proactive pacifism since the end of the Cold War.

On examining Japan's strategic context, comprising institutional inertia, the dynamics of democratic competition, pragmatism, concern about the future of U.S. power, and the shifting regional balances of power, Richard Samuels concludes that these forces 'converge to make the discontinuation of Japan's revisionist course seem likely.'[8] Indeed, the recent revisionist, nationalistic mood in Japanese politics and society is in essence an excessive reaction to the rather extreme pacifist premises of postwar Japanese defence and security policies, and eventually will prove to be a transitional phenomenon. In the same way that the leftist pacifist proposition was unrealistic under the '1955 regime,' reactionary challenges from the 'right' today entail equally unrealistic elements and eventually will be marginalized once again in Japanese society.

In this dynamic process of transition, a somewhat naive nationalism has propelled changes such as transformation in January 2007 of the Japan Defense Agency into the Ministry of Defense, the enactment in May 2007 of procedural laws guiding the legal process of constitutional revision, and the establishment in May 2007 of a panel under then-prime minister Abe to consider the question of the right of collective self-defence with the United States. In essence, however, these changes have not gone beyond the premises of Japan's overall 'postwar consensus.' Even if Japan should recognize the right of collective self-defence and collective security, the outcome should be a much tighter alliance with the Untied States and full participation in multilateral security cooperation. Such a Japan, according to Samuels, 'may never again be as central to world affairs as it was in the 1930s nor as marginal to world affairs as it was during the Cold War.'[9]

In the early 1990s, Yoichi Funabashi presented the concept of a 'global civilian power' as an emerging identity for Japan after the end of the Cold War.[10] A blue-ribbon panel set up in 1999 under then-prime minister Keizo Obuchi also adopted the concept of a 'global civilian power' as a guidepost for Japan's optimal strategy.[11] Despite some confusion in the transitional phase, incurred by the temporary rise of the influence of traditional nationalists, the robust premises of Japan's 'postwar consensus,' the deep cause of Japan's postwar success, will not die away easily; instead, they will be further strengthened by Japan's move toward becoming a 'normal country' – that is, a full-fledged 'middle power.'

In this theorization of Japan's security profile, participation in international security and management of the United States-Japan alliance are important components of the current and future direction of Japanese security policy. It is interesting and important that, in the current Japanese debate, even traditional nationalists do not deny the importance of these basic premises of Japanese security policy, indicating once again that they are not necessarily motivated by any sense of alternative strategy.

Three Dimensions of Post–Cold War Changes

In order to demonstrate the above arguments, in the remainder of this chapter I trace the evolution of changes in Japan's security policy since the end of the Cold War in the domains of international security, the United States-Japan alliance, and national defence. I then examine the Japanese commitment to human security, which demonstrates the value of non-traditional security for Japan's middle power strategy – a sort of niche diplomacy providing an opportunity for a middle power to pursue an 'independent' security policy.

Awakening to International Security

In the domain of international security, the 1991 Gulf War was a critical turning point, awakening the Japanese government to the new realities of the post–Cold War era. After Iraq's invasion of Kuwait in August 1990, the government of Toshiki Kaifu, anticipating a multinational military action led by the United States under the auspices of the United Nations, attempted to pass legislation authorizing the SDF to take part in logistical support for the expected military operations against Iraq. Owing to the still dominantly pacifist culture of Japanese society and politics, however, the Japanese government failed in the attempt, provoking harsh criticism by the international community, particularly the United States, of the 'abnormalcy' of Japanese inaction.

Following the swift victory in the Gulf War by the U.S.-led multinational forces, Japan was again challenged by the Paris Accords on peace in Cambodia, signed in October 1991 under the leadership of the five permanent members of the UN Security Council. The United Nations Transitional Authority in Cambodia (UNTAC) began operations in March 1992 with the arrival of its head, Yasushi Akashi, in Phnom Penh as the special representative of the UN secretary-general. This time, however, the humiliation resulting from the Japanese government's inability, other than through 'chequebook diplomacy,' to contribute to the multinational effort to defeat Iraq, was a central driving force behind the enactment in June 1992 of the International Peace Cooperation Law (known as the PKO law).

The passage of the PKO law enabled the Japanese government to dispatch the SDF for peacekeeping operations under the rubric of UNTAC – the first time Japanese troops had conducted operations on foreign soil since World War Two. This was a dream come true for the Ministry of Foreign Affairs (MOFA), which had been fighting against a set of 'abnormal' elements preventing Japan from taking part in 'normal' multinational security cooperation for a long time. The term widely used in Japan to describe this aspiration was 'international contribution,' which, in effect, expressed Tokyo's eagerness to be a responsible player in the management of international peace and order, and was a strong motivation for Japan's bid to become a permanent member of the UN Security Council.[12]

The SDF's experience in Cambodia under UNTAC proved to be successful, encouraging the Japanese government to dispatch troops to a number of other UN peacekeeping missions, including those in Zaire, Mozambique, the Golan Heights, and East Timor.[13] The rules of engagement for Japanese troops are quite strict, prohibiting them from being involved in the actual use of force except for self-protection in the narrowest sense of the term. This has resulted in the SDF mostly engaging in humanitarian relief activities, which some would dismiss as being more suitable for non-governmental organizations (NGOs). The Japanese government, however, has given top priority to shedding 'sweat,' if not 'blood,' in an effort to 'normalize' Japan's security policy in the post–Cold War era.

As Japan was making this significant engagement in international security for the first time in the postwar era, the LDP's monopoly on power was broken by the formation, in August 1993, of a government led by Morihiro Hosokawa of the short-lived Japan New Party. The desperate LDP returned to power in June 1994 as part of a coalition headed by the Socialist Party's Tomiichi Murayama. In his new role as prime minister, Murayama recognized the constitutionality of the SDF and the legitimacy of the United States-Japan alliance, thus destroying his party's long-standing raison-d'être and leading to its catastrophic demise and the collapse of the '1955 regime.'

The demise of the leftist-pacifist political forces in domestic politics changed the context of political discourse on security matters in a significant way. In particular, it lifted long-standing taboos in the debate about national and international security, including the issue of Article 9 of the postwar Constitution. The combination of successful Japanese participation in peacekeeping activities and the historic change in domestic politics prepared the Japanese public gradually to accept Japan's becoming a 'normal country.' Opinion polls reveal that the percentage of those in favour of revising Article 9 more than doubled from 22.6 per cent in 1986 to 50.4 per cent in 1995, with 59.6 per cent of those in favour in 1995 saying that they supported revision because the Constitution hindered Japan's 'international contribution.'[14] After all, as I stressed at the outset, the emphasis in Ichirō Ozawa's account of Japan's becoming a 'normal country' was more on its participation in international peacekeeping efforts than on anything else.

Reaffirmation of the United States-Japan Alliance

While encouraging Japan's deeper participation in international security, new regional and global security challenges after the end of the Cold War also led to a reaffirmation of the United States-Japan alliance. The new Defense Program Outline, revised in November 1995, stressed, among other things, a new role for the SDF in international peacekeeping efforts and an important role for the United States-Japan alliance in these endeavours.[15] Accordingly, the United States-Japan Joint Declaration on Security, signed by Prime Minister Ryutaro Hashimoto and President Bill Clinton in April 1996, declared that 'the Japan-U.S. security relationship … remains the cornerstone for achieving common security objectives, and for maintaining a stable and prosperous environment for the Asia-Pacific region as we enter the twenty-first century.'[16]

While the end of the Cold War provided the relevant general context for these developments, the immediate trigger for the administrative process reaffirming the alliance, particularly the revision of the 1978 Guidelines for Defense Cooperation, was not a 'China threat,' as many, particularly in China, still tend to believe, but the Korean nuclear crisis of 1994.[17] The crisis came to the verge of a second Korean War, as the Clinton administration seriously considered surgical strikes against North Korean nuclear facilities.[18] At this juncture, Washington warned Tokyo that the failure to plan for military cooperation in the event of war on the Korean peninsula could lead to the end of the alliance.[19] Thus, the 1994 North Korean crisis gave rise to a serious concern about the survivability of the alliance and the prospect that Japan would be left a bystander. The deep and central motive of the reaffirmation process, therefore, was to save the alliance from its possible collapse as a result of Japanese inaction.

The 1996 Joint Declaration on Security – an epochal product of the 'normalization' process – listed five areas in which the two countries would 'undertake efforts to advance cooperation' after the Cold War:

- Continued close consultation on defence policies and military postures, as well as exchange of information and views on the international situation;
- Review of the 1978 Guidelines for United States-Japan Defense Cooperation and studies on bilateral cooperation in response to situations that may arise in areas surrounding Japan and affect Japan's peace and security;
- Promotion of the bilateral cooperative relationship through an Acquisition and Cross-Servicing Agreement, signed on 15 April 1996;
- Promotion of mutual exchange in the areas of military technology and equipment; and
- Prevention of the proliferation of weapons of mass destruction and their delivery systems, and cooperation on the ongoing study on theatre missile defence.

Of particular significance was the agreement to review the Guidelines for Defense Cooperation.[20] The review was conducted in conjunction with 'the peace and security of Japan,' rather than with that of either the United States or the region, because of Japan's constitutional prohibition of the 'use of force' beyond self-defence and for settling international disputes. The type of Japanese cooperation with the United States in 'situations in areas surrounding Japan,' therefore, should not involve Japan's 'use of force,' but relief activities and measures to deal with refugees, search and rescue, non-combatant evacuation operations, ensuring the effectiveness of economic sanctions, the use of military facilities by the United States, rear-area support, surveillance, minesweeping, and sea and air space management. Moreover, what should constitute the 'use of force' was a central issue in Japan's policy-making process and in U.S.-Japanese negotiations on revision of the Guidelines.

All this meant that the alliance was not a 'normal' one compared to U.S. alliances with, say, Australia or South Korea, as mechanisms to act jointly to confront a common danger were entirely missing. The reaffirmation of the alliance, therefore, was an explicit part of efforts to prepare Japan to become a 'normal' middle power.

Having said this, I should note that there is a strong belief among many observers, particularly in China, that this reaffirmation process was triggered by and directed against a 'China threat.' It is not entirely surprising for them to come away with this impression upon observing the Japanese debate and listening to Japanese policy and opinion-makers – anti-China sentiments are prevalent in Japanese society, a fact that nationalists attempt to leverage to advance their agenda. The important point to remember, however, is that the nationalists' agenda is strongly conditioned by their regressive trauma about the Japan's 'postwar consensus,' and not necessarily by a sense of alternative strategy.

A closer look at the actual process reveals that no matter how real anti-China sentiments are among Japanese, the meticulous process of the revision of the Guidelines would not have happened without acute anxiety over the survivability of the alliance at the height of the 1994 North Korean nuclear crisis. The Joint Declaration on Security, which called for revision of the Guidelines, was already complete by fall 1995, and Prime Minister Murayama and President Clinton were scheduled to announce it at the time the Osaka summit of the Asia-Pacific Economic Cooperation group that October. Clinton did not come to Osaka simply for domestic political reasons.

In the meantime, the question of Taiwan's security began to loom large, particularly after a series of Chinese military provocations timed to coincide with the Taiwanese presidential election in March 1996. By that time, former U.S. president Jimmy Carter's trip to Pyongyang had salvaged the North Korean missile quagmire, resulting in an agreement to create the Korean Energy Development Organization to circumvent North Korean missile programs. In the debate about the reaffirmation of the United States-Japan alliance in general and revision of the Guidelines in particular, this unfortunate combination of events shifted people's attention away from North Korea toward Taiwan.

It is fair to say that no responsible policy-makers in either Tokyo or Washington believed that a serious contingency calling for the invocation of the revised Guidelines was imminent over Taiwan,[21] but the revised Guidelines theoretically apply to a Taiwan contingency, which the Japanese government has never denied. Indeed, this stance is implied by the Japanese contention that 'situations in the areas surrounding Japan' are not geographically circumscribed *a priori*.

Yoichi Funabashi describes the role of China in the reaffirmation process as having a 'subliminal' effect.[22] It would be fair to say that both Washington and Tokyo tacitly see the reaffirmed alliance as a way of dealing with the rise of China over the long run. Joseph Nye recalls that he thought the rise of China could be managed more constructively if the United States and Japan were to act jointly on the basis of the alliance.[23] In this regard, the central function of the reaffirmed alliance was to maintain general strategic stability in the face of China's historic rise.

In the end, however, the revised Guidelines could be applicable to a Taiwan contingency, depending on circumstances. China's sensitivity to this, and its strident attacks against Tokyo over the point, may have produced an unwanted result for Beijing, as Tokyo gradually has come to realize the utility of this sort of 'strategic ambiguity.' Legislation passed by the Diet in May 1999 specifying 'situations in areas surrounding Japan' as ones 'that could lead to the nation being the direct target of armed attacks if no action is taken' makes plausible the following interpretation: 'The formula in the legislation would appear to cover the possibility of Japanese support to U.S. forces engaged in combat to "contain" a China-Taiwan military confrontation.'[24]

This evolving dynamism has led to a rather explicit reference to China and Taiwan in a U.S.-Japanese joint statement issued after the 'two-plus-two' meeting of ministers in charge of foreign and defence affairs on 19 February 2005 in Washington. The statement included three relevant points regarding China and Taiwan under the heading, 'Common strategic objectives in the region' – namely, that Japan and the United States would (1) develop a cooperative relationship with China, welcoming a responsible and constructive role regionally as well as globally; (2) encourage the peaceful resolution of issues concerning the Taiwan Strait through dialogue; and (3) encourage China to improve transparency in its military affairs.[25] The substance of the reference to China and Taiwan was not news to anyone, including the Chinese. The fact that it was openly stated in an official document, however, was new, which indicates a stronger political determination for a strengthened alliance relationship on the part of the United States and Japan.

Since it is unlikely that an 'abnormal' Japan would have accepted this set of strategic objectives explicitly in such a joint statement, this development is yet another indication of a 'normalizing' Japan. In fact, contrary to Chinese belief, it was not Tokyo but Washington that proposed and drafted these objectives for the joint statement.[26] A previously 'abnormal' Japan would have shied away from provoking China, but a 'normal' Japan has proven to be ready to engage in long-term hedging diplomacy jointly with the United Sates.

National Defence

The third domain of change in the direction of Japan's becoming a 'normal country,' following active participation in international peacekeeping and humanitarian operations and the reaffirmation of the alliance with the United States, pertains to traditional national defence. In retrospect, Japan has never had an 'independent' national defence policy in the postwar years; rather, Japan has had a de facto 'middle power' defence policy premised on alliance with the United States, a fundamental reality that the end of the Cold War has not essentially changed.

Appropriately enough, the 'National Defense Program Outline' released on 28 November 1995 articulates the purpose of Japan's national defence in the overall context of the alliance with the United States and Japan's 'international contribution': 'Japan, abiding by its Constitution, following the guidelines set forth herein and paying due attention to enhancing the credibility of the Japan-U.S. security arrangements, will strive to ensure its own national defence and contribute to the peace and stability of the international community by appropriately upgrading, maintaining and operating its capability.'[27] Accordingly, the Outline states that Japan's defence capability in the post–Cold War context should contribute to the effective management of the United

States-Japan alliance and deal with a shifting security environment that includes more than just the simple defence of Japanese territory. 'From this perspective,' the document states, 'it is appropriate that Japan's defence capability be restricted, both in scale and functions, by streamlining, making it more efficient and compact, as well as enhancing necessary functions and making qualitative improvements to be able to effectively respond to a variety of situations and simultaneously ensure the appropriate flexibility to smoothly deal with the development of the changing situations.'[28] As a result, the SDF was to become leaner, more mobile, and better able to deal with unconventional dangers such as 'disasters caused by acts of terrorism and other events' and international peace cooperation and disaster relief activities.

While it is no secret that the SDF are equipped with state-of-the-art weapons, thanks to the alliance with the United States, the flipside of the coin is that Japan's defence system is virtually a subsystem of the U.S. military presence and strategy in the Asia-Pacific region. Accordingly, strategic intelligence, command and control, joint war fighting, and missile defence are some of the SDF's weaknesses.[29] All of this makes the 'normalized' defence capabilities of the SDF intrinsically those of a middle power closely bound by the military strategy of the United States – albeit an indispensable ally of Japan as a 'normal country.'

On the basis of these premises, the 'National Defense Program Guidelines' adopted on 10 December 2004[30] continue to emphasize the importance of responsiveness and flexibility in the SDF's capabilities. While arguing that large-scale military aggression against Japan is less likely, and thus that conventional military preparedness for such an event should be reduced, the Guidelines stress the importance of new threats and various situations, including ballistic missile attack, attacks by guerrillas and special forces, aggression against oceanic islands, intrusion into territorial air and maritime space, and large-scale disasters.

This new 'pragmatic realism'[31] concerning national defence is a product of trial and error in dealing with the series of new instabilities and dangers confronting Tokyo since the end of the Cold War, including the North Korean nuclear crisis and the Taiwan Strait crisis in the mid-1990s, a series of violations of Japanese territorial waters by suspected North Korean spy ships in between 1999 and 2001, and threats of terrorism, particularly in the aftermath of the terrorist attacks on the United States on 11 September 2001. In the process, the Japanese public's postwar allergy to anything related to military affairs has been 'normalized' to a certain extent.

A prominent example of this shift is the passage on 6 June 2003 of 'emergency laws' that stipulate legal rules on 'the protection of Japanese nationals, the treatment of prisoners of war, [and] the punishment of inhumane acts' in the event of an armed attack against Japan.[32] Although any 'normal' democracy should have legislation of this kind, postwar Japan overly constraining culture of antimilitarism had found it difficult to enact such measures.[33]

It should be obvious to all that this is evidence neither of the 'remilitarization' of Japan nor of a shift toward the ideological 'right.' In this connection, it is worth repeating that conservative nationalism has provided an impetus for the process of 'normalization,' but has not resulted in the kind of outcome for which doctrinaire nationalists would opt. Nationalism as an antithesis to the 'postwar consensus' effectively has eroded the 'abnormalcy' of excessive 'one-country pacifism,' but the concomitant changes that we witness remain firmly within the framework of that consensus.

The fact that Japan's conservative nationalists do not appreciate the strength of the 'invisible hand' of the 'postwar consensus' is once again a powerful reminder that they are not driven by any sense of alternative strategy. Indeed, this is the most confusing aspect about the changes associated with Japan as an emerging 'normal country.' Capable bureaucrats of the Japanese government, the guardians of the postwar framework of Japanese security policy, are quietly taking advantage of this complex situation, and are not necessarily unhappy about the 'normalization' process for which they have longed for decades.

Human Security as Middle Power Diplomacy

Rectifying 'abnormalcy' should be a normal thing for any sovereign country. This is certainly how central decision- and opinion-makers in Japan perceive it. As a result, it is a non-starter to seek some essence of a 'new Japan' since the end of the Cold War in this normalization process. A 'normal' Japan is a beginning, not a goal. What Japan would actually build on the foundation of its becoming a 'normal country' is really the key to the future course of Japanese security policy, and Japan has just begun this soul-searching journey.

The gaining of a measure of influence on the part of traditional nationalists is perhaps an inevitable, albeit unnecessarily confusing, phenomenon in the transition from the '1955 regime' to something new. The conservative ideological urge is in no way a representation of this something new, even if it has been an important source of change in Japanese domestic politics. What this examination of the three dimensions of change in Japanese security policy demonstrates instead is that Japan is moving in the direction of becoming a full-fledged middle power rather than a traditional great power. Japan's explicit commitment to international peacekeeping and humanitarian relief operations in the domain of international security, as well as to its alliance with the United States, is testimony to this.

The rise of human security as a central pillar of Japan's diplomatic agenda in recent years is another indication that Japan as a 'normal country' is pursuing de facto 'middle power' diplomacy. What is peculiarly Japanese in Japan's approach to human security is that the motivation is closely connected with the desire to play a greater and more proactive role in international society. Clearly, the motivation is pacifism with an internationalist bent. Keizo Takemi, a scholar and former politician of the Japanese legislature's upper house who played a key role through his close ties to Prime Minister Keizo Obuchi in the initial process of the rise of human security, explains as follows:

> Pacifism in Japan evolved into a highly ideological one-country pacifism that repudiated military force, based on deep reflection and contrition for the country's militaristic aggression toward its neighbors. However, with the collapse of the East-West cold war structure, one-country pacifism has been seen to gradually lose its relevance in the face of new realities, and its significance is receding in the minds of the younger generation of Japanese who themselves have had no direct experience of war.
>
> What is now required of Japan is the formulation and projection of a new future-oriented pacifism that enhances and promotes Japan's standing as a responsible member of the international community. In the interconnected and people-oriented 21st century, the nebulous concept of one-country pacifism must be developed into peace diplomacy, where Japan focuses more on individual values. This is a task that the people of Japan themselves can engage in as they enlarge their role at the forefront of the international community based on the pillar of human security.[34]

The 1997 Asian financial crisis was an important catalyst for Japan's human security initiative, just as it provided an impetus for the creation by the Association of Southeast Asian Nations (ASEAN) of ASEAN+3. Takemi, who was an administrative vice-minister of foreign affairs at the time of the financial crisis, became an inspiration for then-foreign minister Keizo Obuchi as his close aide. Obuchi had made the first official reference to the concept of human security as foreign minister in May 1998 in a policy speech in Singapore: 'Economic crisis has its heaviest impact on the poor, the aged, the disabled, women and children, and other socially vulnerable segments of the population. Health and employment being basic 'human security' concerns, Japan has long made social development a major priority in its Official Development Assistance, and we intend to further enhance our cooperation in this area.'[35]

In December 1998, Obuchi, now prime minister, elaborated on the concept of human security as a pillar of Japanese foreign policy at an international conference in Tokyo.[36] Two weeks later in Hanoi, at the ASEAN+3 Summit, Obuchi further advanced his concept of human security, and committed ¥500 million (US$4.2 million) to establish a 'Human Security Fund' under the United Nations – later renamed the Trust Fund for Human Security – to promote human security projects by UN agencies around the world.

Sadako Ogata, who served as the UN High Commissioner for Refugees from 1990 to 2000, is respected in Japan for her dedication to the lofty moral cause of protecting and promoting human dignity in international society. Ogata has served as a critical and effective linchpin connecting Japanese initiatives to developments at the level of international society. The effective linkage between the role of Ogata and initiatives by the Japanese government was established on the occasion of the 'International Symposium on Human Security: From the Kyushu-Okinawa Summit to UN Millennium Summit,' hosted by Japan's Ministry of Foreign Affairs on 28 July 2000. As suggested by the subtitle, the symposium used the opportunity of the Kyushu-Okinawa Summit, held in Okinawa on 21–23 July and anticipated the UN Millennium Summit scheduled for that September. The event was crucial in putting Obuchi's initiatives on human security on the global agenda, particularly at the UN. The two keynote speakers were Sadako Ogata and Professor Amartya Sen, who later became co-chairs of the Commission on Human Security proposed by Prime Minister Yoshiro Mori at the September UN Millennium Summit.

Despite Obuchi's sudden death in May 2000, the momentum on human security was thus sustained by successive Japanese governments. In his speech at the Millennium Summit, Mori emphasized two points: 'the importance of dealing with issues confronting the international community from a human-centered point of view' and 'the need to strengthen the functions of the United Nations in the new century.' He then stressed that, '[w]ith "human security" as one of the pillars of its diplomacy, Japan would spare no effort to make the twenty-first century a human-centered century.'[37] Thus, Japan's bid for permanent membership in the UN Security Council became closely tied to the promotion of human security globally.

Although suspicion lingers about the intention of Japanese security policy, Japan's Asian neighbours have received its human security initiatives relatively well, due in part to the nature of the issue, which, in principle, is 'soft' and does not evoke traditional security concerns. At least as important, however, is the rise of civil society and its evolving networks in many East Asian countries. In this connection, the role of the Japan Center for International Exchange (JCIE) cannot be exaggerated. For almost three decades, the JCIE, under the strong leadership of Tadashi Yamamoto, has promoted intellectual dialogue regionally and globally, involving NGOs, academics, journalists, politicians, bureaucrats, and business leaders. Human security has been one of the priority areas of the activities of JCIE since the time of the Obuchi initiatives, and its impact has been significant both domestically and regionally. In particular, since 1998 the JCIE has hosted, with the support of the Institute of Southeast Asian Studies in Singapore, the 'Intellectual Dialogue on Building Asia's Tomorrow,' at the first gathering of which Prime Minister Obuchi launched the concept of human security as a basic pillar of Japanese foreign policy.[38]

As I argued above, proactive pacifism has been an assumption behind Japanese efforts toward deeper engagement in international security through participation in international peacekeeping and humanitarian relief operations. The same is true for the Japanese approach to human security. In this context, international security and human security can be regarded as the core of Japan's middle power diplomacy, which, in turn, informs an important aspect of Japan's aspiration to become a 'normal country' in international society.

Conclusion: The Case for an East Asian Community

As Japan has aspired to become a 'normal country' since the end of the Cold War, its security profile has developed into that of a de facto middle power, rather than a traditional great power. Sceptics might still view Japan's dedication to international security, the United States-Japan alliance, and human security as fundamentally cosmetic, believing that a more important impulse behind Japan's 'normalization' is the drive to revive its former great power status. The sceptical interpretation, however, cannot help us make sense of what really has been going on in Japan since the end of the Cold War nor enlighten us about the real implications of these changes for Japanese security policy and for an emerging regional order.

In this overall context, it is important to highlight the value of the security partnerships between Japan on the one hand and ASEAN and South Korea on the other. These partnerships have the potential to cause a paradigm shift in East Asian security and regionalism. In a nutshell, these three regional actors could join forces and create genuinely equal middle power networks as the foundation of an East Asian community over the long term.

The development of Japan-ASEAN relations on these basic premises now has a long history.[39] The redefinition of Japan-South Korea relations along the same lines, however, has hardly progressed at all; rather, it is dismissed as unfounded largely because of the prevailing image of Japan as one of the four great powers surrounding the Korean peninsula. The notion of a 'normal' Japan as a middle power is too easily dismissed by believers in the conventional wisdom on Northeast Asian geopolitics. I would argue, however, that the basis of the Japan-South Korea relationship is rooted in the geopolitical reality that these two countries are surrounded by three unilateralist powers – namely, the United States, China, and Russia.

The conventional wisdom does not provide a realistic perspective on Japanese security policy in East Asia, and has even been an important source of confusion in the evolution of a regional order. It has bred, for example, the myth of Japanese-Chinese geopolitical rivalry in East Asia. South Korea's self-understanding as a balancer between Japan and China also appears to be a product of this misconceived conventional wisdom.

A realistic geopolitical perspective suggests that an equal partnership between Japan and South Korea is not a mere political slogan but a potential substantive foundation of the bilateral relationship. It is against the backdrop of this geopolitical reality that democracy in Japan and South Korea, and civil society exchanges between the two peoples, have affected the bilateral relationship in a fundamental way.

The late prime minister Keizo Obuchi placed a special emphasis on the importance of South Korea in his thinking on human security, in addition to the already somewhat comfortable channel of dialogue

Japan enjoys with Southeast Asian nations. This was amply demonstrated by his willingness and determination to make the historic 1998 visit to Japan by South Korean president Kim Dae Jung an unquestionable success.

Obuchi paid a return visit to South Korea in March 1999, and delivered a speech at Korea University, the title of which was translated in English as 'Japan-Korea Relations in the New Millennium: The Creation of a New History.' Obuchi pointed out three areas of Japan-South Korea cooperation: security in Northeast Asia, the revival and prosperity of Asia, and human security.[40] He said that human security should constitute the core of Japanese and South Korean global cooperation, and he called for joint leadership by the two countries to promote international collaboration on the world stage, including at the UN. Obuchi particularly emphasized the intellectual leadership of Japanese and South Koreans in promoting human security. In effect, he was addressing South Korean civil society, while amply recognizing the role of intellectual dialogue in further expanding the concept of human security.

Unfortunately, Japanese-South Korean relations have not evolved as Obuchi had wished. Sage political leadership is required to fill the emotional gap between the two nations that emanates from history and territorial issues, but all too often leaders in both countries have widened rather, than narrowed, the gap, which is clearly based on entirely misplaced assumptions each has about the other. The essence of South Korea's misperception is captured by the erroneous conventional wisdom to which I alluded above. The dominant Japanese misperception is that South Korean leaders use the history card solely for domestic political purposes. The same dynamic of mutual misperception complicates relations between Japan and China, occasionally providing an incentive for South Korea and China to join forces against Japan. If it were not for the prejudices that sustain these emotional and perceptual gaps, South Korea and Japan would be natural partners, cooperating easily on an equal basis to create an East Asian Community for the long-run stability and prosperity of the region.

In this overall context, the East Asian diplomacy advanced by the DPJ government that came into power in September 2009 appears to point in the right direction. Prime Minister Yukio Hatoyama has shifted focus toward the establishment of an East Asian Community by placing a premium on Japan's relations with its neighbours, particularly China and South Korea. When it comes to the components of this overall design, the details are not yet clear. The explicit emphasis on Japan's most troubled relations with its neighbours, however, is appropriate, as these relations have long been in need of closer attention from the Japanese government.

Building an East Asia Community, based on an equal partnership with South Korea, should be a priority for a 'middle power' Japanese security policy. In the same vein, human security should be developed into a common security agenda for a network of middle power countries that might include Japan, South Korea, certain ASEAN countries, Australia, and New Zealand. Changes in Japanese security policies since the end of the Cold War have prepared Japan for such an innovative diplomacy, and it is greatly to be hoped that the DPJ's foreign policy will set Japan even more firmly on the path of a 'normal' middle power.

NOTES

1 Yoshihide Soeya, *Nihon-no Middle Power Gaiko* [Japan's middle power diplomacy] (Tokyo: Chikuma Shobo, 2005). A Korean translation is also available from Oruem publishers.
2 Akihiko Tanaka, *Anzen-hosho* [Security] (Tokyo: Yomiuri Shinbun-Sha, 1997).
3 See the website of the Japanese Ministry of Defense, available at http://www.mod.go.jp/j/approach/kokusai_heiwa/iraq/backup/main.html, accessed 6 December 2010.
4 Shinzo Abe, *Utsukushii Kuni E* [Toward a beautiful country] (Tokyo: Bungeishunju, 2006), p. 160.
5 'On the "Arc of Freedom and Prosperity"' (address by H.E. Tarō Asō, Minister for Foreign Affairs,' 12 March 2007); available online at http://www.mofa.go.jp/policy/pillar/address0703.html, accessed 29 May 2009.
6 Abe, *Utsukushii Kuni E*, p. 29.
7 Yoshihide Soeya, 'The Misconstrued Shift in Japan's Foreign Policy,' *Japan Echo* 33 (3, June 2006): 16–19.
8 Richard J. Samuels, 'Japan's Goldilocks Strategy,' *Washington Quarterly* (Autumn 2006), p. 121.
9 Ibid., p. 125.
10 Yoichi Funabashi, 'Japan and the New World Order,' *Foreign Affairs* 70 (5, 1991/92): 58–74.
11 Prime Minister's Commission on Japan's Goals in the 21st Century, 'The Frontier Within: Individual Empowerment and Better Governance in the

New Millennium' (Tokyo, January 2000); available online at http://www.kantei.go.jp/jp/21century/report/pdfs/index.html, accessed 29 May 2009.

12 L. William Heinrich, Akiho Shibata, and Yoshihide Soeya, *United National Peace-keeping Operations: A Guide to Japanese Policies* (Tokyo: United Nations University Press, 1999), p. 20.

13 Ibid., pp. 24–32.

14 'Yomiuri Poll,' *This Is Yomiuri*, June 1995, p. 149.

15 Japan, Ministry of Foreign Affairs, 'National Defense Program Outline in and after FY 1996' (Tokyo, 28 November 1995); available online at http://www.mofa.go.jp/POLICY/security/defense96/index.html, accessed 29 May 2009.

16 Japan, Ministry of Foreign Affairs, 'Japan-U.S. Joint Declaration on Security: Alliance for the 21st Century' (Tokyo, 17 April 1996); available online at http://www.mofa.go.jp/region/n-america/us/security/security.html, accessed 29 May 2009.

17 Yoshihide Soeya, 'The China Factor in the U.S.-Japan Alliance: The Myth of a China Threat,' *Journal of East Asian Studies* 2 (2, 2002): 37–66.

18 Don Oberdorfer, *The Two Koreas: A Contemporary History* (New York: Basic Books, 1998), pp. 312–16.

19 Yoichi Funabashi, *Alliance Adrift* (New York: Council on Foreign Relations, 1999), p. 280.

20 The review's final report was released on 23 September 1997 as 'Completion of the Review of the Guidelines for U.S.-Japan Defense Cooperation'; available online at http://www.mofa.go.jp/region/n-america/us/security/defense.html, accessed 29 May 2009.

21 For a discussion on the non-strategic nature of Japan's policy toward Taiwan, see Yoshihide Soeya, 'Taiwan in Japan's Security Considerations,' *China Quarterly* 165 (March 2001).

22 Funabashi, *Alliance Adrift*, pp. 393–4.

23 Joseph S. Nye, Jr, 'The Case for Deep Engagement,' *Foreign Affairs* 74 (4, 1995): 90–102.

24 International Crisis Group, 'Taiwan Strait II: The Risk of War,' *Asia Report* 54 (6 June 2003): 39.

25 U.S.-Japan Security Consultative Committee, 'Joint Statement'; available online at http://www.mofa.go.jp/region/n-america/us/security/scc/joint0502.html, accessed 29 May 2009.

26 Masaru Honda, *Nihon-ni Kokka-senryaku wa Arunoka* [Does Japan have a national strategy?] (Tokyo: Asashi Shinsho, 2007), p. 240.

27 Japan, Ministry of Foreign Affairs, 'Security of Japan and Roles of Defense

Capabilities' (Tokyo); available on line at http://www.mofa.go.jp/policy/security/defense96/capability.html, accessed 29 May 2009.

28 Ibid.

29 Alan Dupont, *Unsheathing the Samurai Sword: Japan's Changing Security Policy* (Sydney: Lowy Institute for International Policy, 2004), p. 28.

30 Japan, Ministry of Defense; available online at http://www.mod.go.jp/e/d_act/d_policy/pdf/national_guideline.pdf, accessed 6 December 2010.

31 Dupont, *Unsheathing the Samurai Sword*, p. 12.

32 Japan, Ministry of Foreign Affairs, 'Legislation on the Response in the Case of an Armed Attack and other Such Emergency and Japan's Foreign Policy' (Tokyo, June 2003); available online at http://www.mofa.go.jp/policy/security/legislation.html, accessed 29 May 2009.

33 See, for example, Peter J. Katzenstein and Nobuo Okawara, *Japan's National Security: Structures, Norms and Policy Responses in a Changing World* (Ithaca, NY: Cornell University, East Asia Program, 1993); and Thomas U. Berger, *Cultures of Antimilitarism: National Security in Germany and Japan* (Baltimore: Johns Hopkins University Press, 1998).

34 Keizo Takemi, 'Evolution of the Human Security Concept' (paper presented at 'Session I: Evolution of the Human Security Concept as an Operational Tool for Policy Formulation and Implementation' of the Fourth Intellectual Dialogue on Building Asia's Future, Kisarazu, Japan, 16–17 March 2002), pp. 46–7; available online at http://www.jcie.or.jp/thinknet/pdfs/health_takemi.pdf, accessed 29 May 2009.

35 Keizo Obuchi, 'Statement by Foreign Minister Keizo Obuchi on Japan and East Asia: Outlook for the New Millennium,' Singapore, 4 May 1998; available online at http://www.mofa.go.jp/announce/announce/1998/5/980504.html, accessed 29 May 2009.

36 Keizo Obuchi, 'Opening Remarks by Prime Minister Obuchi at an Intellectual Dialogue on Building Asia's Tomorrow,' Tokyo, 2 December 1998; available online at http://www.mofa.go.jp/policy/culture/intellectual/asia9812.html, accessed 29 July 2009.

37 Yoshiro Mori, 'Statement by H.E. Mr. Yoshiro Mori, Prime Minister of Japan, at the Millennium Summit of the United Nations,' New York, 7 September 2000; available online at http://www.mofa.go.jp/policy/un/summit2000/pmstate.html, accessed 29 May 2009.

38 Japan Center for International Exchange, 'Human Security'; available online at http://www.jcie.or.jp/thinknet/hsecurity.html, accessed 29 May 2009.

39 Japan Center for International Exchange, *ASEAN-Japan Cooperation: A Foundation for East Asian Community* (Tokyo: JCIE, 2003).

40 Keizo Obuchi, 'Shin-seki no Nikkan-kankei: Aratana Rekishi no Sozo' [Japan-Korea relations in the new millennium: The creation of a new history] (Tokyo: Ministry of Foreign Affairs, 20 March 1999); available (in Japanese) online at http://www.mofa.go.jp/mofaj/press/enzetsu/11/eos_0320.html, accessed 29 May 2009.

4 Conservative Conceptions of Japan as a 'Normal Country': Comparing Ozawa, Nakasone, and Ishihara

CHEOL HEE PARK

After the 1991 Gulf War, Ichirō Ozawa advocated the idea of Japan's becoming a 'normal country.'[1] Although Ozawa was not a top leader at the time, his ideas have had considerable impact on Japanese society and politics. Since Ozawa's initial proposition, the notion of remaking Japan into a 'normal country' has dominated Japanese political discourse.[2]

Underlying the 'normal country' discourse is the notion that Japan is presently 'abnormal.' Yet the definitions of both normalcy and abnormalcy remain ambiguous and contested. Among Japan's neighbours, the prevailing perception is that the move toward normalcy reflects an intention to remilitarize Japan. A radical conservative view in Japan that Japan's remilitarization must be a Japanese priority only reinforces this perception. Given Japan's history of imperialism, such attempts at remilitarization raise considerable alarm in the region.[3]

Despite common understanding among Japanese conservatives that Japan should revise its national strategy now that the Cold War has ended, there is no firm consensus on the conception of 'normalcy' itself. In this chapter, I elaborate on the similarities and differences among three dominant conservatives' views of what would constitute a 'normal' Japan. In particular, I look carefully at the understandings of Ichirō Ozawa, Yasuhiro Nakasone, and Shintaro Ishihara. In so doing, I demonstrate that shared views about Japan's 'abnormal' past do not necessarily lead to unified views about Japan's future. This chapter is an attempt to clarify the commonalities and differences among Japanese conservative leaders with respect to their ideals and programs for transforming Japan into a normal country, in order to motivate a richer and more informed public debate about Japanese 'normalization.'

Japanese political and intellectual leaders have devoted much of their energy to fashioning a strategic vision for Japanese foreign and defence policy. Making Japan a 'normal country' is just one – but perhaps the most central element – among many Japanese strategic visions. Therefore, understanding the 'normal country' debate is also important for shedding light on Japan's evolving strategic agenda.

Locating the 'Normal Country' Discourse in Historical Context

Postwar debates on the Japanese state have evolved around two axes.[4] The first concerns the relative importance of Japan's international commitments. Some political leaders and strategists have argued that Japan must expand its international role, particularly in light of the United States-Japan alliance. Others, by contrast, contend that Japanese political priorities must focus on restructuring its unique political and economic system. The second axis revolves around a debate over Japan's reliance on non-military and military means for advancing its national interest. Following the end of World War Two, Japan hesitated to develop and advance its national interest according to conventional metrics of military power. However, after the end of the 1991 Gulf War, Japanese leaders became more proactive in defining their national interest in such terms.

Four Schools of Thought

From the two axes outlined above, four different conceptions of the Japanese national strategy can be identified. The first school, referred to as 'one-country pacifism,' or *heiwa kokkaron,* begins from the premise that Japan must completely repent of its past and build its future on the 'peace clause' (Article 9) of its postwar Constitution.[5] Accordingly, proponents of this school of thought argue that Japan should avoid using military means to realize its goals and abstain from expanding its military capability.[6] This school of thought is best associated with the pacifist orientations of members of the Japan Socialist Party (JSP), as well as doves within the Liberal Democratic Party (LDP).

Similarly, the 'global civilian state' orientation school of thought, or *kokusai simin kokkaron,* delinks Japanese interest and power on the one hand, and military capacity on the other. Proponents of this school argue that pursuing Japan's interests through military means will only provoke its neighbours, as its imperial past will certainly result in a misinterpretation of its motives. Accordingly, they advocate a path of international non-military cooperation. From this perspective, it is not in Japan's interest to expand its military capacity. Instead, Japan should direct its international contributions to the economic and social realms, focusing on such things as overseas development assistance, humanitarian aid, and the promotion of free trade.[7] In short, Japan should aim to be a mercantile civilian state, not a military state.[8] The conservative mainstream (*hoshu honryu*), also called the Yoshida line, often promotes this point of view.[9] It was also prevalent among doves in the LDP in the postwar years.

Advocates of Japan as a 'normal state,' or *futsu no kuniron* – most commonly conservatives in the LDP – emerged in the 1990s. This school of thought contends that Japan's international contributions should not be limited to financial assistance. Rather, as a global economic power, Japan should make military contributions in the form of peacekeeping operations a priority of its foreign policy.[10] Ultimately, from this 'normal country' perspective, for Japan's international prestige to increase, it must participate in the activities of international society as other 'normal' countries do. Military contributions, therefore, should not be taboo, particularly when directed toward international peacekeeping missions.

The other small but vociferous line of thinking about the Japanese state is what I call the 'autonomous state' orientation, or *jishu kokkaron*.[11] This school focuses on re-establishing Japanese identity on the basis of national pride.[12] The postwar mentality of dependence upon the United States should be overcome; a mindset of unwavering independence is needed.[13] Accordingly, Japan should build up its military so that it is able to defend itself. Expanding the Japanese military would serve Japan's interests, according to this view, as it would increase Japanese autonomy in the global political order.

Debating the Japanese State in the Postwar Period

Political debates about Japanese national strategy have shifted over time.[14] Under the '1955 system,' the primary political cleavage was defined by a rift between proponents of 'one-country pacifism' and 'global civilian statism.'[15] The LDP, as the ruling party, favoured developing Japan's economic strength through trade, while relying on the United States when it came to security issues.[16] The JSP, the largest opposition party, by contrast, was strongly committed to the idea of developing a peace state. To this extent, the JSP devoted its energies to promoting a democratic political order based on Article 9 of the postwar Constitution. Despite their differences, however, both parties agreed that military and security issues were of a lower priority than economic growth. To this extent, while the 'global civilian state' mentality defined the prevailing political consensus, the concerns of 'one-country pacifism' were never ignored.

Despite the common reference to the 1990s as the 'lost decade,' it was a major period of regime transformation.[17] The experience of participating in the 1991 Gulf War set a new context for debates about Japanese statehood. Following the Gulf War, Japan came to the realization that its 'chequebook' diplomacy was an insufficient contribution to international politics.[18] The 'normal country' discourse thus emerged as Japan began to reflect on new ways to engage in the global political order. As the 'normal state' orientation began to enter political consciousness, Japanese society was fraught with debates between 'global civilian state' advocates and pacificists. In the end, the traditional schools of thought on Japanese 'global civilian statism' waned and were put on the defensive as the 'normal state' discourse began to define the majority opinion.

As Japan entered the twenty-first century under the political leadership of Junichirō Koizumi, 'normal state' discourse gradually began to contend with the 'autonomous state' school of thought. The latter orientation had long been a controversial, and almost taboo, position, discreetly discussed only by a small minority of Japanese citizens. By the dawn of the new century, however, it was being openly debated by various sectors of the Japanese public.[19] Although the 'autonomous state' position was not a widely held view among the political and intellectual elite, it began to assume legitimacy in the broader public sphere.[20] By the time of Koizumi's leadership, then, all schools of thought on Japanese statism were being publicly debated, although the pacifists increasingly were being pushed to the political margin.

Three Conservative Conceptions of Japan as a 'Normal Country'

Although the 'normal state' began to define the political mainstream in the 1990s, there was no consensus on what exactly would make Japan a normal country. This ambiguity remains today, and despite conservative agreement that Japan must become 'normal,' conservatives themselves cannot agree on what is required for such 'normalization.' Figure

Figure 4.1: A Comparison of Japanese Conservatives

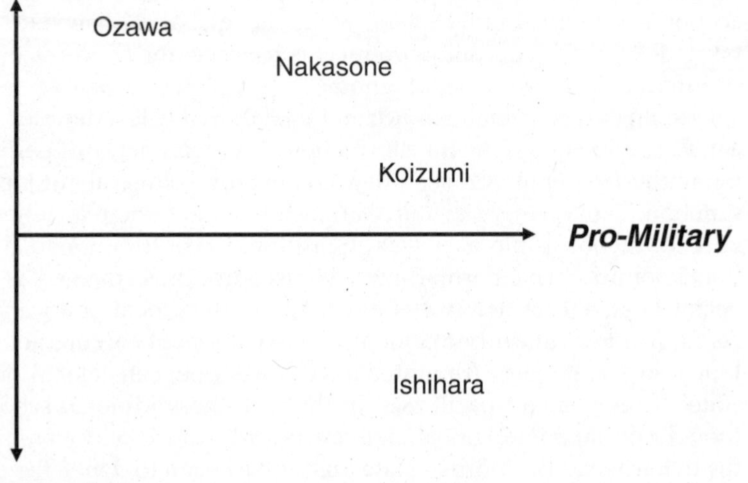

4.1 provides a simplified schematic of the political controversies that have defined Japan's postwar political landscape.[21] Of the conservatives listed there, Ozawa, Nakasone, and Ishihara are of particular note. In the remainder of this chapter, I elaborate on their respective arguments and visions of Japanese normalcy.

Ichirō Ozawa

With the end of the Cold War and the inauguration of a new geopolitical order, Ichirō Ozawa argued against Japan's traditional inward-looking policy. For Ozawa, Japan's economic power necessitated assuming some responsibility for maintaining a stable and peaceful international environment. Accordingly, he argued that Japan should become a truly 'internationalized state.' This due contribution to international society – *kokusai kouken* – would be in the interest not only of international society, but of Japan as well, in view of Japan's reliance on free trade and a peaceful and stable international order.[22] According to Ozawa, in order for Japan's internationalization to come into effect, it must become a 'normal country.'

Ozawa stressed that Japan's normalization would require taking the initiative to contribute to international society. Japan, therefore, should not only respond to demands made on it by other countries or international agencies, but also make collaborative but self-initiated efforts to build and strengthen international society. To this extent, Ozawa argued, Japan should prioritize security cooperation, make the utmost effort to help other countries build prosperous and stable societies, and address global challenges such as environmental protection. In the 'Ozawa Doctrine,' contributions in these areas would transform Japan from a country that pursued only economic growth and domestic consumption into a 'normal country' deeply embedded in the international community.

Ozawa maintained that, during the Cold War era, Japan had relied on the United States to bear the financial burden of defending itself and had failed to contribute sufficiently to the 'cost' of international peace and prosperity. With the end of the Cold War and the collapse of the Soviet Union, however, the reasons for the United States having to bear these costs no longer applied. Japan therefore should assume responsibility for its own security as its contribution to international peace and security, just as other 'normal' countries do.[23]

To achieve the kind of normalization he envisioned, Ozawa advocated an initiative for political reform. The crux of his project was to change the system of political decision-making. From Ozawa's perspective, Japanese politics was marked by a separation of politics and diplomacy that made it very difficult for political leaders to take decisions on foreign policy. Ozawa called this a 'poverty of politics.' Following a program of political reform to overcome this deficiency would be necessary if Japan were to become a 'normal country.'[24]

In order to construct a new style of politics where political leaders could take policy initiatives with a sense of responsibility, two principles would have to be introduced: the concentration of power and competition among political forces.[25] Under these principles, Ozawa suggested a reform agenda that would strengthen the prime minister's office.[26] For the purpose of making the political world more competitive, Ozawa argued that a single-member district system should be introduced, replacing the traditional multi-member district system. Under a single-member district system, two-party competition based on policy differences would be naturally promoted.[27]

On the foreign policy side, Ozawa felt that the 'Yoshida Doctrine,' so long an orthodoxy, had been misunderstood as a policy that prioritized economic growth over defence and security during the Cold War. According to Ozawa, Yoshida clearly intended that Japan should make a substantial contribution to the 'Liberal West.' Ozawa also emphasized Yoshida's claim that it was legitimate to say that a country is a lopsided state if it relies too heavily on others for its self-defence.[28]

Ozawa's advocacy of an active role for Japan in international security as a necessary condition for its 'normalization' implied active participation in the UN collective security framework.[29] Ozawa presumed that, in the post–Cold War period, the United States would strengthen the function of collective security and pursue a 'UN-centered peace strategy.'[30] Ozawa therefore proposed that Japanese forces should be reorganized to create a UN reserve force that could be deployed to respond to peacekeeping situations. Ozawa also argued that Japan should strengthen the alliance with the United States by working with that country to build a new world order under the UN framework, effectively shifting Japan's security policy from defence to international peacekeeping.[31] In line with his support for the UN collective security framework, Ozawa made the case for revising the Japanese Constitution in a way that would permit the creation of UN reserve forces and the peacebuilding activities of the Self-Defense Forces (SDF).[32]

Shintaro Ishihara

At the extreme right of the ideological spectrum, with views that contrast sharply with Ozawa's, is Shintaro Ishihara. Ishihara's conception of Japan becoming a 'normal country' can be categorized virtually as advocating the creation of an autonomous Japanese state. Ishihara agreed that Japan's postwar system had been abnormal and that its system should be revised, but his solution was an extreme one.

Ishihara's position arose from deep-seated resentment and criticism of the way in which the postwar Japanese state had been constructed. From his perspective, Japan had been severely weakened by the U.S. occupation and the subsequent adoption of the 'peace clause' in the postwar Constitution. For Ishihara, Douglas MacArthur had designed a scheme to destroy Japan. In contrast to the German experience of U.S. occupation, in which surrender was conditional – Germany had retained the right to develop its own constitution, had not had to disband its armed forces, and had retained autonomy over its educational system – Japan's had been unconditional, requiring submission to a foreign written constitution that required the dismantling of the Japanese military and the adoption of a new educational program.[33] In particular, Ishihara noted that the new system of education had had the effect of weakening any sense of a distinct Japanese identity.

The collective effect of the postwar surrender, according to Ishihara, had been a concerted effort on the part of the Americans to weaken the Japanese state severely. By fostering an ambiguous sense of trust in a United States-Japan alliance, the United States effectively had found a way to continue its occupation of Japan.[34] What many believed to be a U.S. commitment to defend Japan, Ishihara argued, instead had been a strategy to control it.

Ishihara therefore argued for the reinvigoration of a powerful and self-reliant defence state (*bouei kokka*).[35] As long as Japan continued to rely on the United States for its defence, such invigoration could not occur.[36] At his most earnest, Ishihara criticized leaders such as Ichirō Ozawa for perpetuating Japan's weakness through an inability to say 'no' to the United States.[37]

Ishihara saw international politics as a zero-sum game of relative gains. A staunch realist, Ishihara firmly believed that any country was a potential enemy, and thus that Japan would always have to work to protect its national interest. A truly independent and strong Japan would have no need for alliances or *nakama* – friends/partners.[38] Ishihara argued that there was no guarantee that the United States would come to Japan's rescue, so Japan would have to possess the military capacity to defend itself. The best strategy, in Ishihara's mind, would be to build up Japan's defensive power through a strategy of deterrence. From this perspective, therefore, building Japan's military resources should be a priority. To become the powerful defence state that Ishihara envisioned, Japan would have to abandon or modify Article 9. Ishihara did not feel that Japan had to consult other countries about constitutional change: this was a matter of national sovereignty rather than international diplomacy.[39]

Ishihara was certainly aware that the United States and China might oppose Japanese autonomy, especially if expressed militarily. He contended, however, that it was more important for Japan to restore its prestige as a world power than to worry about its relationships with other countries.[40] Ishihara argued that best way to confront Chinese resistance was to use its official development assistance more strategically as a political weapon against China's biggest weakness, its lack of capital.[41] In the long run, the optimal strategy would be to work to create internal tensions in the Chinese state.[42]

At the end of the day, Ishihara's position derived in large part from a deep-seated pride about Japan's capabilities. Reflecting on Japan's progress in the postwar period, Ishihara argued that Japan should trumpet the fact that it was one of the few non-Western countries to build a modern and prosperous state.[43] Ishihara was unequivocal in his belief that the Japanese success story was a decisive factor in the end of colonial rule in other parts of Asia.[44] From Ishihara's point of view, a nationalist and autonomous Japan should recognize its stature and create a strategic policy that reflected and strengthened its prestige, and should not exclude the strategic option of developing nuclear weapons.

Yasuhiro Nakasone

Falling somewhere in between Ozawa and Ishihara is Yasuhiro Nakasone. Most notably, Nakasone provides a different narrative of Japan's relationship with the United States. From Nakasone's perspective, overconfidence and a mistaken analysis of the international situation by the military in the mid-1930s led to a war that ultimately had started by mistake.[45]

Nakasone's evaluation of Japan's postwar relationship with the United States is strikingly positive. Nakasone argued that Japan's defeat had represented an unprecedented opportunity for the political transformation of Japan. It was only with the reform program initiated by General MacArthur that the democratic system, respect for freedom, and a commitment to human rights had become rooted in Japan. In light of such reforms, the United States and Japan had been able to build a relationship and an amicable alliance based on shared values and interests. By committing Japan to market-based principles of economic reform and growth, the U.S. reform strategy also had enabled Japan to achieve a remarkable level of development and economic prosperity, in part because it had been able to take advantage of the large consumer market in the United States. Nakasone, therefore, in sharp contrast to Ishihara, promoted a continued relationship with the United States.[46]

Nakasone also differed from Ishihara in his interpretation of Japan's relationship with the rest of Asia. While Nakasone argued that the war with the United States and the United Kingdom was an ordinary war among great powers, the war with Asian countries had been an act of aggression by Japan.[47] Despite its having used the rhetoric of liberation, Nakasone argued, Japan's main interest in Asia had been to acquire much-needed resources for its campaign against the United States. Contrary to the legitimating rhetoric of the time, the war had not been one of anti-colonial liberation: if liberation had resulted from Japan's presence in the region, it had been at best an afterthought and an unintended consequence of the war with the United States. In the final analysis, Japan had invaded Asia, an action that should be deeply regretted.[48]

Nakasone also took a more measured view of deterrence as a defensive strategy.[49] While agreeing that Japan should defend itself, Nakasone argued that its self-defence did not require abandoning its relationship with the United States. Unlike Ishihara, Nakasone believed that, while some level of militarization for security would be beneficial, developing nuclear weapons, let alone demonstrating the will to deploy them, would only hurt Japan's mutually profitable security relationship with the United States.[50] With respect to Japan's foreign military endeavours, Nakasone argued that Japan should fight alongside the United States only when its interests and security were severely threatened. In all other situations, it should avoid an armed conflict on foreign soil as much as possible.[51]

Reflecting on the history of the 1940s, when Japan had initiated a war with the United States without serious self-evaluation of its national power and with the intrusion of a politicized military, Nakasone argued that Japan should seek to maintain a stable security relationship with the United States and develop strong multilateral relationships with its Asian neighbours.[52] Japan's foreign policy, he argued, should be guided by four principles: first, Japan should not overreach its national power; second, Japan should not take diplomatic gambles; third, domestic politics should not be mixed with diplomacy; and fourth, Japan should go along with the major trends of the times.

Japan's relationships with North Korea and China were certainly challenges, Nakasone believed. However, unlike Ishihara, who was highly critical of any kind of relationship with either country, Nakasone considered these relationships in a larger historical context. Despite their non-democratic political culture, Nakasone believed that they could still be included in an Asian multilateral community. Although the democratization of a 'rogue' regime such as North Korea was not imminent, Nakasone pointed out that the regime was weakening quickly, and including North Korea in a larger Asia-Pacific community could expedite its 'normalization.'[53] With respect to China and Taiwan, Nakasone suggested that both countries continue to negotiate toward a peaceful unification, without pursuing immediate and drastic changes in the status quo that might destabilize the region.[54]

Nakasone's vision of Japan and the Asia-Pacific was grand and complex. He believed neither in the primacy of economics in regional relations nor in a realist vision of inevitable competition and struggle. Nakasone argued that Asian countries should work to build an 'Asian Security Community,' for which a normalized, multidimensional Japan was a necessary condition.[55]

Similarities among the Three Views

Despite their evident differences, the understandings of Ozawa, Ishihara, and Nakasone of Japanese normalization reveal notable areas of convergence. Although their views of Japanese foreign and strategic policies are strikingly at odds with one another, the three have surprisingly similar views on domestic political issues. Four issues unite them: the need for constitutional change; the need to strengthen political leadership; the need for a crisis management system; and the need to increase Japan's contributions at the international level.

The Need for Constitutional Change

For all three, Japanese normalization requires changing the Constitution. However, despite unanimous agreement on this general point, they differ on why such constitutional change is required.

Ozawa's argument for constitutional reform was pragmatic. Examining the activities of the SDF, he argued that the constitutional stipulations and the actual activities of the SDF, both domestic and international, did not correspond. Accordingly, Ozawa argued that the Constitution, particularly Article 9, had to be amended to reflect the realities of Japan's military activities. He also argued that only when Article 9 had been amended would Japan have genuine control and autonomy over the SDF.[56] The important point here is that Ozawa did not argue for limiting the role of the SDF. Instead, he advocated constitutional reform in order to provide Japan with a more realistic foreign and defence policy.

Rather than focusing on functional correspondence, Nakasone's argument for constitutional change stemmed from the historical context in which the Constitution had been conceived and adopted. The postwar 'Occupation Constitution' had been imposed by the supra-constitutional power of General MacArthur,[57] replacing the Meiji Constitution, which had been bestowed by the emperor. Neither, Nakasone pointed out, had been initiated or written by the Japanese people. Nakasone also agreed with Ozawa that, 50 years after its adoption, the Constitution no longer reflected the realities of Japanese politics and society. Nakasone's understanding of the necessary constitutional changes was quite expansive. He argued that it was necessary for the Japanese people to devise their own Constitution,[58] and that traditions of Japanese community and cultural identity that had been undervalued in the drafting of the postwar Constitution should be the cornerstone of a new one. Nakasone also noted that Japan had been dependent on the United States for its security for too long. A revised Constitution therefore should encompass principles of collective self-defence. He also argued for the direct election of the prime minister as a source of political legitimacy.[59] Hence, Nakasone's conception of constitutional change was not a minor revision of a few clauses but a thoroughgoing revision based on renewed philosophical foundations.

Ishihara took Nakasone's argument for the constitutional reform to an extreme. Like Nakasone, Ishihara questioned the legitimacy of a Constitution that had been imposed on Japan by the United States. However, while Nakasone considered some degree of functional correspondence to be a motivation for recovering Japan's pride, Ishihara categorically denied the legitimacy of the existing postwar Constitution. The Diet, he said, should declare its illegitimacy and quickly move on to rewriting a new and more native – and therefore more legitimate – Constitution.[60]

The Need to Strengthen Political Leadership

Despite their different degrees of conservatism, Ozawa, Nakasone, and Ishihara all agreed that the political leadership in Japan should be strengthened. They argued particularly against the bureaucratization of Japanese politics and, to that end, they supported the greater empowerment of the prime minister's office and the cabinet.

Ozawa claimed that, even if Japan aspired to a greater role in international affairs, its domestic political structure of 'non-decision' stood in the way, for five reasons. First, the Japanese government virtually acted as the lawyer for private corporations in defending their economic interests in the international arena, rather than advocating for Japan's national interest. Second, the 'majority principle' in the Diet was mechanically observed, while resolutions by responsible political leaders were often disregarded. Third, the principle of unanimous decision-making prevented the Diet from making critical decisions. Fourth, the prime minister's office was institutionally too weak to lead. And, fifth, the rigidity of the vertically organized bureaucracy amplified inertia.

To overcome these structural deficiencies, Ozawa argued that the prime minister's office should be endowed with greater responsibility,[61] enlarged to include various 'secretary of state' positions, and be responsible for the overall coordination of domestic and foreign policies. Moreover, bureaucrats should not be subject to questioning by politicians in the Diet. Finally, he suggested that decision-making could be made more efficient by appointing more politicians to positions in various ministries in the government.[62]

Nakasone, for his part, contended that Japan lacked a well-defined national strategy. In order to bring coherence to it, he argued – in line with Ozawa – that the prime minister's office and the cabinet should be strengthened. For Nakasone, the most effective way to empower the prime minister was for him or her to be directly elected by popular vote, rather than by the Diet.[63] In addition, he argued for the creation of a cabinet intelligence bureau, and felt that the Japanese political system should make better use of advisory groups and deliberative councils. Perhaps most important, Nakasone stressed the importance of changing the mindset of the Japanese public. Japan, he said, had long been a 'drifting state,' influenced by a public that favoured a *laissez-faire* approach to politics. Many Japanese also viewed the government with suspicion, which discouraged broader and deeper public interest in politics or engagement with the political system of the kind needed to energize a strong consensus on a national strategy.

The Need for a Crisis Management System

In addition to constitutional and governmental reform, all three conservative leaders argued for the creation of a crisis management system to address external threats and natural disasters.

For Ozawa, indeed, the most important function of any state was crisis management.[64] The fact that Japan had no provision for who should step in for a prime minister who was unable to function was, for Ozawa, a significant weakness in the Japanese political system. He therefore advocated instituting a legal framework for crisis management.

Nakasone attributed the lack of a crisis management facility to the fact that Japan had never seriously considered the possibility of facing a crisis situation some day.[65] To be sure, following the 1995 Kobe earthquake, Japanese policy-makers had begun to consider the necessity of a crisis management unit, but despite the growing discussion and popularity of such a unit, Nakasone argued that much more needed to be done to make it a reality. To move the discussion forward, he advocated the creation of an 'emergency management office' headed by the prime minister.[66]

For Ishihara, clandestine intrusions of North Korean spy ships into Japanese territorial waters were a prime exemplar of why Japan needed a crisis management system. In the absence of a 'national control tower,' Ishihara argued, it took too long for Japanese officials to deal with emerging crisis situations.[67] He deplored the lack of any kind of crisis management system, and felt the need so acutely that, as governor of Tokyo, he carried out several crisis management simulations.

The Need to Increase Japan's International Contributions

Finally, Ozawa, Nakasone, and Ishihara all agreed that Japan should take the initiative to substantially increase its international contributions. In particular, they all argued that such commitments should include increasing the participation of the SDF in international missions.

Ozawa maintained that Japan's international contributions should correspond to its economic wealth. As Japan was able to prosper under relatively peaceful conditions in the postwar period, it had a responsibility to contribute to building international peace and security to ensure that other countries had the same opportunities for political stability and economic growth.[68] Rather than adopt a policy of 'one-country pacifism,' Ozawa proposed that Japan take a leadership role in promoting international peace by supporting the development of a special UN reserve unit within the SDF.[69]

While many interpreters of the Constitution insisted that Article 9 precluded collective self-defence, Nakasone did not. He felt the two were compatible, and that collective self-defence should be actively promoted. To that end, he advocated passing a national security law. For Nakasone, dispatching the SDF overseas to support multilateral peacekeeping and peacebuilding initiatives was a diplomatic affair that failed to contribute to Japan's national security, and that Japan could make a larger contribution to the world notwithstanding the Constitution's peace clause.[70]

Differences among the Three Views

Despite the notable convergence among Ozawa, Nakasone, and Ishihara on several issues, the three disagreed on a number of key areas. In particular, they disagreed significantly about the scope, content, and direction of Japanese foreign policy, the appropriate framework through which to pursue Japanese security, and how Japan should deal with its colonial past.

Foreign Policy

Ozawa articulated a three-pronged approach to Japanese foreign policy: first, Japan should aim to maintain a stable and productive alliance with the United States; second, it should support an international system in which the UN played a seminal role; and finally, Japan should strive to build amicable relationships with its neighbours in the Asia-Pacific region.[71] Ozawa put particular emphasis on support for the UN, as the world strove to redefine the dynamics of world order following the end of the Cold War.[72] For Ozawa, the UN represented the notion of a robust international society. He therefore advocated active Japanese support of and involvement with various UN activities and agencies. Ozawa was also highly sensitive to Japan's relationship with the United States. As Washington increasingly asked for support from its allies, Ozawa perceived U.S. power to be in decline. But Japan, he felt, was indebted to the United States for its postwar prosperity and security, so Japan should cooperate with the United States in its international endeavours.[73]

In contrast to Ozawa's more liberal-internationalist perspective of world politics, Ishihara's was a more neo-realist view.[74] Ishihara was sceptical about the ability of international institutions to mitigate and manage international conflicts. Rather than relying on a UN-sponsored international society to promote international peace – and, by extension, Japan's security – Japan should 'fend for itself,' developing its own capacities for self-defence. In a world system of 'self-help,' Ishihara argued against relying on the United States for its security. In the ultimate test of crisis, there was no guarantee that the United States would come to Japan's rescue, particularly if it were not in the United States' national interest to do so. Ishihara's cynicism was largely directed against China. Not hiding any intention to compete with China for regional supremacy, Ishihara went so far as to say that Japan's national security required China's dissolution.

Like Ozawa, Nakasone promoted a continued and even greater relationship with the United States. Unlike Ozawa, however, he did not put much faith in the UN. Nakasone did not perceive the United States to be in decline; rather, he argued that the United States was the hegemon in the international system. The basic principle of Japanese diplomacy, therefore, should be to strengthen cooperative ties with Washington. From Nakasone's perspective, international organizations could play only a supplementary role in building international order.

Nakasone's support for the United States also distinguished his foreign policy position from that of Ishihara. In contrast to Ishihara's deep suspicion of any kind of alliance with the United States, Nakasone argued that Japan's primary foreign policy priority was to strengthen its bilateral relationship with the United States. Nakasone also disagreed fundamentally with Ishihara's confrontational stance toward Japan's Asian neighbours, advocating a 'pan-Asian security community' that ultimately would comprise not merely Japan's immediate neighbours but the rest of East Asia as well.[75] Nakasone argued that, despite its tragic experience of war and colonialism, Japan should still attempt to construct an 'East Asian Community' that would include South Korea and China, and that other Asian countries – including North Korea – should be embraced, not isolated. For Nakasone, however, the relationship with the United States differed from community building in East Asia. Some non-democratic Asian countries might become members of an East Asian community with a longer-term transformation of them in mind.

Security Policy

Ozawa's security policy was closely linked to his foreign policy framework: an emphasis on maintaining close cooperative ties with the United States in order to foster Asian regional security. Although Ozawa placed greater importance on supporting the UN for the ends of international peace and prosperity, he acknowledged the degree to which Japanese security had been contingent on its close relationship with the United States. Fostering a robust UN, therefore, should be done in conjunction with building a strong and reliable relationship with the United States.[76]

Nakasone's view of Japanese foreign policy was based on five principles: First, Japan should abide by its Constitution and respect the principle of 'exclusive self-defence'; second, a balance should be maintained between foreign and security policy; third, civilian control should be firmly observed; fourth, the 'three non-nuclear principles' should be preserved;[77] and fifth, the SDF should perform the main functions of Japan's defence, with the United States-Japan alliance playing a complementary role.[78]

Not surprisingly, Ishihara's security policy reflected his strong support for a self-reliant, defensive Japanese state. As all countries – including the United States – are potential enemies, Japan should free itself from its postwar dependence on Washington. The U.S. nuclear umbrella, Ishihara maintained, provided nothing more than an illusion of security for Japan.[79] Strengthening Japan's independent capability to defend itself should therefore be the essence of Japanese security policy.

The History Question

Ozawa did not deny the fact that, to put it euphemistically, Japan had unhappy historical experiences with Asian countries. Rather, Ozawa acknowledged it, arguing that it was all the more important to work toward building more friendly and cooperative relations with Asian countries, and that grassroots exchange was critical to the revitalization of those relations.[80] He was inclined to make apologies for Japan's past wrongdoings. Nor did he think that visits to the Yasukuni Shrine were themselves problematic, as they could be seen simply as paying tribute to Japanese who had sacrificed their lives for the nation. He believed, however, that enshrining Class-A war criminals there was wrong because they were not victims but initiators of the war.[81]

In line with Ozawa, Nakasone argued that Japan had to acknowledge and apologize for its wars of aggression in Asia, and strive to overcome its hostile past by building multilateral relations with Asian countries.[82] About Korea, Nakasone said that, while the country had been annexed under an international treaty, the treaty itself had been signed under military coercion. He did not deny that, during the colonial period, Japan had hurt the Korean people's pride. With regard to the United States, however, Nakasone argued that Japan had initiated the war not as an aggression against a weak nation, but as a strategic mistake by a politicized military, and that it thus was not necessary to apologize for it.

For Ishihara, Japan's colonial past could be justified in light of the imperialism other countries had pursued in that period. Ishihara argued that Japanese colonialism, in some ways, had played the role of protector and liberator of Asian countries from Western imperialism. Ishihara asserted that Japan ought to end to its 'repentance diplomacy' with its Asian neighbours. In his view, how history is constructed was a matter of domestic debate, not one that inquired into the views and interpretations of other countries. Stated starkly, he argued that Japan should autonomously decide what and how it chose to remember. Ishihara saw the visits of Japanese leaders to the Yasukuni Shrine as affirming the Japanese state. Paying tribute to ancestors who had died in the war was a basic duty for a state leader, and not subject to international scrutiny.[83] Unlike with Ozawa and Nakasone, one is hard pressed to find any remorse in Ishihara's narrative of Japanese history.

Implications

Looking back on changes in Japanese politics and society since the 1990s, one sees that aspects of the normalization programs Ozawa, Nakasone, and Ishihara advocated are already under way. Significant progress has been made in the areas of constitutional change, governmental reform, and crisis management. While constitutional reform was a taboo issue in Japanese politics prior to the 1990s, today there is a widespread consensus that change of some kind is required. Whereas dispatching the SDF overseas was once considered unthinkable, since 1992 their involvement in foreign missions has slowly increased. The SDF were even sent in a combatant capacity to support the U.S. mission in Iraq. Since the mid-1990s, the prime minister's office has seen its staff grow from 500 to 2000; the intelligence capacity of the cabinet has been expanded and strengthened; bureaucrats have been barred from commenting on political issues in the Diet; and the number of political appointees in each ministry has increased. A new crisis management system is in place, including plans for a U.S.-style National Security Council. Without question, in areas of agreement among these three conservative leaders, significant progress has been made.

Obstacles remain on the issues of disagreement. Japan's relations with the United States are confused and inconsistent, appearing at times almost haphazard, affected as they are by a combination of international, domestic, local, and even personal factors, not all of which are in play at any given time. There is also a great confusion in Japanese policy toward Asia, where pragmatism on functional and economic issues contends with strident emotionalism on the history question. On top of everything, Japan remains divided on the degree to which it should pursue a security strategy that gives a prominent role to the military. Japanese progress toward normalization is therefore difficult to assess. On issues where conservative leaders agree and converge, progress has been made toward significant change; where they disagree or diverge, the lack of consensus continues to block progress. Japanese liberals and progressives could step in whenever gaps appear in conservatives' concepts of a 'normal' Japan.

Despite wide-ranging opinions about what is required for Japan to become a 'normal country,' the surrounding discourse has some distinctive characteristics. First, normalization is always taken to mean the increased Westernization of Japan – in terms of both its institutional structure and its major political relationships. Many consider the United Kingdom a model to emulate.[84] It is beyond doubt that Japan does not want to remain just an Asian country. Nor do Japanese leaders think that Japan can find an appropriate place in Asia alone.[85]

Second, Japanese political leaders put a great deal of emphasis on institutional engineering as a requirement for Japan's normalization. Changing the Constitution, introducing new institutional mechanisms in the political process, and devising a new administrative system are considered essential to 'normalizing' Japan. 'Normalcy' seems to consist more on how Japan operates – in the structure and dynamics of its institutions, in other words – than in what Japan actually does. This leaves an interesting and potentially fateful lacuna in the normalization debate. Despite all the talk of normalization, Japanese leaders have said little about what should happen after Japan has become a 'normal country.' Although outspoken on the need to change Japanese institutions, Japanese leaders remain ambiguous about what Japan should look like – and precisely what it should do – after it has become 'normal.'[86]

NOTES

1 See Ichirō Ozawa, *Nihon Kaizo Keikaku* [Blueprint for a new Japan] (Tokyo: Kodansha, 1993).
2 See Osamu Watanabe, *Seiji Kaikaku to Kenpo Kaisei: Nakasone kara Ozawa he* [Political reform and constitutional revision: From Nakasone to Ozawa] (Tokyo: Aoiki Shoten, 1994). Watanabe describes the historical lineage of political reform from a critical perspective. He links political reform since the Nakasone times to an effort to revise the Constitution.
3 See Ho Sup Kim, Myun Woo Lee, Sang Il Han, and Won Deok Lee, *Ilbon Uik Yonku* [Studies on the Japanese right wing] (Seoul: Joongsim, 2000).
4 See Atsushi Kusano, *Renritsu Seiken* [Coalition governments] (Tokyo: Bungeishunjusha, 1999). Kusano examines political cleavages among coali-

tion partners in Japanese politics in the 1990s, arguing that they ultimately led to a convenient compromise among political forces. I extend this logic to the whole postwar period, adding an axis of controversy.

5 See Yoshikazu Sakamoto, *Sengo Gaiko no* Genten [Starting point of Japanese diplomacy] (Tokyo: Iwanami Shoten, 2004); and Masayoshi Takemura, *Chiisakutomo Kirarito Hikaru Kuni Nihon* [Small but sparkling Japan] (Tokyo: Kobunsha, 1994). According to Takemura, Japan's success following a policy of so-called one-country pacifism suggests that, rather than remilitarizing, it should choose a uniquely Japanese way.

6 Japan's Socialist Party platform has consistently embraced this position since 1955. See Yoshihisa Hara, *Sengoshi no naka no Nihon Shakaito* [The Japanese Socialist Party in postwar history] (Tokyo: Chuko Shinsho, 2000).

7 See Masataka Kosaka, '*Tsusho kokka nihon no unmei* [Japan's fate as a trading state],' *Chuo Koron*, November 1975. Kosaka also argued that Japan should continue to play the role of a global merchant, eschewing international political entanglements and concentrating on commercial activity: Masataka Kosaka, *Bunmei ga suibo suru toki* [When civilizations decline] (Tokyo: Shinchosha, 1981), p. 268.

8 Foreign observers have also characterized Japanese strategy in the postwar period as 'mercantile realism'; see Eric Heginbotham and Richard Samuels, 'Mercantile Realism and Japanese Foreign Policy,' *International Security* 22 (4, 1998): 171–203.

9 For more on conservative mainline policy, or *hoshu honryu*, see Muramatsu Michio and Ellis Krauss, 'The Conservative Policy Line and the Development of Patterned Pluralism,' in *The Political Economy of Japan*, vol. 1, *The Domestic Transformation*, edited by Yamamura Kozo and Yasuba Yasukichi (Palo Alto, CA: Stanford University Press, 1987).

10 Ozawa, *Nihon Kaizo Keikaku.*

11 Shimizu Ikutaro should be considered one of the pioneers who took this line of thinking. He wrote, 'On the one hand Japan should encourage friendly relations with the U.S., the Soviet Union and all other countries, but at the same time we must not forget for an instant that Japan is alone. In the end we can only rely on Japan and the Japanese'; *Nippon yo Kokka tare* [Japan, be a true state] (Tokyo: Bungeishunjusha, 1980), pp. 65–6; cited in Kenneth Pyle, *The Japanese Question: Power and Purpose In a New Era* (Washington, DC: AEI Press, 1996), p. 60.

12 From the standpoint of prioritizing national pride, a social movement for rewriting Japanese national history is emerging; see Kanji Nishio, *Kokumin no Rekishi* [People's history] (Tokyo: Sankei Shimbunsha, 1999).

13 See Shintaro Ishihara, *No to Ieru Nippon* [Japan that can say no] (Tokyo: Kobunsha, 1989).

14 See Pyle, *The Japanese Question*, for an extended discussion on changing discourses about Japan's national strategy.
15 For a discussion on the evolution of political conflicts under the '1955 system,' see Gerald L. Curtis, *The Japanese Way of Politics* (New York: Columbia University Press, 1988); and Shinichi Kitaoka, *Jimintō* [Liberal Democratic Party] (Tokyo: Yomiuri Shimbun-Sha, 1995).
16 Jennifer Lind argues that Japan passed the security buck to the United States in the postwar period: 'Pacifism or Passing the Buck? Testing Theories of Japanese Security Policy,' *International Security* 29 (1, 2004): 92–122.
17 See Cheol Hee Park, 'Political Dynamics of Regime Transformation in Japan in the 1990s,' *Japanese Journal of Political Science* 5 (2, 2004): 311–22.
18 See Takeshige Kunimasa, *Wangansenso toiu Tenkanten* [The Gulf War as a Turning Point] (Tokyo: Iwanami Shoten, 1999).
19 Curtis warns right-wing political forces of the Japanese variation that might emerge; Gerald L. Curtis, *The Logic of Japanese Politics* (New York: Columbia University Press, 1999), chap. 6.
20 See Eiji Oguma and Yoko Ueno, *Iyasi no Nashonarizumu* [Nationalism as an emotional pacifier] (Tokyo: Keio University Press, 2003), for a nuanced discussion of the emergence of Japanese nationalism at the grassroots level.
21 I use this diagram to account for changing discourses about Japanese national strategies in another article; see Cheol Hee Park, '*Koizumi Jungkwon eui Daioi Jungchaek Kyuljung Nonri wa Hankook euo Daieung Chunryak*' [The logic of external policy-making under the Koizumi cabinet and Korea's diplomatic strategy to cope with it], IFANS Policy Research Series 2002–11 (Seoul: Institute of Foreign Affairs and National Security, 2003).
22 Ozawa, *Nihon Kaizo Keikaku*, pp. 102–3.
23 Ibid., p. 107. In this sense, Ozawa assumed that Japan should support the United States.
24 Ibid., p. 108.
25 Ibid., p. 25.
26 Ibid., p. 5.
27 Ibid., pp. 68–9.
28 Ibid., p. 110.
29 Ibid., p. 127.
30 Ibid., p. 116.
31 Ibid., pp. 118–19.
32 Ibid., p. 124.
33 Shintaro Ishihara and SoIchirō Tahara, *Nippon no Chikara* [Japan's power] (Tokyo: Bungeishunjyu, 2005), p. 131.

34 Shintaro Ishihara and Soichirō Tahara, *Katsu Nippon* [Japan that wins] (Tokyo: Bungeishunjyu, 2000), p. 127.
35 Ibid., p. 216.
36 Shintaro Ishihara, *Amerika Sinko wo Suteyo* [Let's give up belief in America] (Tokyo: Kobunsha, 2000), p. 111.
37 Ishihara and Tahara, *Katsu Nippon*, p. 213. In this sense, Ishihara conceived of Japan not only as a supporter, but also as a potential challenger of the United States.
38 Ibid., p. 85.
39 Ibid., p. 207. Ishihara also maintained that, as a country capable of producing high-technology military equipment, Japan should not maintain its prohibition on weapons exports; see Ishihara and Tahara, *Nippon no Chikara*, p. 264.
40 Ibid., p. 79.
41 Ibid., p. 145.
42 Ibid., p. 156.
43 Ibid., p. 51.
44 Yasuhiro Nakasone and Shintaro Ishihara, *Eien Nare Nippon* [Japan forever] (Tokyo: PHP, 2001), pp. 108, 128.
45 Ibid., pp. 113–14.
46 Ibid., pp. 121, 125.
47 Ibid., p. 124.
48 Ibid., p. 126.
49 Ibid., p. 120.
50 Yasuhiro Nakasone, *Nihon no Sorigaku* [A Thesis on the Japanese prime minister] (Tokyo: PHP, 2004), p. 129.
51 Ibid., p. 128.
52 Nakasone and Ishihara, *Eien Nare Nippon*, p. 123.
53 Ibid., p. 181.
54 Ibid., p. 187.
55 Yasuhiro Nakasone, *Nihonjin ni Itteokitai Koto* [What I want to tell my fellow Japanese] (Tokyo: PHP, 1998), pp. 183–94.
56 Ozawa, *Nihon Kaizo Keikaku*, p. 123.
57 Yasuhiro Nakasone, *21 Seki Nihon no Kokka Senryaku* [Japan's national strategy in the twenty-first century] (Tokyo: PHP, 2000), pp. 150–1.
58 Ibid., p. 48.
59 Ibid., pp. 172–81.
60 Ishihara and Tahara, *Nippon no Chikara*, p. 157.
61 Ozawa, *Nihon Kaizo Keikaku*, pp. 40–5.
62 Ibid., pp. 61–4.

63 Nakasone, *21 Seki Nihon no Kokka Senryaku*, pp. 41–51.
64 Ozawa, *Nihon Kaizo Keikaku*, p. 91.
65 Nakasone, *Nihonjin ni Itteokitai Koto*, p. 126.
66 Ibid., pp. 132–4.
67 Shintaro Ishihara, *Nippon yo* [Oh, Japan] (Tokyo: Sankei Shimbunsha, 2002), p. 143.
68 Ozawa, *Nihon Kaizo Keikaku*, p. 107.
69 Ibid., p. 134.
70 Yasuhiro Nakasone, *Jiseiroku* [Self-Reflection] (Tokyo: Shinchosha, 2004), p. 124.
71 Ozawa, *Nihon Kaizo Keikaku*, p. 156.
72 Ibid., p. 127.
73 Ichirō Ozawa, *Kataru* [Say] (Tokyo: Bungeishunju, 1996), p. 53.
74 For an explication of neorealist theory, see Kenneth Waltz, *Theory of International Politics*, (New York: McGraw-Hill, 1979; and Robert Keohane, *Neorealism and Its Critics* (New York: Columbia University Press, 1986).
75 Nakasone, *21 Seki Nihon no Kokka Senryaku*, p. 52.
76 Ozawa, *Nihon Kaizo Keikaku*, p. 114.
77 The three non-nuclear principles are that nuclear weapons should not be 'possessed,' 'produced,' or 'brought in.'
78 Nakasone, *Nihon no souri gaku*, pp. 129–30.
79 Ishihara, *Amerika Sinko wo Suteyo*, p. 203.
80 Ichirō Ozawa, *Ozawa Shugi* [Ozawa-ism] (Tokyo: Shueisha International, 2006), p. 151.
81 Ichirō Ozawa, *Gowan Ishin* [Resolute restoration] (Tokyo: Kakugawa Shoten, 2006), p. 209.
82 Yasuhiro Nakasone and Kiichi Miyazawa, *Kaiken Goken* [Constitutional revision or constitutional preservation] (Tokyo: Asahi Shimbun, 1997), p. 127.
83 Ishihara, *Nippon yo*, p. 113.
84 Jiro Yamaguchi, *Sengo Seiji no Houkai* [Collapse of the postwar politics] (Tokyo: Iwanami Shinsho, 2004), p. 141.
85 In this sense, the discourse on Japan's becoming a normal state resembles Meiji-era intellectual Yukichi Fukuzawa's idea of 'getting out of Asia and entering the West (*Datsu-a nyu-ou*).'
86 This is one reason neighbouring countries have lingering doubts and suspicions about Japanese intentions and preferences. As Japanese intentions are not clearly articulated, neighbouring countries are worried about Japan's potentially playing a bigger politico-military role.

5 Chinese Discourse on Japan as a 'Normal Country'

JIANWEI WANG

Starting in late 2002, the Chinese academic and foreign policy community, as well as the general public, engaged in a heated and sometimes contentious debate about Japan and China's policy toward Japan. A discourse of the so-called new thinking on Japan emerged, with some scholars and analysts beginning to question some of the basic assumptions underlying Beijing's traditional policies toward Japan.[1] Much attention was devoted to this 'new thinking,' with several hundred articles on the subject published in 2003 alone.[2] Although there was no consensus on the meaning or content of 'new thinking,' the debate on China's policy toward Japan was an example of a rare occasion in the history of the People's Republic on which an important foreign policy was discussed and explored publicly and critically. Since the focus was on how China should handle its relations with Japan, the debate inevitably touched on China's perception of Japan as a 'normal' or 'abnormal' country.

There were many reasons for the rise of the 'new thinking' on Japan. First, some Chinese scholars and analysts were alarmed by the increasing mutual dislike, hostility, and suspicion between Chinese and Japanese in recent years. Such a trend, if not checked early enough, could lead the relationship into what the Chinese euphemistically call 'dangerous terrain.'[3] Second, the chronic instability in Sino-U.S. relations, particularly under the Bush administration, prompted some Chinese foreign policy analysts to seek strategic alternatives that could either substitute the pivotal importance of the United States in China's foreign relations or strengthen China's posture vis-à-vis the United States. Just as in the early 1980s, when Sino-U.S. relations soured as a result of the Reagan administration's pro-Taiwan policy, some Chinese turned to Japan to alleviate U.S. pressure on China. Third, the conservative and rightward shift in Japanese domestic politics convinced some Chinese elites that China's traditional policy toward Japan was anachronistic. They argued that Beijing should take note of the new reality in Japanese politics and make necessary adjustments in its Japan policy. Finally, the succession of the PRC leadership from the third to the fourth generation provided an opportunity for wholesale policy review, raising expectations among the Chinese elite for 'new thinking' in Chinese foreign policy in general and in China's policy toward Japan in particular.[4]

The Chinese debate on Japan reached its climax in 2003; by 2004–05, the debate had been gradually overtaken by a downturn in the relationship, and the 'new thinking' school became more subdued. But the seminal change of discourse among China's Japan specialists had already taken place. Bruised but not defeated, the 'new thinking' school did not disappear completely. Rather, it continued among China's Japan scholars, researchers, and retired diplomats in various ways.[5] The recent rapprochement in the relations between the two countries certainly has created a more favourable political circumstance for the 'new thinking' school to reassert itself. With that in mind, this chapter focuses on Chinese perspectives on three questions touched on in the debate and related to the theme of Japan as a normal country: Should Japan become a normal country? How might Japan become a normal country? And, finally, how China should deal with Japan as a normal country?

Should Japan Become a Normal Country?

For a long time, the Chinese public took as 'normal' a Japan without a standing army, an independent security and defence policy, or the right to engage in overseas military conflict. Any small changes along these lines on the Japanese side were considered 'abnormal' and by definition not good for China and Asia.

Chinese intellectuals have begun to question this traditional view of Japan's normalcy. They increasingly define Japan's foreign policy in the postwar period as a process of seeking 'normal country' status, and do not indiscriminately deny the legitimacy of such an objective.[6] Some Chinese scholars are aware of the gap between Japan's status as the second-largest economy and its political status in international affairs, between Japan's contribution to world affairs such as through the United Nations and its influence in international decision-making.[7] Such a gap, many believe, is unsustainable in the long run. Japan's becoming a normal country and in turn a political and military power, according to them, is just a matter of time, irrespective of whether China and other Asian countries like it or not. Furthermore, these scholars argue, given the 65 years since Japan's defeat in World War Two, Japan likely has 'paid the price,' and it is now time to allow it to assume its deserved position in the international community as a normal power. As a pioneer of the 'new thinking' school, Ma Licheng, put it, 'Looking back to history, it is impossible to prevent forever a defeated country from restoring its normal country status. Facing the prospect of Japan to become a political and military major power, we should be psychologically prepared.'[8]

Other scholars have tried to relate the acceptance of Japan as a normal country, with major power status in world politics, to a central objective of China's post–Cold War foreign policy. China, together with Russia and France, in order to offset or modify the unipolar world order dominated by the United States, has been advocating the multipolarization of world politics. The current process of Japanese normalization, these scholars argue, should therefore be seen as part of this process of multipolarization and should be welcomed.[9] If China could be a pole, Japan should also be allowed to be a pole in this multipolar structure.

What does Japan as a 'normal country' mean? It is relative to Japan as a 'special' state after its defeat in World War Two. To be a normal country means that Japan should resume all the rights it so far has been denied but that other countries have – including the right to have a standing armed forces, to engage in war, to exercise collective self-defence, and to have an independent foreign and defence policy.[10] Some Chinese scholars realize that Japan's search for normalcy is the aspiration of the Japanese nation, not merely a result of manipulation of opinion by a small number of right-wing conservatives. The landslide victory of Japan's Liberal Democratic Party (LDP) in 2005, with its policy of normalization, demonstrated the degree to which the idea of a normal Japan resonates with Japanese society at large. This political consensus is even reflected in certain policies advocated by the opposition Socialist Party and the Japanese Communist Party, so even if they were to come to power, they probably would not institute significant policy changes.[11] In short, making Japan a normal country has broad grass roots support in Japan, particularly among the younger generation.[12]

What, then, are the implications of Japan's becoming a normal country? Would Japan once again march on the old track of militarism about which the rest of Asia is so concerned? In this regard, the 'new thinking' school suggests that China should differentiate between Japan's necessary arms buildup as a normal state and its return to traditional militarism, and that it is highly unlikely that Japan would embark once again on such a path.[13] These scholars note that Japan has taken the route of peaceful development for the past half-century. The Japanese people have benefited from this development model and consequently the ideology of pacifism is deeply rooted in the Japanese people's psyche. This pacifism, according to 'new thinkers,' is a valuable common asset of all Asian countries, including China.[14] In addition, so far the right-wing and conservative movement in Japanese politics has not fundamentally changed Japan's liberal democratic political system.[15] Such a system makes it very difficult for extreme positions to become the ideological mainstream. 'New thinking' school scholars therefore caution that China should not overstate the influence of the right-wing conservative movement in Japanese politics.[16] More radically, some even suggest that China's paranoia about the revival of Japanese militarism results from its own ethnocentrism in understanding Japan.[17]

Few Japan-watchers in China publicly oppose Japan's becoming a normal country and securing its proper position under the sun. But uneasiness with the prospect of Japan as a normal power can be detected subtly in some analysts' writings. More sceptical and traditionalist scholars argue that, in many aspects, Japan is already a normal country, with formidable economic and military power. For example, according to a study by Chinese scholars, Japan's military spending surpasses that of other 'normal' major powers such as France, the United Kingdom, and Germany and is second only to that of the United States.[18] Japan's 'abnormalcy,' they argue, therefore does not consist in the absence of military power; indeed, Japan's level of military expenditure goes beyond the need of self-defence and is far from compatible with Japan's constitutionally defined principle of 'exclusive defence.'

Sceptics are also wary of the fact that Japan has failed so far to deal squarely with its imperialistic legacy or take responsibility for its guilt. This is a clear indication that Japan, unlike Germany, lacks the political will and maturity to become a normal country that is not burdened by its historical baggage. The 'normalization' of such a country could hardly benefit the stability of the region.[19]

Based on these observations, what Japan might do to its neighbours after it has become a normal state is far from certain. Unless a country fully recognizes and repents its past wrongdoing, there is no guarantee it would not do the same thing again in the future. Given that Japan has launched wars of aggression many times in its history, Asian countries have maintained a high degree of vigilance against Japanese attempts to expand its military power unduly.[20] Sceptics have serious doubts about whether the current Japanese political system has enough checks and balances to ensure that right-wing militant forces never again usurp state power and launch military aggression against other countries. Unlike 'new thinking' scholars, sceptics contend that Japan's peace Constitution and its postwar pacifist value system have been largely hollowed out and weakened by the surge of right-wing influence in Japanese politics. In their view, there is nothing in current Japanese society to prevent right-wing militant forces from strengthening their influence in Japanese politics. To them, therefore, Japan's transformation into a military power is not 'normal' at all.[21]

The perceived increasing assertiveness of Japanese foreign policy in recent years has sent chilling signals to some Chinese Japan-watchers. For instance, they have been alarmed by Japan's tougher policies toward its territorial disputes with its neighbouring countries, including the Diaoyu (Senkaku) dispute with China, the Northern Territories dispute with Russia, and the Dokdo/Takeshima dispute with South Korea. Some Chinese observers describe such a strategy as 'hitting out in three directions.' They point out that Japan's intensifying its territorial disputes with three countries simultaneously was unprecedented in its postwar diplomacy.[22] If that is what Japan would do even when it is still 'abnormal,' what kinds of policies might Japan pursue if and when it assumed a more normal position in international politics?[23] Once again, Chinese analysts attribute Japan's more assertive foreign policy to a perceived upsurge in right-wing and conservative factions in Japanese politics. Some even suggest that the domestic political climate in today's Japan is quite similar to that on the eve of World War Two, when Japan invaded China and other Asian countries.[24]

Another twist in the discussion about whether Japan should become a normal country is that some Chinese analysts believe that, given Japan's unique geopolitical conditions, its dream of becoming a 'normal' major power might never materialize even it were allowed to. Japan's small territory, highly concentrated population, and lack of natural resources all make the country inherently vulnerable in its national defence and security, a weakness that not even the acquisition of nuclear weaponry could overcome. That is why Japan has to rely on the military protection of the United States.[25] One Chinese scholar bluntly has declared that, given Japan's geographical limitations, Japan lacks the foundational capabilities and resources to become a first-class major power, as is evident by its many failed attempts to ascend to great power status in the prewar period. Today, if Japan were still unable to identify its proper position in East Asian international relations and attempted to renew its old dream of hegemonic power, it certainly would fail again.[26]

Taken together, these different Chinese positions have produced an ambiguous appraisal of the consequences of Japan's 'normalization.' For many Chinese, there is nothing 'normal' about Japan's becoming a normal state. Because of history and the Chinese view of Japan's national character, people might be more at ease if Japan remained an 'abnormal' country, particularly in terms of military power and its role in regional and world security affairs. It would be not just in the interest of Japan's neighbours, but also more beneficial to Japan itself, as its peaceful postwar economic prosperity demonstrates. Put differently, an 'abnormal' Japan would be 'normal' for the rest of Asia, whereas a 'normal' Japan might imply unpredictable risk for China and other Asian countries.

How Could Japan Become a Normal Country?

The worry of some Chinese analysts reveals the historical and political conditions under which China might accept Japan as a normal state. While most Chinese recognize the reality that Japan has been moving steadily toward a normal state in the past two decades or so, very few, even those with 'new thinking' orientation, agree that China and the world should accept Japan as a normal major power without strings attached. First and foremost, can Japan close the book on its war history?[27] On this issue, two views may be distinguished in Chinese academic and policy circles.

The 'new thinking' argues that, while Japan's war history remains an issue in its relations with China and other Asian countries, a further and fuller renunciation of Japan's imperial past should not be treated as a precondition for China and the world to maintain normal cooperative relations with Japan. Ma Licheng, expressing perhaps the most accommodating position, argues that Japan has done enough apologizing for its war history and the issue should now be put to rest.[28] In his highly controversial article on China's Japan policy, Shi Yinhong contends that, to prevent the war history issue from corrupting Sino-Japanese relations, it should be taken off the diplomatic agenda entirely.[29] This view has been endorsed by a number of other Chinese scholars and analysts to varying degrees. Some even quote Deng Xiaoping to justify a 'friendship first, history second' approach. Deng once said that strategic interests should be the priority in the relationship, putting aside the historical enmities and differences in political system and ideology. He also asserted that amity was more important than any other issues in Sino-Japanese relations.[30] From this perspective, resolving tensions between the two countries about historical legacies should not be a prerequisite for recognizing Japan as a normal country and developing good bilateral relations with it. For example, suspending high-level contact between the two countries because of the war history issue is not a sound policy; in fact, it has had the perverse effect of inciting and empowering the Japanese right wing. The underlying rationale behind this approach is that the history issue can be resolved only as overall Sino-Japanese relations continue to make progress.[31]

This position should not be seen as a concession to and acceptance of the Japanese failure to fully denounce their imperial past. Rather, it stems from the recognition of that, on its own, China could do little to change the mindset of the Japanese population. One well-known Japan specialist pointed out that only the Japanese people and government can decide how to perceive the war history. While only a small number of Japanese really want to whitewash war crimes, it is up to the Japanese people eventually to put an end to this issue. In other words, their thinking on this issue should change from within rather than be forced from without. It is not up to foreign governments or peoples but to the Japanese people themselves to get the job done.[32] Moreover, constant criticism and protest from foreign countries cannot help to solve the problem, and it could backfire.

For others, the issue is less whether Japanese perspectives on war can or should be changed by external pressure and more that a large-scale shift in interpretation is unlikely in Japan. More pessimistic observers argue that the historical narratives promoted by Japan's religious and cultural tradition indicate that Japan is unlikely ever to apologize for its war crimes in the way that Germany has – for example, the German prime minister has gone down on his knees in front of a tomb of Jewish victims. China can do little to change this unpleasant fact or force Japan to 'bow its head,' so current Chinese government handling of the history issue can accomplish little but intensify nationalism in both countries. In terms of China's long-term and overall interest, it might be more prudent just to drop the issue and 'swallow this bitter fruit.'[33]

Despite forceful arguments about the need to let go of history, however, the more traditional perspective still sees a resolution of the history issue as necessary for recognizing Japan's status as a normal country. Scholars embracing this position argue that Chinese narratives and memories of the Japanese invasion and occupation cannot easily be discarded even if people wanted to; history exists in the minds of people, and the government has no power to force people to forget.[34] As one analyst vividly puts it, 'History is just like an iron door with a big lock on it. One cannot get around it. One can only open it with the right key. This key is nothing else but the correct understanding of the history of Japan's war of aggression against China.' He goes on to argue that this is a cardinal issue of right and wrong: nobody has the right to ask the Chinese people to give up their right to criticize attempts to understate Japan's war crimes.[35]

Other observers also reject the Japanese claim that the reinterpretation of history rests solely with the Japanese people. Given that other countries were implicated in this history, they argue it transcends boundaries, and those who suffered from Japanese aggression should have a say.[36] Chinese leaders evidently have favoured this approach of 'history first, normal state second.' This was perhaps best reflected by Chinese leader Hu Jintao's personally telling Japanese prime minister Junichirō Koizumi that the crux of the problem in Sino-Japanese political relations was the visits of Japanese leaders to Yasukuni Shrine, a gesture regarding the war history that the Chinese regarded not merely as unacceptable, but offensive.[37] Accordingly, the Chinese leadership at that time explicitly stated that, if Japan intended to play a more important role in international affairs, it would have to renounce its history of aggressive warfare. Otherwise, it would be difficult, if not impossible, for Asian countries to accept Japan's status as a normal state.[38]

Although Chinese scholars and analysts disagree about whether acknowledging Japan's war history is a necessary precondition for its transformation into a normal country, they all equally deplore Prime Minister Koizumi's repeated visits to Yasukuni Shrine, arguing that such tributes to Japan's war history sit uneasily with Asian countries, especially in light of discussion about reforming the UN Security Council to give Japan, among others, a permanent seat.[39] Despite widespread disapproval of Koizumi's actions, analysts offered different explanations for Koizumi's motivation to do so. Some attributed it to serving the needs of domestic politics. Others blamed Koizumi's personal beliefs and character for his intransigence on this issue. Still others regarded it as yet another expression of Japan's determination to become a major power, one that does not yield to international pressure on an 'internal issue.'

In stark contrast to these views, some 'new thinking' scholars caution against reading too much into the visits, arguing that merely visiting the shrine should not be simplistically seen as evidence of denying a history of war crimes and militarism.[40] Indeed, visiting the shrine was not Koizumi's only activity and it would be wrong to judge him solely by this single event.[41] Although regrettable, Koizumi's visits, and various remarks about Japan's war history by Japanese politicians, should not negate the fact that the Japanese government has made significant progress toward apologizing for its war history to China and other Asian countries.[42]

For some Chinese analysts, in addition to the resolution of historical tensions, another precondition for Japan's transition to normal country status in the Asia-Pacific is a change in its overall foreign policy orientation and its related self-identification. They point out that Japan historically always desired to escape from Asia to join Europe. Japanese look down on other Asian nations because of their feeling of superiority that makes them able to be on par with European and Western countries. That sense of superiority has alienated other Asian countries that seldom see Japan as a truly indigenous 'normal country' in the region. Therefore, for Japan to become a normal country in the region, it should 'return' to Asia both politically and psychologically.

But historically Japan has displayed a pattern of collaborating with a non-Asian power to confront its peripheral countries.[43] Japan always desires to be in alliance with the stronger to deal with the weaker.[44] In particular, concerns have been raised about Japan's effort to strengthen its alliance with the United States in the post–Cold War period. Not only is this seen as a sign that Japan has yet to demonstrate a capacity for a more independent foreign policy, it also shows that Japan relies on the United States to increase its influence and exert power in East Asia as well as in the world. For these Chinese scholars, if Japan is serious about becoming a normal country in East Asia, it is time for Tokyo to pursue a different strategy.[45] Many Chinese observers notice that the United States is the most important international driving force behind the push for Japan's normalcy as a regional and global power.[46] In this respect, Chinese observers did not view favourably Koizumi's strong pro-American impulse in his foreign policy. They took as seriously mistaken the notion of some Japanese strategists that, so long as Japan-

United States relations were in good shape, other relationships would fall into place automatically.[47] Such an assumption, from the Chinese perspective, was a serious and dangerous 'strategic misjudgment.'[48] Moreover, Chinese analysts were quick to point out that Japan's pro-U.S. policies and gestures were not always fully rewarded by its patron. For instance, Japan had counted on the United States to support its bid for a permanent seat on the UN Security Council but instead received only half-hearted support and, at times, active resistance from the United States, which still puts its own interests above everything else.[49]

More broadly, the Chinese were very upset by Japan's perceived strategy of 'befriending distant states while attacking those nearby' in seeking its permanent seat on the Security Council. Japan's campaign tactics of bypassing its neighbours, including China, and 'surrounding East Asia with other regions' raised many eyebrows in China.[50] For many Chinese, to offend Asian nations by Koizumi's repeated visits to the notorious Yasukuni Shrine while prematurely attempting to push itself onto the Security Council with the backing of the United States was not a smart way for Japan to obtain major power status.[51] Such a behavioural pattern further indicated that Japan still did not take its Asian neighbours seriously. Japan simply cannot have it both ways: if it is to become a permanent member of the Security Council, it first must reach an understanding with its Asian neighbours and win their endorsement.[52]

Related to Tokyo's UN bid, China's Japan-watchers pointed out that, for Japan to become a genuine normal power, it was not sufficient for it to use money to 'buy' votes; Japan had to show more independence in its diplomacy. Some Chinese analysts described Japan's international political and security policy as 'blindly following the United States.' To the dismay of many Chinese, the 'lack of autonomy' in Japan's foreign policy had been reinforced rather than reduced since the mid-1990s. On many international issues, such as the War in Iraq, Japan displayed its 'small country diplomacy' rather than 'major country diplomacy.' If Japan did get a permanent seat on the Security Council, they wondered whether it would have the guts to 'hold justice' and the ability to differentiate right from wrong.[53]

Needless to say, Japanese autonomy comes with its own danger for China. If Japan were to distance itself from the United States, Japan might well develop a more independent foreign policy, requiring a more autonomous military force. Is China ready to accept such a 'normal' Japan? This dilemma has not been clearly reconciled in the minds of many Chinese Japan-watchers. For some, the ideal would be for

Japan to pursue a more independent foreign policy while restraining from strengthening its own military forces. But, as some other Chinese scholars have pointed out, China cannot have it both ways either. It cannot oppose Japan's strengthening its security alliance with the United States while also opposing its movement toward becoming a normal country with a more independent and assertive foreign policy.[54]

Reading between the lines of Chinese analysis of Japan as a normal power, an unspoken consensus can be detected: Japan's transformation into a normal country should not be achieved at the expense of China's interests. Some Chinese analysts perceive a sort of zero-sum game in which Japan is neglecting, if not deliberately jeopardizing, China's important interests in its rise as a normal country. They see an inclination in Japanese foreign policy to raise its status in international relations by being confrontational toward China on those issues on which Japan used to take a low profile.[55]

One symptom of Japan's 'normalization' is its incremental redefinition of its relationship with Taiwan, which Beijing views with alarm. For example, Japanese officials have publicly advocated the 'internationalization' of the Taiwan issue; Japan supports Taiwan's accession to the World Health Organization; is following in the footsteps of the United States in strengthening its security and military relations with Taiwan; and has agreed to include the Taiwan issue among United States-Japan 'joint strategic objectives.' All these moves, according to some Chinese observers, indicate that Japan is determined to stall China's eventual reunification with Taiwan. Indeed, to some extent, Japan is even more reluctant than the United States to see Taiwan become an integral part of China.[56] A series of legislation passed in recent years by the Japanese Diet to deal with emergency situations surrounding Japan is perceived by Chinese observers as paving the way for Japan's joint military intervention with the United States in the event of conflict in the Taiwan Strait. Some even wonder if Japan eventually would abandon its nominal 'One China' policy.[57] Another symptom of Japan's 'normalization' is its increasing awareness of 'the ocean interest,' which would also bring it into conflict with China, as reflected in Japan's noticeably hardened positions on the Diaoyu (Senkaku) Islands and the East China Sea disputes.[58]

How Should China Adjust to Japan as a 'Normal Country'?

Japan's move toward normal country status thus has significant implications for Sino-Japanese relations. The issue, however, is not only about the conditions under which Japan could or should become a normal country, but also about how China should respond to, and interact with, a Japan that aspires to normal major power status. For some Chinese scholars, how China manages its relationship with this transformation in Japan's international status will be the ultimate test of China's diplomatic sophistication and savvy. Here the most difficult issue is how to define the nature of Japan as a nation-state and the nature of Sino-Japanese relations.[59]

One approach is to understand Japan's aspiration to become a normal state in the context of China's own rise. Many scholars and analysts draw attention to the fact that both China and Japan are growing giants.[60] One is transforming itself from an economic power to a political and military power. The other is changing from a political power to an economic and military power.[61] In a sense, both countries want to become 'normal' states. Whereas Japan aims to become a normal country with political influence that is commensurate with its economic might and a standing army capable of defending itself and projecting power overseas, China's goal is to broaden its political influence by fully integrating into the international community and becoming a responsible and respectable economic and military player.[62] Thus, considering their respective goals and ambitions, rather than viewing the relationship between the two countries as antagonistic and competitive, it would be better to cultivate mutual empathy and work cooperatively by adjusting the standards by which each judges the other's behaviour.[63] While most Chinese analysts acknowledge the economic and technological gap between the two countries, some already accept the notion that China and Japan are about equal in terms of their respective comprehensive national power.[64] This means that, for the first time in history, Sino-Japanese relations have turned into a so-called strong-strong relationship. If one takes the broad perspective that China and Japan face a similar historical mission, then, if China is sincere about the desirability of multipolarity, it should welcome Japan's rise as a normal major power, just as the Japanese should learn to live alongside a rising China.[65]

Needless to say, the road to multipolarity will not be without complications.[66] For instance, one scholar points out the mutual dislike of Japan and the United States in the 1980s when Japan was a rising global economic power. Frictions between China and Japan therefore should not be surprising – but neither should they lead to panic.[67] Of course, that does not mean that Sino-Japanese relations do not need careful management. How to make sure that friction does not escalate into all-out conflict is the key challenge to Sino-Japanese strategic planners.[68] Both countries need to make some adjustments to the new reality in Sino-Japanese relations. Both sides should be willing to go beyond traditional assumptions and approaches and move toward not simply managing the relationship, but making a concerted effort to promote more amicable relations. Related to the debate about whether China should take Japan's 'correct' understanding of the war history as a precondition for normal political relations, some Chinese scholars hold that Beijing should not wait passively for the Japanese government to change its attitude and to become friendlier. Instead, China should take initiatives to cultivate a more favourable peripheral security environment that includes Japan.[69]

The steady deterioration of the political relationship since the emergence of the Japan debate in 2002, however, unfortunately suggests that both countries have failed to manage the relationship well. Put differently, the desire of both sides to seek 'normal country' status has caused some 'abnormalcy' in the relationship, which is now in need of 're-normalization.'[70] Some Chinese analysts have described the stagnant political relationship as 'cold peace,' probably just one step short of 'cold war,' and they offer competing diagnoses of and solutions to the problem. Mainstream opinion is that, while the Chinese government has not been flawless, the Koizumi government's policy and behaviour were responsible for the stalemate in the relationship.[71] Even some 'new thinkers' largely blame the Japanese for the 'icy' relationship between the two countries. More specifically, criticism was lodged against the Koizumi government's overall assertiveness in foreign policy, particularly in military and defence; its increasingly proactive role in the United States-Japan security alliance and related stands on Taiwan; its more provocative policy toward the Diaoyu (Senkaku) Islands and the East China Sea disputes; and, finally, what some perceive as Japan's unwillingness to acknowledge its history of aggression in the region. As a shorthand, some have summarized the outstanding problems between China and Japan as the five 'Ts': territory, Taiwan, textbook, theatre missile defence, and trade.[72] The issues surrounding Japan's war history and its position on Taiwan raise the greatest concern among the Chinese, as Japan appears to have shifted its low-profile approach toward an assertive willingness to say 'no' to China.[73]

Analysts differ, however, about who should take the blame and to what extent. Those with more radical views argue that the responsibility for the recent deterioration of Sino-Japanese relations lies squarely with Japan's misconduct. From this perspective, the history issue has arisen not from China's constant demands for apology, but from deliberate provocations by certain Japanese politicians to which China has had no choice but to respond. If that is the case, then it is Japan, not China, that needs 'new thinking' to improve relations.[74] Other analysts suggest, however, that, while the Koizumi government should shoulder much of the blame, China's policy and practice also require improvement. For example, prominent America-watcher Zhi Zhongyun argues that China's own inconsistency and utility-oriented policy and practice have made it difficult for Japan to address its war history in a way that adequately satisfies the Chinese population.[75] If China is partly to blame for the bad relations, then some 'new thinking' on the part of the Chinese side is necessary.

Another America expert, Shi Yinhong, offers the most dramatic and systematic set of recommendations to remedy Sino-Japanese relations. In a widely circulated essay published in 2003, he argues that China should seek a 'diplomatic revolution' to increase its 'closeness with Japan.' More specifically, he suggests that China put the history issue on hold, take measures to further increase Japan's imports and investment in China, take a more tolerant attitude toward Japan's military build-up, treat Japan as a normal major power, and support Japan's bid to become a permanent member of the Security Council. The rationale behind this view is that, for a lengthy period, China's main strategic concern will be the United States, not Japan. Significantly improving relations with Japan would considerably improve China's position vis-à-vis the United States.[76]

Shi's article triggered an interesting exchange about China's Japan strategy among Chinese international relations professionals. Traditionalists charged that his prescriptions were tantamount to an 'unconditional surrender' to Japan, one unlikely to garner the support of the majority of the Chinese people. They further criticized the practicality of his recommendations. Together with another prominent 'new thinker,' Ma Licheng, Shi has been described as a 'quack,' doling out prescriptions without a clear diagnosis.[77] Critics argued that the appropriate solution is for China to lay down clear conditions under which Japan would be considered and accepted as a normal country with major power status, rather than to grant recognition as a free lunch. First, on the war history issue, Japan should sign a formal statement of apology similar to the one it offered South Korea in 1998. The satisfaction of this provision would fully resolve the issue, leaving China with no need to ask for future apologies. In addition, visits by Japanese prime ministers to Yasukuni Shrine should be prohibited, and textbooks should not downplay Japanese war crimes. Second, Japan should make a commitment not to interfere in China's unification with Taiwan; to this end, Japan should sever its relations with the pro-independent constituencies in Taiwan. Third, Japan should relinquish its effort unilaterally to control the Diaoyu (Senkaku) Islands, respect China's sovereignty in the area, and resolve the dispute through negotiation. If Japan agreed to these conditions, China could recognize Japan's political power status and support its bid for a Security Council position. Otherwise, China should use its veto power without hesitation.[78]

Though they fall short of advocating such a crude, power-driven response, more moderate scholars also express reservations about Shi Yinhong's goodwill strategy. Their main concern is whether Japan would reciprocate with a goodwill strategy of its own. Most analysts are not sure.[79] From their point of view, while China has changed its attitude and strategy toward Japan significantly in recent years, incorporating some elements of the 'new thinking,'[80] Japan's reciprocal change in attitude has been limited. To the contrary, the Koizumi government turned out to be more assertive and more oppositional in its stance toward China. This has convinced many observers that, without reciprocal 'new thinking' on the Japanese side, the unilateral 'new thinking' on the Chinese side will not bear much fruit,[81] limiting the prospects for Sino-Japanese 'closeness.' Moderates thus dismiss as wishful thinking Shi Yinhong's expectation that a friendlier attitude toward Japan would elicit Japan's cooperation in China's dealings with the United States.

The most significant weakness of Shi Yinhong's position, from the moderate perspective, is its failure to take into account Japan's grand strategy. According to some analysts, Japan's basic strategy is quite clear: to ally with the United States in order to hedge China's rise. Understanding Japan's position in this way explains why the Koizumi government took such an unyielding stance toward China and why Koizumi kept visiting the shrine, totally ignoring China's strong feelings. For Japan's future status, the best scenario is that it becomes Asia's United Kingdom. It is unlikely that Japan would become Asia's Germany or France. In this context, it will be nearly impossible for China and Japan to achieve genuine strategic cooperation similar to that between Germany and France.[82] Thus, moderates contend that China will never be in a position to use Sino-Japanese relations to hedge against the

United States or cast as a bone between the United States and Japan because the alliance between those two countries is much more solid than either United States-China relations or China-Japan relations.[83] Indeed, some predict that, in the event of a future conflict between China and the United States, Japan should be seen as an ally of the United States rather than as neutral.[84]

Since a bilateral solution to the tepid relations between China and Japan does not look very promising, some Chinese scholars have turned to alternative methods to help 'renormalize' the relationship. One possibility is to view the relationship in a broader multilateral context that might facilitate more productive communication and negotiations between the two countries. Examples include the Six-Party Talks on the Korean nuclear crisis, the multilateral security framework in the Asia-Pacific, and multilateral regional financial and economic mechanisms. Given the evident willingness of Japan to cooperate in a broader East Asian regional framework, Chinese analysts argue that this is the best way, and possibly the only way, to resolve China's differences with Japan over the history issue and to alleviate the pressures of a security dilemma. Within the larger East Asian regional context, both countries will become more conscious about their responsibility as regional powers as the smaller partners in the region more carefully monitor their behaviour.[85] By the same token, some analysts also argue that, in order for China to get 'closer' to Japan, ironically China must first 'drift apart' from Japan. Only by focusing on integrating with other East Asian and Southeast Asian countries economically and politically can China attain the degree of regional influence necessary to force Japan to join the process of integration – something for which an improved relationship with China would clearly be a prerequisite.[86]

Conclusion

Chinese discourse on Japan as a 'normal country' is far more complex and nuanced than the simple message conveyed by the anti-Japanese street demonstrations in China in 2005. Generally speaking, most Chinese scholars and analysts, to varying degrees, accept the reality that a 'normal' Japan is already emerging, to which China must respond. They disagree, however, on what that response should be. At the risk of being somewhat overly simplistic, we can discern the emergence of two major schools of thought during this debate. The 'new thinking' school advocates significant change in China's conceptualization of and strategy toward Japan. Since the birth of a normal Japan is inevitable, China should follow the trend rather than go against it.[87] This school holds that it is high time for China to put the issue of Japan's war history to rest lest it exacerbate tensions in China's relationship with Japan that will do more harm than good to China's fundamental national interest.

The 'traditionalist' school, in contrast, argues that the basic principles and assumptions of China's Japan policy should remain unchanged. It is not China but Japan that needs 'new thinking.' Without a proper resolution of the controversy surrounding Japan's war history, Sino-Japanese relations will lack a solid ethical foundation. China should not accept a normal Japan automatically, but make it contingent upon Japan's accommodating to China's vital national interests. Against those who argue that this position would only bring the two countries closer to conflict, traditionalists maintain that such worries are unwarranted: Japan needs China at least as much as China needs Japan. Conflict is in neither country's interest.

Clearly, there is a gap between the discourse on Japan as a normal country espoused by the Chinese elite and the one articulated by the general public. In the battle to win public support, the traditionalists seem to have made greater headway during the period of the Koizumi government, while the 'new thinking' school appeared unable to transform some of its ideas into a consensus of the general public. Wary of this trend, many Chinese Japan-specialists urged the government and academia to cultivate more positive and balanced views about Japan among the public.[88] The Koizumi government's rigid China policy made the 'new thinking' perspective an even tougher sell. Anti-Japanese demonstrations in China in 2005 and the consequent vicious action-reaction between the two countries made the 'new thinkers' seem out of touch and placed them on the defensive.[89] In this instance, the words and deeds of the Japanese side definitely changed the balance between the two schools' respective influence on the Chinese public's perception of Japan as a normal country.

The dynamic interaction between China's discourse on Japan and Sino-Japanese relations on the ground took another dramatic turn after Koizumi stepped down as prime minister in 2006. The change of government in Japan seemed to bring new hope for advocates of China's 'new thinking' on Japan. Indeed, a quick turnabout in Sino-Japanese relations resulted after both governments incorporated some 'new thinking' into their policy toward each other. On the Chinese side, the leadership began to move away from requiring Japan to change its attitude on the war history as a precondition to normalizing the relationship. Without a firm commitment from the new Japanese prime minister, Shinzo Abe, not to visit Yasukuni Shrine – previously considered a must for a summit to take place – Hu Jintao made a courageous political decision to invite Abe to visit China. On the Japanese side, Abe moved away from Koizumi's lopsided pro-U.S. policy by visiting China and South Korea to improve relations with Japan's Asian neighbours as his first diplomatic priority. He also cleverly decided to put the issue of a symbolic shrine visit on hold for the sake of realizing broader interests between the two counties. Taking this historical opportunity, both leaders agreed to raise Japan-China relations to a higher level by building 'a strategic relationship of mutual benefits.'[90] To deal with the conflicting interpretation of the war history, they agreed to a joint study of the history by academics from both countries.

With the thaw in Sino-Japanese relations, there were calls for a revival of 'new thinking' in China's Japan policy.[91] Although many Chinese observers soon realized that Abe was no less determined than Koizumi to make Japan a normal state, his modest goodwill on the symbolic shrine visit seemed to have moved relations forward a great distance. On a series of Japanese moves toward 'normalization' – such as the formal upgrading of the Japanese defence agency into a ministry and a security pact with Australia – Beijing reacted moderately. Even on the very sensitive World War Two issue of 'comfort women,' Chinese leaders did not show a strong desire to take on Japan. All these developments indicate that positive gestures from Japan, even though symbolic, could be the catalyst for changing Chinese opinions and perceptions of the implications of Japan as a 'normal country.'

The consecutive visits to Japan of top Chinese leaders Hu Jintao and Wen Jiabao in 2007 and 2008 moved China even closer to accepting Japan as a 'normal country.' Premier Wen Jiabao's historic speech before the Japanese Diet, in particular, introduced some important conceptual changes regarding Japan. Never before had Chinese leaders used such explicit language in such a public fashion to praise Japanese politicians' remorse and apology for the war of aggression against China and other Asian countries, to acknowledge Japan's assistance and contribution to China's economic modernization, and to affirm Japan's postwar path of peaceful development.[92] These new positions were what the Japanese public and politicians had waited a long time to hear, and Wen uttered them with feeling and sincerity. The 'new thinking' on Japan suggested by China's more open-mined Japan scholars and analysts now became the formal position of the Chinese government.

Wen's speech was also widely broadcast in China, indicating that the leadership wanted the general public to absorb the new discourse and reduce hostility toward Japan. Some subtle changes in the Chinese public's perception of Japan did take place. The tragic Sichuan earthquake in 2008 provided another unique moment for China's 'new thinking' to spread from the elite to the general public. Japanese rescue teams' dedication and respect of the Chinese dead touched many Chinese citizens and began to melt their otherwise negative image of Japan and the Japanese.[93] Ma Licheng, the initiator of the 'new thinking' school, commented with much relief that 'new thinking' was becoming a reality.[94]

Needless to say, discussion and debate in China about Japan as a normal country are far from over – some continue to worry about the implications of 'new thinking.'[95] While the Chinese people appreciate that Japanese hands reached out during a natural disaster, they still feel uncomfortable about such signs of Japan's normalization as dispatching a Self-Defense Forces airplane to China to carry out relief efforts.[96]

The 'regime' change from LDP to the Democratic Party of Japan (DJP) in August 2009 presents another test of China's new thinking on Japan. For one thing, the new Japanese prime minister, Yukio Hatoyama, and particularly Secretary General of DPJ Ichirō Ozawa had long been leading proponents for a 'normal' Japan. In his provocative book, *Blueprint for a New Japan*, Ozawa for the first time set out the objective of transforming Japan into a 'normal country.' For that purpose, Japan should, among other things, reform its political system, amend its Constitution, and have a formal military force to play a more active role in international security affairs. While the vision of Hatoyama and Ozawa of Japan as a normal country might have had some parallels with China's policy interest and preferences, such as reversing the pro-U.S. policy of the previous government, issues such as the overseas role of the Japanese military and Japan's aspiration to become a permanent member of the Security Council also tested the bottom line of China's acceptance of Japan as a normal country. As some Chinese analysts acutely observed, without China's support and understanding, it would be very difficult, if not impossible, for Japan to join the ranks of normal countries. But is China ready to accept a fully fledged 'normal' Japan?[97]

NOTES

1 Although the term 'new thinking on Japan' was first used by Ma Licheng in 2002, some Chinese scholars advocated change and adjustment of China's Japan policy as early as 1997; see Feng Zhaokui, 'The Difficult Exploration of the Relationship with Japan,' *World Economics and Politics* 5 (2004): 26 (original in Chinese).
2 Ibid., 27.
3 Shi Yinhong, 'Sino-Japanese Rapprochement and "Diplomatic Revolution",' *Strategy and Management* 2 (2003): 71–2.
4 Feng Zhaokui, 'On New Thinking toward Japan,' *Strategy and Management* 4 (2003): 1–2.
5 Feng Zhaokui, 'Micro Sino-Japanese Relations: A Review of China's "New Thinking" on Japan'; 31 January 2007; available online at http://www.jnocnews.jp/news/show.aspx?id=8943, accessed 9 August 2008.
6 Zha Daojun, 'The Change in Japan's Post-Cold War China Policy and China's Response,' *China's Foreign Affairs* 3 (2005): 45.
7 Feng Zhaokui, 'On New Thinking toward Japan,' p. 6.
8 Ma Licheng, 'New Thinking toward Japan – An Apprehension between Chinese and Japanese People,' *Strategy and Management* 6 (2002): 43.
9 Zhou Guiyin, 'Understanding "Diplomatic Revolution" toward Japan,' *Strategy and Management* 4 (2003): 21; and Feng Zhaokui, 'Micro Sino-Japanese Relations.'
10 One Chinese commentator has the following reading of the meaning of the 'ordinary' country in the Japanese political dictionary. First, it means that Japan should completely get rid of the status of 'defeated country' in the UN Charter and other international treaties and all its related constraints on Japan. Second, to be 'ordinary' also means to be 'normal.' For Japan, to be 'normal' actually means to be above 'ordinary.' That is, 'normal' means that Japan needs to become a political and military major power. See Liu Ning, 'How to Get Along with Japan as a Political Major Power'; available online at http://www.ncn.org/asp/zwginfo/da.asp?ID=65452&ad=8/22/2005, accessed 12 August 2005.
11 Lu Zhongwei, 'China-Japan Relations: Understanding and Promotion,' *Chinese Diplomacy* (2004/01): 20–1.

12 Luo Xiaojun, 'The 'grass roots opinion' in Japan is worrisome,' *South Wind Window,* 15 September 2005; available online at http://www.nfcmag.com/ReadNews.asp?NewsID=3262, accessed 19 September 2005.
13 He Degong, 'Four big factors that affect Japan's China policy,' *Outlook Newsweek,* 24 January 2005, p. 50.
14 Lu Zhongwei, 'China-Japan Relations,' 20.
15 Zhang Wang, 'Is Japan Returning to the Old Track of Militarism?' *Strategy and Management* 4 (2003): 26.
16 Xue Li, 'Could Sino-Japanese Relations Go beyond History?' *Strategy and Management* 4 (2003): 30.
17 Zhang Wang, 'Is Japan Returning to the Old Track of Militarism?' 23.
18 'Comparing the military power of China, United States, Japan, and India,' http://www.dhbc.net/datalib/Life/2005/2005_05/life.2005-05-20.5360316255.
19 Pang Zhongying, 'Disturbing historical intransigence,' *Oriental Morning Post*, 3 March 2004.
20 Lin Zhibo, 'Another Critical Look at the "New Thinking toward Japan"'; available online at http://news.xinhuanet.com/newscenter/2003-08/15/content_1027372.3.htm, p. 1, accessed 17 August 2003.
21 Lin Zhibo, 'My Views on Several Issues in Current Sino-Japanese Relations,' *Strategy and Management* 4 (2004): 91.
22 Duan Tingzhi and Zhou Qingjian, 'Behind Japan's "hitting out in three directions,"' *Outlook Newsweek*, 28 March 2005, pp. 8–9.
23 Pan Yan, 'One can only be responsible to future when one is able to deal with the past seriously,' *Outlook Newsweek*, 11 April 2005, p. 11.
24 Ibid.
25 Duan Tingzhi, 'Three basic tendencies in Japan's effort to become a military major power,' *Outlook Newsweek,* 28 February 2005, p. 57.
26 Shen Dingli, 'Japan made a wrong strategic choice a century ago,' *Oriental Morning Post,* 15 August 2005.
27 Public opinion shows that 80 per cent of Chinese regard the war history as the number one issue in Sino-Japanese relations; see Xue Li, 'Could Sino-Japanese relations go beyond history?' p. 28.
28 Ma Licheng, 'New Thinking toward Japan,' 47.
29 Shi Yinhong, 'Sino-Japanese Rapprochement and "Diplomatic Revolution,"' 71–2.
30 Feng Zhaokui, 'On New Thinking toward Japan,' 7.
31 Ibid., 8.
32 Ibid., 9.

33 Xue Li, 'Could Sino-Japanese Relations Go beyond History?' 28, 30, 32.
34 'Recommendations on Improving China-Japan Relations,' *Contemporary International Relations* 6 (2004): 8.
35 Lin Zhibo, 'Another Critical Look at the "New Thinking toward Japan."'
36 Zhang Jinshan, 'My opinion on how difficulties could be overcome in China-Japan relations,' *Outlook Newsweek*, 24 January 2005, p. 54.
37 'Hu Jintao puts forward guidelines for developing healthy and stable bilateral relations,' in *Current Affairs and Sino-Japanese Relations – A Reader* (Beijing: Red Flag Press, 2005), p. 2.
38 'Wen Jiabao answers questions from the Associated Press reporter during his visit to India,' in *Current Affairs and Sino-Japanese Relations*, p. 4.
39 Chinese senior leader Tang Jiaxuan remarked that it is beyond the comprehension of the Chinese public why Japan wants to do these two things simultaneously. 'State Councilor Tang Jiaxuan met Japanese guests,' in *Current Affairs and Sino-Japanese Relations*, p. 6.
40 Zhang Wang, 'Is Japan Returning to the Old Track of Militarism?' 25–6.
41 Feng Zhaokui, 'Second Take on New Thinking toward Japan,' *Strategy and Management* 5 (2003): 79.
42 'China-Japan Relations: Is It Possible to Go beyond History?' *World Affairs* 16 (2003): 23–4.
43 He Degong, 'The motivations behind Japan's keen interest in the Taiwan issue,' *Outlook Newsweek*, 28 February 2005, p. 56.
44 Duan Tingzhi, 'Three basic tendencies,' p. 57.
45 Lin Zhipo, 'On Some Issues in Current China-Japan Relations,' *Strategy and Management* 2 (2004): 92.
46 Lu Zhongwei, 'China-Japan Relations,' 20.
47 Feng Zhaokui, 'Koizumi should reflect on five issues in his China diplomacy'; available online at http://news.sino.com.cn/c/2005-05-23/11055963008s.shtml, accessed 30 May 2005.
48 Wang Cong, 'Japan has made a strategic misjudgment about China,' *China Youth Daily*, 7 August 2005.
49 Indeed, some Chinese believe that the United States will never let a country that inflicted 'Pearl Harbor' upon it enjoy a truly independent foreign policy. See Qiu Yongzhen, 'The United States helps Japan expand its military to challenge China, ROK and DPRK,' *Youth Reference*, 14 April 2005.
50 Jin Xide, 'The Identification and Evolution of Japan's UN Diplomacy,' *World Economics and Politics* 5 (2005): 24.
51 Zhu Xinfu, 'Why the United States supports Japan not Germany to enter the UN Security Council,' *Wenhui News*, 10 June 2005.

52 'Li Zhaoxing on current Sino-Japanese relations,' in *Current Affairs and Sino-Japanese Relations*, p. 23.
53 Jin Xide, 'The Identification and Evolution of Japan's UN Diplomacy,' 23, 25.
54 Feng Zhaokui, 'A Third Take on New Thinking towards Japan,' *Strategy and Management* 2 (2004): 91.
55 Li Shu, 'The strategic dilemma in Sino-Japanese relations: The key problem is the dispute between unipolarization and multipolarization,' *South Wind Window*; available online at http://www.nfcmag.com/Read/News.asp?NewsID=72, accessed 18 August 2005.
56 He Degong, 'Four big factors that affect Japan's China policy,' p. 56.
57 Zhao Jieji, 'The trends in Japan's Taiwan policy deserves attention,' *China's Foreign Affairs*, No. 3, 2005, p. 49.
58 Duan Tingzhi and Zhou Qingjian, 'Behind Japan's "hitting out in three directions,"' pp. 10–11.
59 'Some recommendations on improving Sino-Japanese relations,' *Contemporary International Relations*, No. 6, 2004, p. 7.
60 Some Chinese scholars made some systematic comparison of the similarities and differences in China and Japan's rise and the interaction between the two countries during the process. See Li Xudong, 'A comparison of the strategic frameworks for China and Japan's rise and the options for security interaction,' *International Survey*, No. 3, 2005, pp. 36–41.
61 Lu Zhongwei, 'China-Japan Relations: Understanding and Promotion,' p. 23.
62 'China-Japan Relations: Is It Possible to Go beyond History?' 23.
63 'Sino-Japanese relations have fallen into a political ice age,' *Chinese Newsweek*, 26 May 2005.
64 Feng Zhaokui, 'On New Thinking toward Japan,' 7–9.
65 Some Chinese analysts attributed the recent troubles in the relationship to the fundamental inability on the Japanese side to face the reality of China's rise; see Xu Yi, 'Japan is willing to be America's pawn,' *Chinese Industrial and Commercial Daily*, 4 June 2005.
66 He Degong, 'Four big factors that affect Japan's China policy,' p. 51.
67 Lu Zhongwei, 'China-Japan Relations.'
68 'China-Japan Relations: Is It Possible to Go beyond History?' 18.
69 Zha Daojun, 'The Change in Japan's Post-Cold War China Policy and China's Response,' 46.
70 'China and Japan debate about the Yasukuni Shrine and textbook, '*Southern Metropolitan Daily*, 12 August 2005.

71 Many Japan specialists agree that frictions in the relationship in recent years were initiated by the Japanese side without exception; see Wu Jinan, 'Sino-Japanese Relations Are at a Turning Point,' *International Survey* 2 (2005): 9.
72 'Some Recommendations on Improving Sino-Japanese Relations,' *Contemporary International Relations* 6 (2004): 3–4.
73 Li Shu, 'The strategic dilemma in Sino-Japanese relations,' *China Youth Daily*, 20 March 2005.
74 Lin Zhipo, 'On Some Issues in Current China-Japan Relations,' 92.
75 Zhi Zhongyun, 'Why Is It So Difficult for Japan to Admit Its Guilt?' *World Affairs* 20 (2003): 39.
76 Shi Yinhong, 'Sino-Japanese Rapprochement and "Diplomatic Revolution,"' 71–5.
77 Lin Zhipo, 'On Some Issues in Current China-Japan Relations,' 93.
78 Lin Zhibo, 'Another Critical Look at the "New Thinking toward Japan,"' 2–3.
79 'China-Japan Relations: Is It Possible to Go beyond History?' 22.
80 The change in China's Japan policy is described as a 'silent revolution'; see Lu Zhongwei, 'China-Japan relations,' 17.
81 One prominent Japan-watcher pointed out that China's 'new thinking' diplomacy in recent years has worked quite well in dealing with all the major powers except Japan; see Feng Zhaokui, 'The Difficult Exploration of the Relationship with Japan,' 28.
82 'Some recommendations on improving China-Japan relations,' *Contemporary International Relations*, No. 6, 2004, p. 9.
83 Feng Zhaokui, 'On the new thinking toward Japan,' p. 6.
84 'China-Japan Relations: Is It Possible to Go beyond History?' 22.
85 Wang Yong, 'To Use Regional Cooperation to Alleviate the China-Japan Structural Contradictions,' *Strategy and Management* 1 (2004): 45–7.
86 Chen Yawen, 'How to make Japan "need" China,' *Window of South Wind*, 11 March 2005; available online at http://www.nfcmag.com/RealNews.asp?NewsID=458, accessed 12 March 2005.
87 As an independent Chinese journalist puts it: 'Since we do not have enough power to prevent Japan from becoming a political and military power, from now on we have to learn how to get along with a powerful neighbour that is increasingly moving towards an "ordinary" state.' See Liu Ning, 'How to Get Along with Japan as a Political Major Power.'
88 Xue Li, 'Could Sino-Japanese Relations Go beyond History?' 31; and Zhou Guiyin, 'Understanding "Diplomatic Revolution" toward Japan,' p. 21.
89 Some Chinese observers complained that the Japanese reaction, at both

the public and governmental level, to the 'new thinking' on Japan' put its advocates in a very difficult position. The Koizumi government's 'getting tough' policy toward China did not give any 'face' to the Chinese 'new thinkers.' Feng Zhaokui, 'The Difficult Exploration of the Relationship with Japan,' pp. 27–8.

90 'Press conference by Prime Minister Shinzo Abe following his visit to China,' 8 October 2006; available online at http://www.kantei.go.jp/foreign/abespeech/2006/10/08chinapress_e.html, accessed 12 October 2006.

91 Wang Liang, 'Coping with Abe: Time for 'new thinking' in China's Japan policy,' PacNet 3B, 24 January 2007.

92 'For Friendship and Cooperation,' speech by Premier Wen Jiahao of the State Council of the People's Republic of China at the Japanese Diet, 13 April 2007.

93 'Chinese public embraces new thinking on Japan and collectively expressed its gratitude to Japan,' *China Review News*, 3 June 2008.

94 'Ma Licheng dismissed the title of "number one traitor" with laugh: new thinking on Japan is becoming a reality,' *Economic Observer*, 17 November 2008.

95 Ping Daxia, 'Maintain a high vigilance against the return of new thinking on Japan'; available online at http://ido.3mt.com.cn/Article/200609/show490226c32p1.html, accessed 30 September 2006.

96 'Chinese public embraces new thinking on Japan and collectively expresses its gratitude to Japan,' *China Review News*, 3 June 2008.

97 Nan Zhimo, 'Can Hatoyama lead Japan to realize the state normalization?' 10 September 2009; available online at http://zaobao.com, accessed 12 September 2009.

6 The Limits to 'Normalcy': Japanese-Korean Post–Cold War Interactions

JOHN SWENSON-WRIGHT[1]

The contemporary international relations of East Asia are in a state of flux. China's emerging status as a great power; the dramatic growth of the Indian economy; persistent territorial disputes and competition over access to scare oil and natural gas reserves; newly negotiated bilateral and multilateral trade agreements between some of the key states in the region and the wider impetus to establish a new East Asian Community; the efforts by Putin's Russia to reinvent itself as a player in the geopolitics of Northeast Asia; signs of an incipient arms race in the region – fuelled, in part, by the nuclear status of India and Pakistan, and most dramatically by North Korea's emergence since October 2006 as the latest addition to the nuclear club and by Pyongyang's second nuclear test in May 2009: all of these developments pose critical challenges and opportunities for states in the region. This is particularly true for Japan and South Korea – two modern, vibrant democracies that are flexing their political and economic muscles and seeking to maintain and extend their traditional strategic alliances while also reaching out to other powers with which they have traditionally not had particularly close or well-developed relations.

For Japan, during the early part of the twenty-first century, this shift in direction has been reflected in the domestic debate over Japan's status as a 'normal country,' as political elites and public opinion have begun to engage with the practical challenges of constitutional revision,[2] the redefinition of the role and status of Japan's defence forces, and the difficult issue of the legacy of World War Two and the experience of the 1930s. In South Korea, between 2002 and 2007, the administration of President Roh Moo Hyun similarly engaged with contentious historical issues – particularly colonial-era collaboration between Koreans and their Japanese administrators – as a means of encouraging more open and, by implication, more accountable government, and also (according to some critics) as a means of shifting the domestic power balance towards progressive and away from conservative political forces. In Korea under Roh, the talk was less of acquiring a 'normal' status and more of acting as a pivotal, balancing force – or hub – reconciling and accommodating the interests of larger states in the region. While Japanese policy elites have long been concerned to find a mechanism to translate Japan's extensive economic capabilities – those of the world's second-largest economy – into commensurate political influence, South Korean leaders have been taxed more with the challenge of leveraging relatively limited economic clout into disproportionate and in some senses inflated or exaggerated strategic authority. In the former case, the problem has been one of unrealized or unfulfilled potential; in the latter, it is arguably a case of international ambition running ahead of national capabilities.

The following analysis focuses on the recent North Korean nuclear crisis in order to assess the relative abilities of the Japanese and South Korean governments to meet some of these new challenges and to place Japan's post–Cold War relationship with the Korean peninsula in context. It does not attempt to provide a comprehensive assessment of the strengths and weaknesses of the political decision-making process in both countries. Rather, it uses the nuclear crisis as a two-part case study to analyse the motives of national leaders in both countries and the mechanics of policy-making in Tokyo and Seoul. It concentrates, in the first instance, on the Japanese response to North Korea's emerging nuclear weapons program during the administration of Prime Minister Junichirō Koizumi between 2001 and late 2006. In the second, it examines the factors – cultural, political, personal, institutional, and historical – that might have limited active cooperation between Seoul and Tokyo not only in dealing with the challenge of the North, but in fostering a more cooperative and mutually beneficial relationship with each another – two key, democratic Asian allies of the United States.

In the course of considering the Koizumi administration's policies, the following analysis contrasts a Japanese approach that seemingly has shifted from accommodation with the North to a hard-line posture of confrontation with a South Korean approach that apparently has been focused more consistently on engagement. Examining policy options in this way helps to address the question of whether, in its actions, the Japanese state is becoming more 'normal' – whether, to use

David Welch's formulation,[3] Japan's 'behaviour,' primarily in the field of foreign policy-making, has evolved in a more conventional or unexceptional direction.

The evidence presented here – particularly in terms of signs of a more independent Japanese foreign and security policy, less conditioned by or dependent on the United States – suggests that, over time and incrementally, Japan's regional and global actions are becoming akin to those of other states, shaped by the national interest broadly defined and articulated in a manner that hints at the pursuit of a coherent strategy.[4] In this regard, the record of Japan-Korea relations since the turn of the twenty-first century confirms the observations of other contributors to this volume. However, in terms of Welch's second formulation, 'normalcy' defined in terms of 'status' – how the nation 'is' rather than how it 'acts' – the record is less clear cut. Here, the point to keep in mind is that a country's identity – its sense of itself – is shaped by both internal phenomena – its institutions, its domestic social and political evolution over time, its national narratives and mythologies – and by external elements, most notably its history of engagement with others.

In the case of Japan and the two Koreas, a range of factors – historical, cultural, as well as the distinctive quality of the regional context and the impact of national division on the Korean peninsula – has contributed to a comparatively fraught and volatile state of affairs. Japanese and Korean attitudes towards each other both define and distort a bilateral relationship that is arguably peculiarly emotional and tense and at odds with the rational interests of peoples who, in terms of their shared history, culture, and language, should have much to bring them together. Whether such a relationship should be defined as 'abnormal' in terms of either contemporary international relations or modern diplomatic history, and whether the parties to the relationship see each other as atypical or unusual, is difficult to answer. Indeed, a convincing response to this question would require an exhaustive (if not exhausting) comparative study of comparable bilateral relationships between geographic neighbours and between formerly colonizing states and colonized dependencies (one thinks, for example, of the parallels with the Anglo-Irish relationship). This is something that is beyond the scope of this chapter, but it is clear that exploring normalcy in this context requires us to recognize that a nation's status is invariably defined in relational terms and cannot be separated from the perceptions of others – whether other states, institutions, or individuals. Methodologically this inevitably makes the search for definitive conclusions tricky and often frustrating; however, the merit of such an approach is that it can reveal much that is of interest not only about Japan, but also about its neighbours and the countries with which it has had a particular close and longstanding relationship.

In many respects, Japan's relations with both Koreas since the middle of the twentieth century have been strikingly abnormal. In the case of North Korea, this abnormalcy has manifested itself straightforwardly in the absence of formal diplomatic relations – a consequence of the adversarial standoff of the Cold War and the persistent state of simmering conflict symbolized by the 1953 armistice that suspended, but did not end, the Korean War. In the case of South Korea, Japan's distorted relationship has been more complicated and is less readily explained. Formal reconciliation between Tokyo and Seoul occurred in 1965 with the signing of a bilateral Normalization Treaty, but the two countries arguably remain fundamentally divided from each another in a manner that seems contrary to the rational interests of not only their elites and publics, but also of both countries' most important senior partner and patron, the United States. Various explanations have been offered for this anomalous state of affairs. Some stress the bitter legacy of Japan's colonial dominance of the peninsula from 1905 to 1945;[5] some point to the political and ideological differences separating, at least up until 1993, an essentially authoritarian from a democratic polity; others highlight the critical role of the United States, which, by its fluctuating engagement with the East Asian region, has acted like a powerful alternating electromagnet, sometimes pulling its two allies closer together, sometimes driving them apart from each another, but in both instances in a manner that has potentially qualified or constrained the autonomy and self-interests of political actors in Seoul and Tokyo.[6]

By the early part of the twenty-first century, there seemed good reason – at least superficially – to question the inhibiting effect of these different factors. Japan and South Korea were headed by similarly radical, young, reform-minded democratic leaders, intent in their early years in power on carving out a distinctive and effective role for themselves and their countries, especially in the field of foreign affairs. Democratic convergence and generational change might have been expected to compensate for the tensions and estrangement of the past. Seen from the vantage point of 2008, however, these high expectations have not been realized. The following analysis attempts to explain why this is the case and in the process reveals the abnormalities that continue to hamper Japan's relations with two of its most important neighbours.

The Historical Context for Japan-Korea Relations since 1945

Japan's postwar historical relationship with Korea in general and North Korea in particular has been, for the most part, a limited and attenuated one. During the Cold War, relations with the peninsula were refracted through the lens of the United States-Japan security partnership, with decision-makers in Tokyo playing the role of interested but nonetheless semi-detached bystanders to the conflict taking place across the Sea of Japan, or East Sea as it is known in Korea. While Japanese minesweepers provided a valuable (albeit understated and infrequently commented on) supporting role for allied United Nations forces during the Korean War from 1950 to 1953, for the most part Korea's impact on Japan during this period was primarily economic.[7] To Japan's early postwar prime minister, Shigeru Yoshida, the war was a 'gift from the gods'[8] that provided a valuable and timely economic stimulus, acting, through the expanded military procurements program of support for the U.S. war effort, as a major injection of demand pulling Japan out of the economic sluggishness of the postwar Occupation period.

The indirectness of Japan's relationship with the peninsula did not, it should be stressed, imply a lack of contact, but rather an informal, semi-official pattern of engagement, at least where North Korea was concerned. Full diplomatic normalization of relations with South Korea came relatively late in the day in 1965, in part because of bitter personal rivalry between Yoshida and his South Korean counterpart, President Syngman Rhee, as well as difficult and seemingly persistent tensions over territorial claims, fishing disputes, and the fractious question of compensation for Japan's colonial domination of Korea from 1905 to 1945. In the case of Japan-North Korea relations, Japan's leaders mirrored their experience of dealing with mainland China, relying on low-profile, semi-formal bilateral contact via political intermediaries and, in particular, business contacts. This was part of a 'dual-track' approach[9] that survived until the late 1980s and that kept relations with Seoul and Pyongyang equally alive, and through which Japan's leaders shied away from whole-hearted endorsement or criticism of either side in a conflict that to some represented a bitter, internecine civil war[10] as much as an ideological proxy war in the larger international Cold War conflict between East and West.

Part of the reason for Japan's studied official ambivalence towards the two Koreas has been the presence of large numbers of ethnic Koreans in Japan – by the 1990s still numbering some 600,000 in all – the direct consequence and living reminder of the colonial period. In the early postwar period, the existence of this large community of foreign residents was a huge source of potential insecurity – indeed, in that period, 'foreigner,' with all the suspicion and anxiety the term connoted, was almost synonymous with 'Korean,' such was the high profile and numerical dominance of this single ethnic community within Japan.[11] Yoshida, in particular, worried that Koreans represented a potential fifth column of sedition and dissent that might prove a far greater threat to political stability at home than the risk of a direct assault on Japan by either Soviet or Chinese-supported military forces. Moreover, while members of Japan's Korean community aligned themselves in two competing groups – the pro–North Korean General Association of Korean Residents in Japan (*Chosen Soren* or *Chongryon*) and the South Korea–leaning Korean Residents Union in Japan (*Mindan*) – in the 1950s *Chosen Soren* was the overwhelmingly dominant group, with some 90 per cent of all Korean residents in Japan identifying with the North.

In an effort to devise a crude sociological safety valve to minimize the pressure from this potential hostile community, the Japanese government, in conjunction with the Red Cross in Geneva, negotiated an agreement with North Korea in 1958 to allow the voluntary repatriation of Koreans in Japan to the North. Some six and a half thousand or so Koreans returned to the North, but the flow of returnees was short lived, drying up in the 1960s as news of the difficult economic and political conditions in the North filtered back to Japan.[12] Over time, the political and demographic balance between the pro–North and South Korean constituencies in Japan has shifted, recalibrated by demographic trends within Japan, by intermarriage between Koreans and Japanese, and by the growing economic prosperity and political liberalism of South Korea that emerged over time and accelerated in the 1980s and 1990s – so much so that *Mindan* affiliates now outnumber their *Chosen Soren* counterparts by some four to one.[13]

Paralleling these important trends has been a shift of attitudes towards the two Koreas among key political constituencies within Japan. For much of the postwar period, Japan's political leaders were hesitant to be seen to align too closely with the authoritarian administrations that dominated South Korean politics at least until the late 1980s. Although a number of prominent figures in Japan's Liberal Democratic Party (LDP), such as prime ministers Nobusuke Kishi and his brother Eisaku Sato, worked closely with their South Korean counterparts, they faced resistance from colleagues within the ranks of the

LDP – most notably the Ikeda-Ohira line of politicians closely identified with Prime Minister Yoshida. This latter group, often referred to collectively as the *Kochikai* faction, preferred to view relations with South Korea almost exclusively in economic terms, and in some instances this qualified engagement reflected ambivalence, if not guilt or at the very least regret, over Japan's record of excesses during the colonial period.[14]

This sense of discomfort was arguably even more pronounced among Japan's opposition politicians, particularly within the Japan Socialist Party (JSP), until the early 1990s the country's most prominent opposition party. The Socialists, and the left in general, opposed alignment with South Korea, expressing misgivings about the authoritarian nature of military government in the South and reflecting their sense of partial responsibility for the division of the peninsula and a deeply felt desire to avoid embroilment in the wider Cold War conflict. Moreover, for much of the post-1945 period, the North was able to exploit these sentiments by representing itself as the legitimate representative of the Korean people. This was in part accomplished by presenting the North as a model of successful and dynamic economic modernization – an argument buttressed by the relatively higher economic growth rates that the North enjoyed over its Southern rival until the early 1970s. It was also reinforced by the North's careful management of the historical record to present a contentious, inflated, and in many respects mythologized portrayal of the North's leader, Kim Il Sung, as the single-handed vanquisher of the Japanese colonial occupiers. This image of principled independence, although exaggerated (given the substantial political and material support that the North received from its Soviet and Chinese allies), was not entirely without foundation. The North's leadership could point (as it still does today) to the presence of U.S. troops in the South and the absence of foreign forces in the North as evidence of the strength of the North's claim to represent the authentic voice of the Korean people.[15]

Over time, as the North's economic success story was replaced by one of economic failure and the crippling inefficiencies of central planning, reinforced by the famines and floods of the 1990s and most powerfully by the phenomenal economic growth record of South Korea, the North's relative standing in Japan diminished. Equally important, the experience of democratic transition in the South from the military rule of General Chun Do Hwan to Roh Tae Woo in 1988, from Roh to Kim Young Sam in 1993, and perhaps most powerfully of all from Kim Young Sam to Kim Dae Jung in 1997, clearly demonstrated the deep and increasingly secure roots of representative government in South Korea.

In the absence of a political consensus within Japan about how best to interact with the two Koreas, it was natural for Japan's political leadership to adopt a strategy of qualified pragmatism. Consistent with a general pattern of separating economic from security concerns (*seikei bunri*) that has long been a hallmark of Japan's post-1945 foreign policy posture, Japanese governments concentrated particularly during the 1960s and early 1970s on developing modest trade ties with the North – an approach reinforced by the commitment on the part of *Chosen Soren* to send regular cash remittances to the North. For North Korea, this trading relationship became a valuable source of support, so much so that, by the 1990s, Japan had become the North's second-largest trading partner after China. For Japan, the relative importance of the North economically has been much less – the country ranked ninety-eighth among Japan's trading partners in the early 1990s. This limited role reflects in part the small size of the North Korean economy; it also reflects the strong and persistent perception in Japanese financial and business circles that the North is an unreliable economic partner. In 1979, the North defaulted on payments to Kyowa Busan Trading Company, a conglomerate of some 20 Japanese firms involved in trade with the North, prompting the then Ministry of International Trade and Industry (MITI) to suspend all export credits to the North. Today, North Korean companies still reportedly owe Japanese firms some US$667 million from various economic deals dating from the 1970s and 1980s.[16]

Economic unreliability coupled with increased tension between the North and the international community during the 1980s following evidence of the North's active involvement in terrorist activities – most dramatically the partially successful effort to assassinate much of the South Korean cabinet in the Rangoon bombing of 1983 and the shooting down of a South Korean civilian airliner, KAL 858, in 1987 – ensured that Japan-North Korea relations remained largely underdeveloped. In the 1990s, however, this limited relationship began to change, particularly with the ending of the Cold War and the first signs that politicians in South Korea, most notably the administration of Roh Tae Woo through its new policy of *Nordpolitik*, were beginning to reach out to the North. Decision-makers in Japan worried that they risked isolation if they failed to address one of the few remaining bilateral issues left over from the post–World War Two period.[17] The governing LDP in this period, under the leadership of Prime Minister Toshiki Kaifu, was in a relatively weak position, criticized at home for poor economic management and for a string of damaging corruption scandals that first surfaced in the late 1980s. In an effort to develop a new bipartisan approach to relations with the North, a joint delegation, headed by Shin Kanemaru, a senior LDP figure, and Makoto Tanabe, his counterpart from the JSP, travelled to Pyongyang in September 1990 and announced with some fanfare an eight-point declaration that suggested a breakthrough in bilateral relations. In particular, the declaration appeared to indicate that the Japanese authorities were prepared to compensate North Korea for the excesses of the colonial period and for losses experienced by the North since World War Two to the tune of some US$10 billion.[18] The problem with the declaration was twofold: first, the Kanemaru mission was a private initiative and lacked the official support or authorization either of the cabinet or the *Gaimusho* – the Japanese foreign ministry; second, it met with opposition from the South Korean government which baulked at a compensation deal that seemed far more generous than the Japan-South Korea package that had been negotiated in 1965.[19]

In the face of these difficulties, but prompted by this first, important albeit unauthorized initiative, the Japanese government sought to re-engage with the North. A flurry of important official contacts started in January 1991, leading to some eight rounds of talks over a 22-month period. The talks focused on a range of issues, including the question of compensation and reparations, but also the troubling question of the fate of Japanese citizens whom the Japanese authorities claimed had been kidnapped and abducted from Japan by North Korean agents in the 1970s and 1980s. Ultimately, the bilateral talks stalled in the eighth round following controversies surrounding the role of Yi Un Hye, a Korean-Japanese kidnapped by the North and allegedly involved in training the operatives who carried out the bombing of KAL 858.[20]

Despite the failure of these discussions to deliver an immediate breakthrough, their importance is as a marker highlighting the evolving pragmatism of the Japanese authorities in dealing with the North. At the beginning of the 1990s, there were some encouraging, albeit tentative indications that the leadership in Pyongyang might be receptive to a more accommodating approach on the part of Japan. To begin with, the North, having already signed the Nuclear Non-proliferation Treaty in 1985, signed with South Korea a Declaration on the Denuclearization of the Korean Peninsula in December 1991.[21] Under the terms of the declaration, both countries underlined their commitment to a non-nuclear Korea, their willingness to eschew plutonium or any highly enriched uranium reprocessing for military purposes, and acceptance of International Atomic Energy Agency (IAEA) inspections to ensure compliance with this and earlier agreements.

Barely a year later, these encouraging signs had been replaced by more worrying developments. At the end of 1992, the IAEA expressed its concern at indications that the North Korean authorities might have been trying to conceal the existence of two nuclear waste sites and its worries that the North might be seeking to weaponize plutonium withdrawn between 1989 and 1991 from its 5 megawatt civilian nuclear reactor at Yongbyon.[22] These concerns, in turn, prompted the North abruptly to withdraw from the Nuclear Non-proliferation Treaty in March 1993, triggering the first nuclear crisis on the Korean peninsula, and pushing the United States and the North into high-stakes brinkmanship in which the Clinton administration came perilously close to authorizing military action against the North. Ultimately, the situation was resolved diplomatically, in no small measure thanks to the eleventh-hour intervention of former president Jimmy Carter, who travelled to Pyongyang in June 1994 and secured an agreement by the North to allow the IAEA to continue its monitoring work, opening the door to a negotiated settlement.[23]

Amid this crisis, which threatened to spark a hot war of potentially devastating consequences for the wider Northeast Asian region, arguably what was most remarkable was the relatively limited involvement or influence of the Japanese authorities. The Clinton administration, in an effort to devise a multilateral solution to the crisis, did attempt to bring Japan and its other regional allies into its decision-making councils.[24] Yet Japan's ability to shape materially the choices and policies of the key players was conspicuously weak, with the Japanese government confined to a supporting rather than decisive role in shaping a response to a security crisis that, in light of the proximity of the peninsula and the magnitude of the military threat posed by the North, unquestionably affected its vital national interests.

Part of this weakness was, undoubtedly, a function of domestic political confusion within Japan. Between March 1993 and June 1994 – the chronological bookends marking the start and end of the crisis – Japan went through no fewer than four prime ministers, a reflection of the political instability and uncertainty generated by the LDP's first formal loss of power (marked by its defeat in the lower house election of 1993) since the party's formation in 1955. Part of the difficulty for Japan's decision-makers was the Japanese public's inability or unwillingness to view the crisis with the seriousness it deserved. In general, the government had few policy tools or resources with which to respond to the North Korean challenge. While the coalition government headed by Prime Minister Morihiro Hosokawa that took over from the LDP in August 1993 contemplated introducing economic sanctions against the North, these were given at best partial, half-hearted consideration, mainly because of the anemic response of the Japanese public: in October 1993, only 54 per cent of Japanese polled backed sanctions; by the end of the year, those in favour had dropped to 49 per cent.[25]

More generally, Japan appeared remarkably ill-prepared to deal with a security contingency on the Korean peninsula, despite past statements by Japanese leaders (most notably by Prime Minister Sato in 1969) that it would provide support to the United States in the event of an attack on South Korea. Even when Prime Minister Hosokawa took the precautionary step of ordering the drafting of temporary legislation for submission to the Diet providing for Japanese logistical support for the United States and possible participation in a future blockade of the North, public opinion in Japan remained highly sceptical about the merits of cooperation with Washington. According to one survey, some 70 per cent of Japan's public opposed the use of U.S. bases in Japan for the defence of South Korea even in the event of a North Korean attack.[26]

The Japanese political establishment's constructive response to the Korean crisis really only became apparent after the crisis had peaked. As has often been the case in past international crises, postwar Japan's diplomatic comparative advantage is in the provision of aid and economic assistance. As part of the Agreed Framework – the multifaceted and detailed package of measures put in place in 1994 to resolve the first nuclear crisis – Japan played a critical role, agreeing to provide some US$1 billion of support towards the cost of two light-water reactors intended to meet the North's energy needs. In March 1995, the Korean Peninsula Energy Development Organization (KEDO) was established, with Japan, South Korea, and the United States as its core members (the European Union joined its executive board later).[27] Similarly, in an effort to address the basic needs of the North Korean people, Japan in 1995 began donating food aid to offset the effects of famine in the North, and between 1995 and 2005 provided more than US$250 million worth of humanitarian aid to the North.[28]

It was only later in the decade, following the North's August 1998 launch of a Taepodong medium-range ballistic missile over Japan, that signs of a more muscular Japanese response to the North Korean security challenge began to become apparent. The missile launch, by highlighting Japan's strategic vulnerability, had a catalyzing effect on Japanese public opinion, abruptly shaking it out of the postwar psychological cocoon that had encouraged voters to assume mistakenly that Japan could play the role of disinterested spectator in regional and global security crises.

The government of Prime Minister Keizo Obuchi responded swiftly, temporarily suspending support for both KEDO and food and humanitarian assistance to the North.[29] More fundamentally, the government put in train a series of policy initiatives intended to bolster Japan's security preparedness to deal with the North Korean security challenge. In December 1998, the government agreed to introduce intelligence satellites by 2003 that could be used to monitor North Korean military preparations; it also signalled Japan's intention to participate in an ambitious program of research and development with the United States on Missile Defence. Similarly, in April 1999, Japan joined with South Korea and the United States in establishing the Trilateral Coordination and Oversight Group, a critical collaborative body bringing together key foreign and defence personnel to address on a regular basis common security challenges, particularly those in Northeast Asia. Enhanced minilateral cooperation of this sort was also bolstered by important legislative initiatives. An important first step had been taken in 1997 with the approval and passage of the Joint United States-Japan Defense Cooperation Guidelines, intended to enhance logistical cooperation between the U.S. and Japanese militaries in 'situations in areas surrounding Japan' – an intentionally ambiguous reference designed to maximize the strategic flexibility of the United States-Japan security partnership, but still allowing Tokyo and Washington to respond pragmatically to the North Korean challenge. Japan's government went beyond this with the passage of a new law in 1999, the Contingency in Surrounding Areas Act, clarifying the circumstances in which Japan's forces could be used in conjunction with the U.S. military.[30] Similarly, in 2000, the government passed new legislation authorizing Japan's Maritime Self-Defense Forces to investigate foreign vessels on the high seas – another measure intended to address possible hostile activity emanating from the North.[31]

It would be a mistake to assume that Japan's response to the North Korean challenge was primarily a defensive one. By the end of the 1990s, there were tentative signs that Japan's political elites were ready to explore the possibility of restarting talks with their North Korean counterparts. In 1999, former prime minister Tomiichi Murayama visited Pyongyang with a bipartisan delegation and suggested in the course of discussions that Japan would be willing to provide additional rice aid if Pyongyang were willing to restart normalization talks.[32] Japan's government had good reason to push the envelope on talks with the North. North Korea's ballistic missile threat, as well as its stockpiles of chemical and biological weapons, represented a real and present danger to Japan. Moreover, officials in Tokyo had reason to believe that the Clinton administration's approach towards the North risked leaving Japan out in the cold on key negotiating issues, most notably the fate of Japan's abducted citizens.

By the end of 2000, there were indications that the United States, in an effort to induce the North to be more compliant in bilateral negotiations, was willing to consider dropping the long-standing characterization of the North as a state sponsor of terror – a step that potentially would have removed a broad list of economic and political sanctions against the North and (importantly for Japan) without requiring a resolution of the abduction issue.[33] This sense of narrowing negotiating room for Japan was reinforced following the June 2000 bilateral summit between the leaders of North and South Korea – an important diplomatic initiative for which the Japanese government received no advance notice from their South Korean counterparts. To the Japanese government, there was then ample evidence that its ability to influence events on the peninsula was dwindling.[34] Fortunately for the Japanese, the North Koreans had concluded independently that talking to their century-old enemy might be worthwhile. In August 2000, worried about signs of military modernization in Japan, the North Koreans began to suggest that they would be willing to see the same economic formula employed in the South Korea-Japan 1965 normalization talks applied to any future negotiations between Pyongyang and Tokyo, discussions in which the issue of 'reparations' could now be replaced by the less diplomatically and politically contentious talk of 'compensation.'[35]

This hint of flexibility from the North opened the door for a new initiative on the part of Japan, one conveniently timed to coincide in spring 2001 with the emergence of a new type of political leadership in Japan in the guise of Prime Minister Junichirō Koizumi – a confident leader who appeared eager to embrace a more active and assertive diplomacy in tackling global security threats in general and those of Northeast Asia in particular.

Diplomatic Deficiencies: The Limits to Japan's Policy of Pragmatic Engagement with North Korea

Postwar Japanese administrations have often adopted a mediating role in dealing with regional challenges. Self-consciously defining themselves in a Janus-like relationship with both the United States and Asia – the latter an area where Japan's cultural and historical ties have been strong and its strategic interests critical – Japan's governments have often sought to play the role of regional brokers, albeit with mixed success. This was evident in the attempts under prime ministers Ikeda and Sato in the early 1960s to mediate between Indonesia and Malaysia,[36] or under Takeo Fukuda in the late 1970s to develop a more active role in Southeast Asia. Since the end of the Cold War, a similar pattern can be seen in Japan's policy towards Cambodia, in raising much needed international resources to deal with the post-conflict situation in Afghanistan, and in helping to assemble an international aid initiative to deal with the Southeast Asian tsunami of 2004.[37]

Foreign Policy under Koizumi

When Koizumi became prime minister in 2001, there was some evidence to suggest that the new young, telegenic leader saw himself as playing just such a mediating role. Japan has long pursued, in the words of Richard Samuels, a 'dual-hedge' strategy, balancing its relationship with the United States with a UN-focused diplomacy that stresses collective, internationally sanctioned initiatives in dealing with global and regional security challenges.[38] Koizumi's early foreign policies certainly appeared to reflect this tradition – underpinned most dramatically by the Japanese government's unwavering support for the Bush administration in the war against Iraq and, from September 2004, in the government's attempts – ultimately unsuccessful – to secure a permanent UN Security Council seat for Japan. The signal from Tokyo – one that continues to be reflected in Japanese national strategy documents today – was of a Japanese government that wanted to balance its traditionally strong pro-U.S. stance with an increasingly active and assertive internationalism. The same hedging approach arguably helps to explain the motives of the Koizumi administration in its two critical overtures towards the government of North Korea: Koizumi's dramatic September 2002 visit of Pyongyang, the first ever by a Japanese premier, and his second visit in May 2004.

The notion that Tokyo might play a brokering role in the North Korean context is a novel one, in some respects at odds with the conventional wisdom. Some analysts, most notably, Victor Cha in his path-breaking work, *Alignment Despite Antagonism*, present the United States, rather than Japan, as the key reconciler of diverging approaches – creating common purpose between the United States' two most important Asian allies and helping to reconcile often bitter and divisive differences separating South Korea and Japan. The key mechanism for securing alliance cooperation has been the variation in U.S. commitment to the region. Crudely put, fear of U.S. disengagement – according to Cha – has often compelled the leaderships of both Japan and South Korea to overcome their instinctive suspicions and mutual hostility and develop an effective pragmatic relationship. Conversely, when the U.S. presence in and commitment to the region has appeared secure, bilateral tensions between the United States' two key Asian allies have tended to flare up.[39]

It is debatable, however, whether this model of quasi-alliance coordination adequately describes the situation between 2001 and 2007. During a period when the Bush administration appeared, at least until late 2006, to have been remarkably detached from events on the Korean peninsula – or at least apparently unconcerned to develop coherent and effective solutions to the North Korean problem – officials in Tokyo and Seoul found it difficult to work effectively together to overcome key bilateral differences: either over persistent sovereignty disputes surrounding the contested island territories of Dokdo/Takeshima, unresolved differences over history textbooks, slow progress in free trade negotiations, and, most recently, over the sensitive question of wartime 'comfort women' – Korean and Chinese individuals forced by the Japanese military into state-sanctioned prostitution. This situation appears to be at odds with the Cha hypothesis. At a time when the United States appeared to be treading diplomatic water, one might have expected the emergence of a much more effective and meaningful alliance relationship – albeit a virtual one – between Seoul and Tokyo. Yet, the evidence for such cooperation is hard to find. Instead, personality clashes, most notably between President Roh Moo Hyun and Prime Minister Koizumi, lingering historical tensions, and mutual misperceptions appeared to have been the order of the day.

However difficult the relationship between Seoul and Tokyo may have been, there is no doubt that, under Koizumi, Japan sought to enhance substantially its efforts to confront the North Korean challenge. Part of the explanation for this change of emphasis can be attributed to the personality and temperament of the prime minister, part also to important institutional changes. The decline in the influence and power of Japan's dominant LDP following its electoral setback in 1993, and innovations such as the introduction of a new electoral system designed to foster policy debate and the emergence of a more competitive two-party system, opened the door to a new style of political leadership.

Koizumi defined himself as an iconoclastic politician, self-consciously pitting himself against the LDP's old guard by embracing radical new domestic policy initiatives, such as structural reform, deregulation, and the marginalization of vested interests in the construction industry and the postal service. This radicalism was also reflected in the prime minister's involvement in foreign policy matters. Just as in South Korea, where the emergence of the new 386-generation of younger, progressive politicians helped propel President Roh into power,[40] so too in Japan, a younger, more internationally minded, U.S.-educated, and less deferential cohort of government and opposition politicians encouraged a prime minister – who before assuming office had had only limited foreign experience – to turn his attention to diplomatic matters. This interest tended to manifest itself in a somewhat ad hoc manner, without much evidence of strategic coordination, but there was no doubting the prime minister's willingness to devote significant time and effort, and occasionally substantial amounts of political capital, to advancing particular foreign policy goals.

Institutionally, Koizumi was also operating in a more flexible and adaptive environment than that faced by his predecessors. In South Korea, President Roh sought to delegate responsibility for domestic affairs to his prime minister and to the governing party structure in the National Assembly, while simultaneously giving greater decision-making authority over foreign affairs to the Blue House and National Security Council – often at the expense of the authority of the Ministry of Foreign Affairs and Trade.[41] In Japan, too, Koizumi turned to non-party structures and informal advisory commissions, as well as his cabinet advisers, in developing specific foreign policy initiatives.[42] Japan's Policy Affairs Research Council (the *Seichoukai*), the key party policy-making body, saw its influence decline under Koizumi – a trend that continued under his successor, Shinzo Abe. Instead, the prime minister depended heavily on advice from key members of his personal kitchen cabinet: individuals such as former chief cabinet secretary Yasuo Fukuda and, most notable of all, Isao Iijima, Koizumi's personal secretary, were a key influence on Japan's North Korea policy.

For Japan's policy elites, the two principal worries over Korea are, first, the risk of war on the peninsula, a risk exacerbated by the nuclear standoff with the North; and, second, the possibility – admittedly a distant one over the past few years – of rapprochement between the United States and the North. In either case, Japan's decision-makers fear that Japan will be left out of the loop, inadequately consulted by the main players, especially its principal ally, the United States. Japanese decision-makers argue, in private, that this concern is amply justified by past events. In 1993–94, during the first nuclear crisis, when the Clinton administration appeared ready to risk catastrophic war on the peninsula to thwart the North's nuclear ambitions, Japan's leaders worried about entrapment – that they might be sucked into a devastating conflict that they were unable to influence and for which they would be completely unprepared. By contrast, in late 2000, when then-secretary of state Madeline Albright visited Pyongyang, Tokyo was more concerned about abandonment: the risk that an overly eager and sanguine U.S. government would rush to secure a deal on nuclear proliferation without adequately taking into account either Japanese concerns regarding the ballistic missile threat from the North or the unresolved question of the fate of Japanese citizens abducted by North Korean agents from Japan in the 1970s and '80s.

Following the events of the 1990s, U.S. and Japanese policy-makers took positive measures to minimize both these sets of fears, first by the drafting and passing of the Joint United States-Japan Security Guidelines of 1997, and second by the sustained effort by 'Japan hands' in the first post-2001 Bush administration – individuals such as Deputy Secretary of State Richard Armitage and Michael Green, Northeast Asian head on the National Security Council (NSC) – to enhance the status, effectiveness, and regional and global scope of the United States-Japan alliance.

Positive and valuable though these changes were, they were not sufficient to resolve the Koizumi administration's concerns over North Korea. During 2001 and 2002, the prime minister faced important pressures and incentives encouraging him to seize the initiative on North Korean matters.

The First Pyongyang Summit, September 2002

When first selected as LDP leader and, by extension, prime minister in April 2001, Koizumi enjoyed record high approval rates of between 70 and 80 per cent. In contrast to his lacklustre predecessor, Yoshiro Mori, Koizumi appeared to offer new leadership, both in terms of style and substance, appealing directly to the electorate and challenging the old guard within the LDP by conspicuously refusing to adhere to the traditional practice of allocating senior positions in cabinet on the basis of the numerical clout of individual party factions. A credible performance by the government in the July 2001 upper house elections, when it secured 64 seats – ahead of its pre-election target of 61 – was indicative of the popularity of the new prime minister.[43] This popularity would prove hard to sustain, at least in the short run.

In late 2001, early 2002, Koizumi confronted sluggish economic growth that made a foreign policy success abroad particularly attractive as a potential means of distracting public attention from difficult circumstances at home. Tension with his outspoken and undiplomatic foreign minister, Makiko Tanaka, damaged Koizumi's reputation for administrative competence; he was forced to fire Tanaka in January 2002, in the process sharply denting his reputation as a reforming premier and producing in matter of weeks a marked decline in his approval ratings from the 80 per cent mark to the low 50s. Adding to the prime minister's woes was a damaging corruption case involving Muneo Suzuki, a senior LDP politician with influence in policy-making on Russia, and a tax-evasion scandal that surfaced in March 2002, involving Koichi Kato, a leading LDP figure closely associated with, or at least sympathetic to, Koizumi's economic reform agenda.[44]

North Korea, in the early part of the new century, also appeared to be undergoing important changes that hinted at new policy opportunities for a bold and imaginative Japanese leader willing to take some political risks. The 2000 North-South summit – facilitated, as we now know, by covert financial inducements from the South – suggested a significant thaw in North-South relations. Economic desperation in the North, exacerbated by natural disasters and the failures of central planning, had prompted the partial economic liberalizations of 2002. On the international stage, the opening of new North Korean diplomatic missions in Europe pointed towards more flexibility on the part of the leadership in Pyongyang.

Japan's political and foreign policy elites also had begun to worry by 2002 that Washington, then under the first Bush administration, had embraced a hard-line approach to the North, symbolized by the president's 'Axis of Evil' reference in his January 2002 State of the Union address, which closed the door to negotiation with the North. Animated by an 'anything but Clinton' (or ABC) approach towards foreign affairs that made Bush and his associates implacably opposed to the policy initiatives of the previous administration, the United States appeared unwilling to consider constructive means of dealing with the multiple security challenges posed by the North – either its ballistic missiles and conventional capabilities with respect to weapons of mass destruction (WMD), or its incipient nuclear program. Negotiation and engagement as favoured by the Clinton administration seemingly had been replaced by political and economic isolation, fostering regime change and possible military pre-emption as preferred tactics for dealing with the North. In the context of the emergence of new nuclear weapons states, most notably India and Pakistan in the late 1990s, senior foreign ministry officials in Tokyo were understandably worried, feeling the need for a new more pragmatic and independent Japanese initiative to address the growing regional security challenge from North Korea.[45]

Importantly, a new mechanism had been put in place within a tight circle of associates around the prime minister, to push forward the normalization process with the North. Key LDP political players such as Nonaka Hiromu and Taku Yamazaki had received back-channel overtures from North Korean officials suggesting that Pyongyang was seriously interested in talks.[46] Moreover, a leading *Gaimusho* official, Hitoshi Tanaka, the director general of the Asian and Oceanian Affairs Division, and Foreign Ministry colleagues who favoured a modest change of emphasis in Japan's diplomacy towards greater focus on Asian matters and less overt dependence on the United States took the lead in advancing the normalization agenda.[47] Tanaka benefited from personal ties and access to the prime minister[48] and was able to coordinate the initiatives towards the North with considerable secrecy – a quality to these early talks that the prime minister's office saw as essential to offset potential opposition to the negotiations from hardliners in the LDP such as former prime minister Ryutaro Hashimoto.[49]

Against the backdrop of these pressures and incentives, it was easy to see why Koizumi chose to seize the risk of an autumn summit in North Korea in 2002, travelling to the North to announce jointly with Kim Jong Il on 17 September the Pyongyang Declaration.[50] Superficially, the prime minister's gamble appeared to have paid off handsomely. The North agreed to waive its traditional demand for formal compensation for the Japanese colonial period, in return for the possibility of substantial amounts of Japanese economic assistance; it extended its 1999 missile-testing moratorium; and it agreed to abide by international agreements – indirectly a commitment to observe the terms of the Agreed Framework of 1994 that had helped to resolve the first nuclear crisis in the 1990s. Most dramatically of all, Kim Jong Il admitted in his discussion with the prime minister – although, in the formal declaration, this was an implicit rather than an explicit admission – to the North's role in the kidnapping of some 13 Japanese citizens in the 1970s and 1980s and apologized for these past actions.[51]

The dividends from these negotiations were immediate and dramatic: a much-needed bounce for Koizumi in the opinion polls,[52] and talk of possible normalization of relations with North Korea within three months. Yet Japanese critics of the prime minister soon argued that he had overreached himself and had not paid sufficient attention to fundamental security issues. In particular, there were four core areas in which Koizumi and his wider negotiating team were arguably guilty of misjudgment.

First, Japanese officials had acted unilaterally and, by briefing the United States late in the day about the September summit, had generated irritation and resentment in Washington.

Second, despite having been informed in advance of the September summit by the United States of a covert North Korean Highly Enriched Uranium (HEU) program dating from the 1990s, the Japanese side had failed to raise this matter in direct talks with the North. As a consequence, the Pyongyang Declaration referred only indirectly to the Agreed Framework of 1994 and not at all to the equally important and earlier 1991 North-South Denuclearization Declaration – an agreement that, if reiterated, would have put added pressure on the North to come clean on its putative HEU program.

Third, Japan's discussions in Pyongyang had focused on missile testing and deployment but not on the question of missile exports. This suggested a limited and not especially sophisticated Japanese position – focusing only on narrow threats to Japanese security rather than wider regional and global challenges. Some saw this in turn as worrying evidence of a possible gap in U.S. and Japanese security cooperation.

Finally, Koizumi had failed to anticipate the later Japanese public backlash on the abductee issue. While Kim Jong Il's revelations ultimately led to the return of five surviving abductees to Japan, their North Korean relatives remained in the North and the fate of as many as 80 others – most notably, Megumi Yokota, abducted from Japan in 1977 at age 13 – remained unclear. The public fallout from these unresolved issues quickly reversed the prime minister's positive ratings and provoked a sustained public relations campaign by a number of high-profile and well-organized Japanese interest groups representing the families of the abductees calling for more progress on the abduction issue.[53]

The question of advance consultation with the United States became a particular problem for Koizumi publicly. In October, a month after the Pyongyang Declaration, James Kelly, then assistant secretary for East Asian Affairs, travelled to North Korea and confronted it with evidence of its HEU program. To some observers – such as veteran U.S. journalist Selig Harrison – this was not only an effort to derail any prospect of progress in U.S. talks with the North, but also an attempt to block any hope of rapprochement between Tokyo and Pyongyang. The Americans had distorted their own intelligence on the HEU issue – 'sexing up' their information as the British media liked to call it – to scuttle any hope of progress.[54]

Whether the White House, via the Kelly visit, wanted to set back talks with North Korea in general is not entirely clear. Certainly there is strong circumstantial evidence that suggests hawks in the Bush administration were looking for proof of the unreliability of the North Korean government. Moreover, there is little doubt that, at the time, many U.S. officials — including politicians, representatives of the intelligence community, and bureaucrats in the State Department and the NSC – felt that the evidence of a covert North Korean HEU program was credible.[55] However, the charge that the October surprise was designed to block an improvement in Japanese-North Korean relations is harder to sustain. Discussions with U.S., Japanese, and South Korean officials suggest a more complicated picture: that the United States may have been more relaxed about the Japanese overture than appeared to be the case at the time.

For Japan hands in the Bush administration who had been trying to build a more genuinely cooperative relationship with Tokyo for some time, risking alienating the Koizumi administration by such blocking tactics would have been at odds with their efforts to enhance the bilateral security partnership. It is true that the United States was officially informed by Japan of Koizumi's visit to the North relatively late in the day – in August 2002, during a visit to Tokyo by Deputy Secretary of State Richard Armitage. However, Tanaka Hitoshi had attempted to brief the Americans on the visit earlier in the summer at a Washington meeting with James Kelly. According to Jack Pritchard, then NSC representative for Northeast Asian affairs, poor reading of Tanaka's intentions on the part of U.S. officials during the meeting led the Americans to miss the subtle effort by the Japanese side to solicit their support in opening negotiations with the North.[56] In any event, any irritation on the U.S. side about the timing of the notification appears to have been confined to the working level, among State Department and Pentagon officials. At more senior levels, there appears to have been close cooperation between the two governments. President Bush personally endorsed Koizumi's visit in a telephone conversation with the prime minister before his departure for Pyongyang,[57] and Koizumi reportedly delivered a personal message to Kim Jong Il from President Bush during the 17 September meeting.[58]

The notion also that the Americans had deployed the HEU issue to undercut the Japanese negotiation position with the North is also implausible given the extensive sharing of intelligence on this issue among U.S., Japanese, and South Korean officials in advance of Koizumi's visit.[59] While it is true that the Japanese side chose not to refer directly to the HEU issue in talks with the North Koreans, this appears to some observers to have reflected a deliberate division of labour among the various negotiating parties. The Americans were willing to share their intelligence with their allies, but the assumption was that the United States would take primary responsibility for presenting this argument to the North.[60] The South Korean, Japanese, and U.S. governments, according to one senior South Korean official, routinely shared information on the HEU issue and all were aware of this concern well in advance of Koizumi's September visit. Even the argument that the U.S. mission to Pyongyang in October was an attempt to short-circuit further negotiations is questionable. Kelly's negotiating points were tightly – some might argue, overly rigidly – circumscribed, but this was not, according to some observers, intended to close off further talks with the North Korean side.[61]

Perhaps most important, the substantial Japanese economic aid package of US$5–10 billion discussed in the context of the 2002 September summit represented a valuable negotiating card that neither the Americans nor the Japanese would have wanted to discard by foreclosing any long-term hope of reconciliation between Tokyo and Pyongyang.

Yet the suspicion of underhand action by the Americans at this critical juncture still remains. How else might we explain it? Here, interestingly, the evidence reveals tensions that were more pronounced between Washington and Seoul than they were between Washington and Tokyo. South Korean official irritation with the Bush administration was based on the firm belief that domestic politics might have been the key factor explaining the Kelly revelation. The Roh Moo Hyun administration had already known of the HEU claims from the Americans well before October, and had specifically requested that these details not be released prematurely. Consequently, senior South Korean officials were particularly irritated when the White House chose to publicise the HEU claims in advance of the mid-term November congressional elections. To some in Seoul, it looked as if the Bush administration, in an effort to look tough in its dealings with the North, was placing its narrow domestic interests ahead of any larger diplomatic goals.[62]

Domestic and International Fallout

Whatever the precise motives on the U.S. side, the consequences of the Kelly visit proved very destabilizing. North Korean officials appeared – at least in the judgment of the members of the Kelly delegation – to have acknowledged the HEU program,[63] then denied they had made any such admission. The HEU revelation, in turn, prompted KEDO to suspend heavy fuel-oil shipments to the North in November 2002, generating a tit-for-tat retaliation by the North in the form of the expulsion of IAEA inspectors from the North in December, leading ultimately in 2003 to North Korea's withdrawal from the Nuclear Non-proliferation Treaty and the reprocessing of fuel rods from the North's Yongbyon reactor, which set in train the second North Korean nuclear crisis.

In turn, Japan appeared to recoil from its earlier accommodating overtures towards the North – toughening its rhetoric, reaffirming its security relationship with the United States, and signing up in May 2003 to the Proliferation Security Initiative, a multilateral based effort to contain the export of WMD by the North.[64]

In part, this shift by the Koizumi administration was an effort to insulate itself from sharp criticism at home. Lurid media reports in Japan of North Korean money-laundering activities, of illegal remittances flowing to the North from North Korean residents in Japan, of North Korean amphetamines flooding into Japan, and rumours of a North Korean espionage ring in Japan all served to discredit or at the very least limit the prospects for the normalization of relations with the North.[65]

In the wake of criticism of its conciliatory approach by conservative legislators[66] and an attempt in September 2003 by Japanese right-wing extremists to detonate a bomb in the residence of Hitoshi Tanaka, the head Foreign Ministry official handling the government's North Korea policy, the government sought to manage the public relations fallout from these developments without unduly jeopardizing its relations with the North.

The government arguably walked this precarious tightrope with some skill. Koizumi talked publicly about the possibility of embracing full economic sanctions against the North, but carefully avoided formally committing the administration to any such strategy. In an effort to play for time, the government passed symbolic legislation limiting port visits to Japan by North Korean ships, while all the while using back-channel meetings[67] and the establishment of a telephone hotline to Pyongyang in 2004 to keep bilateral discussions alive behind the scenes. Koizumi also astutely appointed Shinzo Abe – a noted hawk on North Korean issues – as party secretary general in 2003 – as a means of insulating himself from conservative criticism at home.[68] In grappling with the second nuclear crisis, the Koizumi government recognized the important distinction between talking tough in public while pursuing diplomatic openings and opportunities in private. The clearest expression of this was its official commitment from 2003 onwards to a combined strategy of 'pressure and dialogue' (*atsuryoku to taiwa*). In detail, this approach was based on a three-stage process in which the government concentrated on, first, resolving the abduction and nuclear issues; second, normalizing bilateral relations and providing economic aid while also addressing the North's ballistic missile threat; and third, fully engaging the North politically, economically, and militarily to attempt to make it a full-fledged member of the international community and secure a more stable Northeast Asia.[69]

The Second Pyongyang Summit, May 2004

Most important of all, Koizumi remained willing to pursue a second dramatic diplomatic opening to North Korea – which emerged during his unexpected May 2004 follow-up visit to Pyongyang. Critics of this second visit suggested that the prime minister was motivated in this instance primarily by political calculations, in particular a desire to secure a good showing for the governing LDP in the July 2004 upper house elections by realizing another foreign policy coup.[70] Yet, this seems at best a partial explanation. Certainly, for senior Foreign Ministry officials, the more immediate cause was frustration with the Bush administration's inertia on North Korean matters. By early 2004, the *Gaimusho* had become worried by what it saw as an overly complacent U.S. 'containment' strategy towards the North.[71] The Bush

White House seemed happy to use the Proliferation Security Initiative – together with the threat of catastrophic retaliation against the North if it were caught proliferating nuclear material – to keep the North's nuclear genie safely in its bottle.

By contrast, Japan's government, while sharing the proliferation concerns of the United States, was much more concerned by the immediate threat to Japan of a possible nuclear North Korea, equipped with ballistic missiles capable of delivering nuclear material – either sophisticated bombs or 'dirty' fissile material – onto Japanese territory. This difference in outlook – or so-called strategic asymmetry – helps to explain why the Koizumi administration at this point had a much greater sense of urgency than Washington for the need to resolve the standoff with the North.

The May visit, as it turned out, was another high-risk political gamble that delivered only partial gains for Prime Minister Koizumi. He helped to secure the release of all but three of the remaining family members of the five abductees first revealed in 2002, while Kim Jong Il admitted that a nuclear freeze would be the first step to dismantling nuclear weapons programs and signalled his willingness to find a way to resolve the abductee issue. In return, Japan offered emergency food and medical aid to the North and the prospect of further economic support if the North were willing to demonstrate its commitment to the terms of the original 2002 Pyongyang Declaration.[72]

Yet there were very real limits to how far Japan's professional diplomats could push this process of accommodation with the North. There is strong evidence that Koizumi, in part because of his closeness to the U.S. president, might have been instrumental at a personal meeting on the sidelines of the June 2004 G8 Georgia summit in persuading Bush to present a serious negotiating proposal to the North in the third round of the six-party talks that took place subsequently in Beijing.[73] Here was an opportunity for Japan to play a mediating, constructive role, nudging the United States towards engagement, and one that Koizumi appears to have seized. How decisive Koizumi's intervention was at this stage is not fully clear; we probably will have to await the opening of the diplomatic archives before we can make a complete assessment of the degree of influence he exerted. Influential or not, the Japanese prime minister had to contend with other obstacles – not least of which was the U.S. presidential cycle, which intervened in fall 2004 to delay any prospect of a breakthrough with the North. Moreover, fresh U.S. intelligence revelations in February 2005 of a North Korean role in providing uranium hexafluoride to Libya acted much in the same way as the Kelly intervention of 2002 to heighten tensions between the North and the international community.

Koizumi's flexibility on the North Korean issue was also restricted by opinion at home. Increasingly in 2004 and 2005, conservative politicians and Japanese armchair military strategists pointed to the North Korean threat as grounds for a more assertive Japanese security stance. They argued that this might include the nuclearization of Japan's defence policy – particularly in the context of a build-down of U.S. forces on the Korean peninsula as part of the United States' Global Posture Review. Such views were, and remain, very much non-mainstream opinion,[74] but they were symptomatic of the narrowing of the policy options open to Koizumi. Equally important, the Japanese media – both print and television outlets – became increasingly preoccupied with the experience of Japan's abductees – in particular, the fate of Megumi Yokota – fuelling a growing public mood of hostility towards the North.[75] The issue was further inflamed in December 2004 when Pyongyang attempted to pass off a collection of allegedly fake remains as the bones of Yokota. Senior Japanese Foreign Ministry officials had already assumed – in the face of North Korean claims that she had committed suicide in 1994 – that Yokota was almost certainly dead. But the revelation – thanks to DNA testing by a private Japanese research institute – that the bones were not genuine led to a further deterioration in relations between the Japanese and North Korean governments.[76]

The Koizumi government found its hands tied both by its inability to restrict the dissemination of the results of the DNA testing and by the practical realities of local politics in Japan. Responsibility for investigating the disappearance of Yokota rested with the police authorities in Niigata prefecture, from where Yokota was abducted. For this reason, the central government in Tokyo could not control the way in which the information relating to this emotional and controversial case was either managed or disseminated.[77] To North Korea, however, such subtle distinctions were unlikely to have been readily apparent, and North Korean officials took umbrage at the Japanese reaction, assuming erroneously that the Koizumi government was intentionally proving uncooperative on this issue. Unsurprisingly, the fallout from this controversy led to a sharp deterioration in relations between the two governments and a reversal of much of the bilateral progress that had been achieved in 2004 – including earlier ministerial meetings and the suspension of the direct telephone hotline between Tokyo and Pyongyang.[78]

In the wake of such problems at home, one might have anticipated that the Koizumi government would turn to other regional parties to enhance its negotiating position with the North. The challenge for Tokyo was – and arguably still is – the absence of any immediately obvious partner in promoting its interests directly with the North. China, while increasingly impatient with the North Korean leadership, could hardly have been counted on to lobby on behalf of Japan at a time when rising popular nationalism in both China and Japan, as well as Koizumi's personal commitment to visit the controversial Yasukuni Shrine commemorating Japan's war dead, had led to a serious deterioration in Sino-Japanese relations.

One might have expected the Japanese government to turn to South Korea as an obvious partner in reopening relations with the North, especially given the conventional and nuclear challenge the North posed to both countries and in light of efforts by elites in Seoul and Tokyo to persuade a reluctant Bush administration to engage constructively with the North. However, mutual rational interest appears to have had little traction during this period. Instead, historical and territorial disputes, personal tensions between Prime Minister Koizumi and President Roh, and the vagaries of domestic politics in both countries appear to have been more powerful than geopolitical considerations or any putative balancing or brokering role for the United States in explaining the absence of effective bilateral cooperation between Japan and South Korea.

History, National Identity, and the Power of Local Interests in Japan's Relations with South Korea

At the heart of tensions between Japan and South Korea since World War Two are disagreements about the past. Japan's colonial experience on the Korean peninsula has acted like a historical millstone weighing down the reputation of Japanese leaders in the eyes of contemporary Koreans, who tend to see Japan as at best only partially contrite and remorseful for its past excesses and transgressions. Koreans of whichever political persuasion, progressive or conservative, embrace a common narrative of the past in which two key dates – namely, 1 March, the anniversary of the abortive independence movement of 1919, and 15 August, marking the end of the Pacific War and liberation from Japanese rule – have powerful emotional resonance. Korean national identity is, in some respects, defined by resistance against Japan, and it is no accident perhaps that one of the greatest heroes of Korean nationalism is Ahn Joong Kun, a political activist who in 1909 assassinated Hirobumi Ito, Japan's resident-general of Korea.[79]

While Japanese politicians routinely and repeatedly seek to express regret or remorse for Japan's past actions in Korea, many Koreans question the sincerity of such remarks. The earliest instance of an apparently qualified admission of responsibility on the part of Japan came in 1953, when Kanichirō Kubota, the head Japanese official involved in normalization talks with South Korea, declared publicly that 'Japanese rule over Korea was not entirely without positive benefits.' Kubota's statement was intended to enhance Japan's negotiating leverage in talks over property rights with the Koreans, but to many in Korea it seemed to represent an effort to evade responsibility for the past.[80] Similarly, in 1958, Kazuo Yatsugi, as a personal envoy to Seoul of Prime Minister Kishi, declared in discussions with the South Korean government his desire to 'atone for the wrongs committed by Hirobumi Ito,' only to have his remarks repudiated subsequently by Kishi. Likewise, in 1965, Foreign Minister Etsusaburo Shiina arrived in Seoul and issued what seemed like an apology for the past, expressing his 'sincere regret' for an 'unfortunate period in bilateral relations' – remarks that were very well received at the time by south Korean public opinion, but that were not matched by any comparable expression of regret in the eventual communiqué signed by Prime Minister Sato formally establishing bilateral normalization.[81]

From the South Korean perspective, the shortcoming of Japanese expressions of regret has either been their apparently qualified nature or the sharp political backlash from conservative opinion they have produced in Japan.[82] Japanese prime ministers frequently find their ability to speak for the nation on the issue of colonial and wartime responsibility circumscribed if not directly undercut by conservative rivals at home. In the 1980s, Prime Minister Yasuhiro Nakasone went out of his way to promote positive ties with South Korea, selecting Seoul as the symbolically important first destination for his initial travel abroad as premier in 1983. During the visit, he had offered the administration of Chun Do Hwan some US$4 billion worth of economic assistance, and sought to create a climate of amity and reconciliation by both talking and, in one instance, singing in Korean. This form of olive-branch diplomacy opened the way for further accommodation when Chun travelled to Tokyo in 1986 and met Emperor Showa, who broke new ground by expressing his 'regret' for Japan's colonial rule. This positive initiative was undercut, however, by Nakasone's own education minister, Masayuki Fujio, who promptly and controversially published an article in a monthly magazine asserting that the Koreans in part bore both legal and political responsibility for the Japanese annexation of their country in 1910.[83]

Even when Japan's leaders grapple directly and authoritatively with the issue of wartime responsibility, they find it especially difficult to reassure the South Koreans that they speak for the nation as a whole. In 1995, for example, Prime Minister Murayama chose the symbolically important date of 15 August to characterize Japanese aggression during the Pacific War as a 'mistaken national policy,' and expressed his 'heartfelt remorse' for Japan's colonial rule – perhaps the boldest and most unambiguous expression of regret by a Japanese leader to date. Yet the impact of Murayama's admission was almost immediately weakened by the unwillingness of the Diet to follow through with a similarly unambiguous statement, offering instead a more watered-down apology appearing to rationalize aspects of Japan's colonial and wartime experience.[84]

Despite these difficulties, by the time Koizumi took over as prime minister in 2001, there was a well-documented set of statements by past Japanese premiers reflecting a desire to address bilateral relations with South Korea positively, most notably the breakthrough apology for the past in October 1998 by then prime minister Obuchi on the occasion of President Kim Dae Jung's visit to Tokyo. Obuchi not only expressed deep remorse and sincere apologies for the past, but the Japanese government also provided some US$3 billion in aid, an offer that materially enhanced bilateral relations.[85]

In the early years of his premiership, Koizumi went out of his way to reinforce this positive message. In 2001 he visited Seodaemun Prison in Seoul, the notorious facility formerly used by the Japanese colonial authorities to incarcerate and brutalize anti-colonial activists, and commented empathetically, '[W]hen I looked at things put on display, I strongly felt ... regret for the pains Korean people suffered during Japanese colonial rule. As a politician and a man, I believe we must not forget the pain of [Korean] people.'[86] With the joint hosting of the World Cup in 2002 it seemed, at first glance, as if the two countries were on track to forging an effective and mutually beneficial relationship.

Despite these positive indicators, there were clouds on the horizon. One especially problematic issue was the controversy surrounding history textbook reform in Japan. Since the mid-1990s, conservative factions within the LDP and revisionist historians and commentators in activist groups such as the Japanese Society for Text Book Reform (*Tsukurukai*)[87] had sought to promote a highly contentious view of the past, one that challenged the notion of Japanese war guilt and responsibility, questioned the victim status of 'comfort women,' and argued against a view of the past that was unduly masochistic and self-critical. These new, polemical, and empirically questionable views prompted interest groups in both South Korea and Japan to mobilize and lobby their respective governments to prevent the adoption of a junior high school history textbook that embraced these revisionist viewpoints. This interest group activism was successful in the sense that it helped to limit local adoption of the offending textbook in question to a mere 0.4 per cent of all school districts in Japan.

Nevertheless, the controversy associated with this issue demonstrated to many critical observers in South Korea that intolerant nationalist opinion, while still a minority view, was on the increase in Japan and in a manner that appeared to foreclose informed and balanced discussion about the past.[88] In an effort to address these and similar historical controversies, the Koizumi and Roh administrations agreed in 2001 to establish a new joint committee to study common historical issues. Although the committee met regularly and produced a substantial body of written material, overall the initiative appears to have been singularly unsuccessful in generating a consensus among Japanese and Korean historians on how to view the past. Its concluding report in June 2005 was conspicuous in its admission of the continuing differences between the two sides, particularly surrounding Japan's early twentieth-century annexation of Korea.[89]

Controversies over the past were not limited to academic debates among historians and their political supporters. At the very highest level of government, national leaders injected themselves into the center of these controversies – in Koizumi's case, via his decision annually to visit the Yasukuni Shrine; in Roh's case, through his support for the declassification of controversial postwar historical archival records that cast new light on Japan-South Korea relations. In autumn 2004, the South Korean government released documents detailing the terms of the bilateral 1965 normalization negotiations. The disclosure was controversial since it revealed that substantial amounts of Japanese money (some US$500 million in total) intended to serve as compensation for the Korean victims of the colonial period had been channelled to South Korea's conservative elites and used to support the economic development initiative of President Park Chung Hee.[90] To some observers, the disclosure appeared intended to undermine contemporary South Korea-Japan relations either by exposing past collusion or by indirectly weakening Japan's bargaining position in its continuing normalization negotiations with the North. To others, the disclosure appeared to be a political gambit by Roh intended to embarrass Park Geun Hye, the daughter of former president Park and a leading potential presidential candidate for the opposition Grand National Party. President Roh appeared especially eager to court popular controversy by fostering a wider debate within South Korea on the sensitive question of colonial era collaboration between Koreans and their former Japanese overseers. This became starkly apparent in late 2004 when the South Korean National Assembly passed a 'Special Law on Truths Concerning Anti-Korean activities during the forcible [sic] Japanese Occupation,' and on 15 August 2005, when Roh personally intervened and urged the Assembly to pass legislation confiscating the property of former colonial collaborators.

Although it is easy to discern hidden motives or conspiracies behind these disclosure initiatives, it is unlikely that Roh was seeking directly to destabilize relations with Japan. As a self-educated lawyer and unambiguous outsider, excluded for most of his professional career from the mainstream of elite society in South Korea,[91] Roh's political identity had been shaped by his desire to challenge conservative norms and foster a more open political climate at home. This appears to have been the primary motivation behind these initiatives, rather than any putative desire to score points against political rivals either at home or abroad.[92]

Notwithstanding the president's intentions, there was always the risk that an issue only indirectly related to diplomacy might spill over unpredictably to destabilize the bilateral relationship. This became a particularly potent concern in 2005, the fortieth anniversary of the normalization of relations between Japan and South Korea, officially designated as a Year of Friendship between the two countries. Ironically, 2005 witnessed some of the most bitter and divisive controversies between the two governments and a new low point in bilateral relations.

Two key events acted as triggers for the tension that emerged during the course of the year. The first was a public remark in February by Toshiyuki Takano, Japan's ambassador to South Korea, reiterating the long-standing official Japanese territorial claim over the island of Takeshima. South Korea, which refers to the island as Dokdo, rejects this claim and asserts its own legal claim to the island and has occupied the territory since the end of World War Two. The second trigger was the 16 March announcement by Shimane prefecture, in Japan's southwest, declaring its formal designation of 22 February as 'Takeshima Day.' Both events immediately generated a firestorm of protest in South Korea. Both progressive and conservative opinion there has long been united in the unshakeable belief in the legitimacy of Korea's sovereignty over the territory, and popular and elite representatives were quick to condemn Japan. South Korean protestors symbolically burnt the Japanese flag outside the Japanese embassy in Seoul, and some demonstrators went so far as to cut off their fingers to underscore the intensity of their hostility to the Japanese actions. For its part, the South Korean government cancelled a trip to Japan by then foreign minister Ban Ki Moon, and on 17 March Roh publicly called on Japan to apologize and demanded compensation for its wartime and colonial actions. Very emotively, Roh referred to the reiteration of the Japanese territorial claim as 'a second dispossession of the Korean peninsula that denies the history of Korean liberation.'[93]

While the intensity of these protests was conspicuous, to the disinterested observer perhaps the most striking element in this controversy was the gap in understanding between the two sides to the dispute. Each government, in particular, appeared to see the worst possible motivations underpinning the actions of the other. From Seoul's perspective, the prefectural declaration bore all the hallmarks of an orchestrated central government effort to humiliate South Korea. The Roh administration remained convinced that the Japanese government was disingenuous in suggesting that this was an exclusively local affair. In Tokyo, senior Foreign Ministry officials viewed Roh's public criticisms of the Koizumi government as opportunistic demagoguery – in the words of one official, 'behaviour as bad as that of North Korea'[94] – and motivated simply by the desire to bolster President Roh's flagging public opinion ratings at home.

Neither side's criticism was justified. Shimane's actions were, it appears, at best only partially influenced by national territorial ambitions or revisionist historical claims. Instead, the prefecture was motivated by two sets of factors: economic interests on the part of the prefecture's aging fishermen, who wished to solicit backing from Tokyo in the daily battle with their younger South Korean counterparts to secure fish catches in the waters close to the contested islands; and, second, local-national political tensions within the LDP. A prominent local assemblyman and cousin to then chief cabinet secretary Hiroyuki Hosoda had recently been passed over for selection as a candidate for the national upper house elections, and raising the volatile territorial issue was a way of thumbing his nose at both the cabinet – which had sought unsuccessfully to dissuade Shimane from making the controversial declaration – and the national party.[95]

On the South Korean side, Roh's actions and language should be seen in the Korean cultural context. While to Japanese ears, the rhetorical salvo against Japan on 17 March might have seemed provocative and confrontational, by South Korean norms of political discourse they were arguably relatively restrained.[96] Indeed, in a follow-up announcement on 23 March, in the form of an open letter to his fellow South Korean citizens, Roh used notably emollient and non-confrontational language, noting that 'the Government [would] not take a hard-line stance emotionally' and calling on the Korean people to 'keep calm and respond with composure.' Indeed, the president appeared to backtrack from his 17 March statement when he stressed that South Korea had not 'demanded that Japan make a new apology.' Although, Roh continued to see the hidden hand of the Koizumi government behind Shimane's announcement, he appears, to his credit, to have recognized the range of opinion in Japan on this and other related controversial issues. As he noted, '[W]e must never condone the aggressive intent of some Japanese ultra-nationalists, but this does not mean that we should distrust or antagonize the entire Japanese people.'[97]

Mutual misunderstanding, then, and the intervention of local political issues appear to have undermined the bilateral relationship seriously. The crisis was compounded by the absence of an effective network of close personal connections (or 'pipes' as they are often referred to in Japan) linking together the political constituencies of both countries. Much of this can be attributed to rise to political prominence of the 386-generation of younger politicians in South Korea. This cohort has tended to be more critical of Japan than are older political cohorts, and the 2002 parliamentary elections led to an appreciable drop in the number of legislators with close ties to Japan – in 2005, there were fewer than 20 National Assembly members with an active interest in Japan.[98]

Overall, tension over historical and territorial concerns and the attenuation of personal ties has been reflected in growing hostility and a lack of trust between the two countries, with South Koreans in particular registering high levels of antipathy and suspicion towards Japan. In 2001, for example, when asked to name the country in East Asia they disliked the most, 68.9 per cent of South Koreans polled answered Japan – a sizable increase on the figures recorded in 1984 (38.9 per cent) and 1988 (50.6 per cent).[99] Similar trends were reflected among South Korean politicians in 2002, with 66 per cent of members of the National Assembly identifying Japan as the biggest potential threat to security in East Asia, second only to the North.[100] Distrust, in turn, has encouraged many South Koreans to believe, almost as an article of faith, that, out of fear of a stronger and more assertive Korea, Japan actively welcomes the continuing division of the peninsula between North and South. Yet a close reading of Japanese commentary on this issue reveals widely diverging opinion, even though many policy-makers would be concerned if a future, unified Korea embraced aggressive weaponry, including nuclear weapons, and severed its political and military ties with the United States.[101]

The consequences of this antipathy and lack of trust have been not only the difficulty of managing the bilateral relationship, but also the relative lack of any significant security or strategic cooperation between political and security elites in the two countries. South Korea under Roh remained resolutely outside the Proliferation Security Initiative structure and chose not to explore opportunities for missile defence development either separately or in conjunction with the United States. The president for much of this time in office was personally inclined to focus diplomatic initiatives on regional cooperation, demonstrating in the process a keen interest in the relevance of European models of successful multilateral decision-making and conflict resolution. Bilateral or trilateral security arrangements by contrast appear to have been of relatively limited interest to Roh.[102]

Conclusion

In light of the real and substantive differences and tensions outlined above, should one conclude that the relationship between Japan and the two Koreas is 'abnormal'? Only, I argue, if we take a too narrow view of what constitutes 'normalcy' in international relations. Many relations between states are coloured by historical tensions and the legacy of the past – think of Germany and France, or, for that matter, the United States and the two Koreas. However, just as historical controversies can intrude in domestic politics to limit debate, polarize political parties, or act as a check on constitutional revision, so too in foreign policy, where the same controversies can impede successful policy-making and bilateral cooperation. This undoubtedly was the case for the South Korea-Japan relationship during the Koizumi and Roh administrations.

In the long term, what would it take to normalize Japan's relationship with the two Koreas? Clearly, establishing diplomatic relations and ending any formal state of conflict is a necessary first step. As the post-1965 experience of South Korea-Japan relations demonstrates, however, this is not sufficient. Far more is required to break down mutual mistrust and overcome the challenges of the past. Some of this could be accomplished through educational initiatives of the type seen in the field of textbook reform and the creation of bilateral academic panels to explore contentious historical events. Some could also be realized by building on past successes in improving people-to-people connections between states via student and tourist exchanges, and by bolstering the political friendship associations that exist to enhance dialogue between professional politicians and bureaucrats. Indeed, in South Korea, some of the traditional left-right, conservative-progressive distinctions that have shaped contemporary political life appear to be breaking down,[103] which could foster a new pragmatism that would open the door to greater dialogue and cooperation between new Korean and Japanese administrations.

The election of a new Democratic Party of Japan (DPJ) administration in August 2009 seemed to herald a new era in inter-Asian relations. In dramatically supplanting the conservative LDP Party, the DPJ articulated a foreign policy vision oriented towards a more Asia-centric diplomacy and reduced reliance on Japan's traditional alliance with the United States. Some of this, it could be fairly argued, represents rhetorical gamesmanship, rather than an ambiguous reorientation of Japan's diplomatic posture, and it might well have been conditioned by the electoral requirements of drawing a stark dividing line between the positions of the DPJ and the LDP.[104]

Judged in terms of the new governments' policy decisions, however, there does appear to have been a modest backpedalling away from the incremental realist tilt of past administrations. Ending the deployment of Maritime Self-Defense Forces personnel to the Indian Ocean in January 2010 as non-combatant logistical support of Operation Enduring Freedom (the joint U.S.-UK-Afghan anti-Taliban operation) and replacing this with a US$5 billion assistance package to Afghanistan had the hallmarks of a reversion to a more low-profile diplomatic posture.

A Japan less beholden to a more powerful senior U.S. ally also might be expected to strengthen its ties with its regional neighbours, including South Korea. Indeed, even before the advent of the DPJ government, there were signs of the start of such a change. Under both Tarō Asō and Yasuo Fukuda, Hatoyama's two immediate predecessors, the Seoul-Tokyo relationship appeared to be strengthening. Then prime minister Fukuda was one of the first foreign leaders to meet President Lee following his inauguration in 2008, and as an indication of the weight Japan placed on positive ties with South Korea, the LDP government invited South Korea to participate as an observer in the G8 summit meeting in Hokkaido in July 2008.[105] In a whole raft of areas – the revitalization of mid-level defence dialogue among Japan, South Korea, and the United States via the Trilateral Coordination and Oversight Group, discussions of a possible bilateral free trade agreement or economic partnership agreement, and Japanese and South Korean participation in the Proliferation Security Initiative – there were important opportunities for enhanced cooperation.

The clearest expression of this new goodwill is the trilateral Asian summit of the leaders of Japan, China, and South Korea. In the past, such events were always held on the margins of the ASEAN summit; since December 2008, however, when the three leaders met in Dazaifu, in Fukuoka, Japan, the gathering has become a stand-alone meeting in its own right. The institutionalization of such meetings suggests to some positively minded observers that Asia is finding its own distinctive voice, and in this context there could be added incentives for Japan and South Korea to work more closely together. Of course, important as new institutions are, they depend ultimately on far-sighted and politically dextrous leadership. In this regard, President Lee has played an important role, and his close personal ties with Japan – he was born in Osaka in 1941 – could help to explain his commitment to ensuring the bilateral relationship works well. Shortly after taking office, Lee talked about the importance of promoting a 'future-oriented relationship'[106] – an encouraging indication of a willingness to move beyond past historical controversies. Indeed, in general, it is surely important to recognize that historical tensions are not immutable and persistent. The example of post-1945 Franco-German reconciliation is a powerful reminder that the legacy of the past, while sometimes bitter, can be overcome.[107]

Historical problems are, it should be emphasized, only one part of the challenge of improving relations between Japan and the Korean peninsula. As Japan's experience of interacting with the North so clearly demonstrates, there are real, substantive national interests at stake

– the well-being of individual citizens, concerns about the conventional, nuclear, and ballistic missile threat posed by the North, and wider issues to do with the developmental priorities of the North and how Japan can best deploy its economic and aid resources to meet these priorities in a mutually beneficial manner.

These are complex and challenging issues. One thing is clear, however, from examining the experience of Japan's post-1945 relationship with the Korean peninsula in general, and the specific record of the Koizumi administration's diplomacy between 2001 and 2006 in particular: Japan's policy-makers have been anything but passive in confronting such challenges. Japan's politicians and bureaucrats, especially within the Ministry of Foreign Affairs, have often taken the initiative in seeking to develop feasible and imaginative policy solutions, albeit with mixed success, and without the encouragement or brokering role of the United States. South Korea, too, under Roh's leadership, by continuing the Sunshine Policy of Kim Dae Jung, has promoted closer engagement with the North.

The tragedy, or at the very least the disappointment in this context, has been the absence of a clear means of harmonizing these two sets of initiatives to ensure that the policies of governments in Seoul and Tokyo can be more than the sum of their individual parts. Indeed, at a time when the United States, under George Bush's presidency, had been curiously ineffectual in handling the North Korean nuclear crisis and simultaneously at odds with decision-makers in Tokyo and Seoul,[108] it is the absence of more extensive and sustained cooperation between Japan and South Korea that is most striking. Personal leadership preferences, interest group pressures, and the power of public opinion, not to mention the divided nature of authority between national and local governments, all have had a role to play in shaping policy outcomes. These factors suggest the very real limits to Cha's theory of quasi-alliances, as well as the danger of looking for methodologically neat or – as they are sometimes characterized by social scientists – 'parsimonious' explanations for the complicated and sometimes convoluted decisions of national leaders. The lack of cooperation between Seoul and Tokyo is not so much a fundamental aberration or abnormalcy as it is a glaring deficiency. With time, patience, and the maturing of political constituencies on all sides, cooperation may grow, opening the door to a more successful and harmonious relationship between Japan and the Korean peninsula as a whole.

NOTES

1 The research for this article was made possible thanks to a grant provided by the Korea Research Foundation. Additionally, the author would also like to express his gratitude to Yonsei University's Graduate School of International Studies, the Institute for Foreign Affairs and National Security in Seoul, and the Japan Institute for International Affairs in Tokyo for providing a stimulating environment between October 2004 and March 2005 that facilitated the initial research and interviews on which the analysis in this chapter is based.

2 See Masayuki Tadokoro, in this volume.

3 See David A. Welch, in this volume.

4 Ibid.

5 See, for example, Samuel S. Kim, *The Two Koreas and the Great Powers* (Cambridge: Cambridge University Press, 2006), pp. 164, 223.

6 Victor Cha, *Alignment Despite Antagonism: The U.S.-Korea-Japan Security Triangle* (Palo Alto, CA: Stanford University Press, 1991), p. 49.

7 John Swenson-Wright, *Unequal Allies? United States Security and Alliance Policy Towards Japan, 1945–1960* (Palo Alto, CA: Stanford University Press, 2005), p. 56.

8 Aaron Forsberg, *America and the Japanese Miracle: The Cold War Context of Japan's Postwar Economic Revival, 1950–1960* (Chapel Hill: University of North Carolina Press, 2000), p. 13.

9 Cheol Hee Park, 'Japanese Strategic Thinking toward Korea,' in *Japanese Strategic Thought Toward Asia*, edited by Gilbert Rozman, Kazuhiko Togo, and Joseph P. Ferguson (Basingstoke, UK: Palgrave Macmillan, 2007), p. 186.

10 The most detailed exposition of the civil war thesis is the two volume study by Bruce Cumings, *The Origins of the Korean War* (Princeton, NJ: Princeton University Press, 1989).

11 Mika Mervio, 'Koreans in Japan: A Research Update,' in *Proceedings of the International Conference on Globalization, Migration and Human Security: Challenges in Northeast Asia*, October 2003; available online at http://gsti.miis.edu/CEAS-PUB/2003_Mervio.pdf, accessed 13 April 2010.

12 Yoshibumi Wakamiya, *The Postwar Conservative View of Asia* (Tokyo: LTCB International Library Foundation, 1998), p. 189. For a detailed recent study of the repatriation issue, see Tessa Morris-Suzuki, *Exodus to North Korea: Shadows from Japan's Cold War* (Lanham, MD: Rowman and Littlefield, 2007).

13 International Crisis Group, *Japan and North Korea: Bones of Contention*, Asia Report 100 (Brussels, 2005), p. 14.
14 See, for example, the role of Tokuma Utsunomiya, a conservative politician with close ties to former prime minister Tanzan Ishibashi and who argued vigorously for closer ties with the North in the 1970s. Utsunomiya's role and that of the Kochikai are documented in Wakamiya, *The Postwar Conservative View of Asia*, p. 211.
15 Chaibong Hahm and Seog Gun Kim, 'Remembering Japan and North Korea,' in *Memory and History in East and South East Asia: Issues of Identity and International Relations*, edited by Gerrit W. Gong (Washington, DC: Center for Strategic and International Studies, 2001), pp. 106–8.
16 Kim, *The Two Koreas and the Great Powers*, pp. 205–10.
17 Park, 'Japanese Strategic Thinking toward Korea,' p. 187.
18 Kim, *The Two Koreas and the Great Powers*, p. 176.
19 Isa Ducke, *Status Power: Japanese Foreign Policy Making toward Korea* (New York: Routledge, 2002), p. 157.
20 Kim, *The Two Koreas and the Great Powers*.
21 Richard P. Cronin, 'The North Korean Nuclear Threat and the U.S.-Japan Security Alliance: Perceived Interests, Approaches and Prospects,' *The Fletcher Forum of World Affairs* 29 (1, 2005): 55.
22 International Crisis Group, *North Korea: Where Next for the Nuclear Talks?* Asia Report 87 (Brussels, 2004).
23 The most detailed and authoritative study of this crisis is Joel S. Wit, Daniel B. Poneman, and Robert L. Gallucci, *Going Critical: The First North Korean Nuclear Crisis* (Washington, DC: Brookings Institution, 2004).
24 Ibid., p. 194.
25 Ibid., p. 38.
26 Ibid., p. 178.
27 Charles L. Pritchard, *Failed Diplomacy: The Tragic Story of How North Korea Got the Bomb* (Washington, DC: Brookings Institution Press, 2007), p. 41.
28 International Crisis Group, *Japan and North Korea*, p. 3.
29 Kim, *The Two Koreas and the Great Powers*, p. 182.
30 Hong Suk Yoon, 'Japan's Legislation on the New Defense Guidelines: Building a Normal State?' *East Asian Review* 11 (3, 1999); available online at http://www.ieas.or.kr/vol11_3/yoonhongsuk.htm#6, accessed 13 April 2010.
31 Park, 'Japanese Strategic Thinking toward Korea,' p. 191.
32 International Crisis Group, *Japan and North Korea*, p. 4.
33 Pritchard, *Failed Diplomacy*, p. 86.
34 Park, 'Japanese Strategic Thinking toward Korea,' p. 192.

35 Kim, *The Two Koreas and the Great Powers*, p. 182; see also Hajime Izumi, 'Remembering and Forgetting: Japan-Korea Dimensions,' in *Memory and History in East and South East Asia: Issues of Identity and International Relations*, edited by Gerrit W. Gong (Washington, DC: Center for Strategic and International Studies, 2001), pp. 88–97.
36 James Llewellyn, 'Japan's Diplomatic Response to Indonesia's Policy of Confronting Malaysia (Konfrontasi) 1963–1966,' *Kobe University Law Review* 39 (2006): 39–68; available online at http://www.law.kobe-u.ac.jp/lawrev/2006.james.pdf, accessed 13 April 2010.
37 Peng Er Lam, in this volume, discusses this Japanese mediating role in Southeast Asia more extensively.
38 For an extended elaboration of this theme, see Eric Heginbotham and Richard J. Samuels, 'Japan's Dual Hedge,' *Foreign Affairs* 81 (5, 2002): 110–21.
39 Cha, *Alignment Despite Antagonism*, pp. 202–5.
40 Sun Hyuk Kim and Won Hyuk Lim, 'How to Deal with South Korea,' *Washington Quarterly* 30 (2, 2007): 74. The early years of the twenty-first century revealed a growing polarization of South Korean politics along ideological and generational lines as well as the emergence of a more strident anti-Americanism. For an especially informative analysis of these changes, see Sook Jong Lee, 'The Transformation of South Korean Politics: Implications for U.S.-Korean Relations' (Washington, DC: Brookings Institution, Center for Northeast Asian Studies, September 2004); available online at http://www.nautilus.org/fora/security/0438A_Lee.pdf, accessed 13 April 2010.
41 Mid-ranking official, Office of Strategy Planning, National Security Council, Republic of Korea; personal interview, Seoul, 31 January 2005.
42 One of the most detailed and authoritative recent accounts of this enhancement in the power of Japan's prime ministerial decision-making process is Tomohito Shinoda's *Koizumi Diplomacy: Japan's Kantei Approach to Foreign and Defense Affairs* (Seattle: University of Washington Press, 2007).
43 International Institute for Strategic Studies, *Strategic Survey 2001/2002* (Oxford: Oxford University Press, 2002), p. 286.
44 Ibid., p. 287.
45 Senior Japanese Foreign Ministry official, Japan Institute of International Affairs; personal interview, Tokyo, 9 March 2005.
46 Celeste Powell, 'The Dynamics of Japan's Foreign Policy-Making Process: The Case of Tokyo's Post-Cold War North Korea Policy' (unpublished MPhil dissertation, University of Cambridge, 2004), p. 48. Reliance on such informal back-channels of contact has been a characteristic feature

of Japan's postwar diplomacy and was especially pronounced during the Okinawa reversion talks with the United States in the 1960s. See, for example, Kei Wakaizumi, *The Best Course Available: a Personal Account of the Secret U.S.-Japan Okinawa Reversion Negotiations*, edited by John Swenson-Wright (Honolulu: University of Hawai'i Press, 2002).

47 International Crisis Group, *Japan and North Korea*, p. 4.

48 Senior Japanese Foreign Ministry official, North America Bureau; personal interview, Tokyo, 29 March 2005.

49 Powell, *The Dynamics of Japan's Foreign Policy-Making Process*, p. 48.

50 There was little doubt that Koizumi's bold initiative was seen by the prime minister and those around him as a radical and high-stakes break from past diplomatic convention. In the immediate run up to the visit to the North, internal Japanese cabinet memoranda speculated that Koizumi's visit might be as momentous as U.S. president Nixon's path-breaking 1972 visit to China, which paved the way for Sino-U.S. normalization. See International Institute for Strategic Studies, *Strategic Survey 2002–2003* (Oxford: Oxford University Press, 2004), p. 261.

51 The text of the declaration can be found online at http://www.mofa.go.jp/region/asia-paci/n_korea/pmv0209/pyongyang.html, accessed 13 April 2010.

52 Koizumi's popularity had risen to 61 per cent by October 2002, a sharp increase from the 44 per cent recorded in August 2002. See International Crisis Group, *Japan and North Korea*, p. 5.

53 Conservative LDP Diet members such as Yuriko Koike and Shigeru Ishiba – both of whom subsequently went on to serve as minister of defense under Koizumi's two successors, Shinzo Abe and Yasuo Fukuda, respectively – helped form a Parliamentarian League for the Early Repatriation of Japanese Citizens Kidnapped by North Korea. This new organization cooperated with existing groups representing the abductees' relatives, such as the National Association for the Rescue of Japanese Kidnapped by North Korea, and the Association of Families of Victims Kidnapped by North Korea, to make the case for further progress on the abductee question. See Powell, *The Dynamics of Japan's Foreign Policy-Making Process*, pp. 50–1. Not all interest groups in Japan were instinctively hostile to interacting with the North. Industrial associations, such as *Keidanren*, for example, took a far more pragmatic approach, arguing that a breakthrough on the abduction issue would help to dilute public animus towards the North and open the door to closer, pragmatic cooperation. See David C. Kang, 'Japan: U.S. Partner or Focused on Abductees?' *Washington Quarterly* 28 (4, 2005): 114.

54 Selig Harrison, 'Did North Korea Really Cheat?' *Foreign Affairs* 84 (1, 2005), p. 101.
55 Pritchard, *Failed Diplomacy*, pp. 27–8. Subsequently, U.S. officials, most notably Joseph DeTrani – mission manager for North Korea at the Directorate of National Intelligence – appeared to downgrade the reliability of the original HEU evidence. Questioned at a 27 February 2007 session of the U.S. Senate Armed Services Committee, DeTrani admitted U.S. authorities had shifted from 'high' to 'mid-confidence' belief in the existence of a North Korean HEU program. See Jon Fox, 'U.S. Lowers Confidence in North Korean HEU Program,' *Global Security Newswire*, 28 February 2007; available online at http://www.nti.org/d_newswire/issues/2007/2/28/7e044a37-4e8e-44e5-86e3-7d3d40ad5a29.html, accessed 13 April 2010.
56 Pritchard, *Failed Diplomacy*, p. 87.
57 Ibid., p. 88.
58 International Institute for Strategic Studies, *Strategic Survey 2001/2002*, p. 260.
59 Senior official, South Korean Ministry of Foreign Affairs and Trade; personal interview, Seoul, 1 February 2005; senior South Korean foreign ministry/government official; personal interview, Tokyo, 25 October 2004.
60 Sung Han Kim, Institute for Foreign Affairs and National Security; personal interview, Seoul, 31 January 2005.
61 Senior official, Northeast Asia Division, Asian and Oceanian Affairs Bureau, Japanese Ministry of Foreign Affairs; personal interview, Tokyo, 23 March 2005.
62 Senior former adviser to the Roh administration; personal interview, Seoul, 29 January 2005.
63 Pritchard, *Failed Diplomacy*, pp. 38–9.
64 International Institute for Strategic Studies, *Strategic Survey 2003/4* (Oxford: Oxford University Press, 2004), p. 270.
65 International Institute for Strategic Studies, *Strategic Survey 2002–2003*, p. 262.
66 For example, in early February 2003, young conservative legislators hostile to the North pushed for new legislation allowing for the confiscation of private-sector disbursements to North Korea and measures intended to prevent North Korean ships from entering Japanese ports; see ibid., p. 257.
67 Key officials and politicians who were deployed via these informal channels in 2003 and 2004 included Hitoshi Tanaka, Mitoji Yabunaka, Taku Yamazaki, and Katsuei Hirasawa; see International Institute for Strategic Studies, *Strategic Survey 2003/4*, p. 271.

68 Ibid., p. 275.

69 Project for Northeast Asian Security, *Resolving the North Korean Nuclear Problem: A Regional Approach and the Role of Japan* (Tokyo: Japan Institute of International Affairs, 2005), p. 20.

70 In March 2003, the cabinet's popularity had dropped to 49 per cent, significantly below the 61 per cent approval it enjoyed in September 2002 immediately after the first Pyongyang visit. The economy was still performing poorly in 2003, consumer spending was sluggish, deregulation and structural reform were contentious issues, the financial sector was still weighed down by US$1 trillion worth of non-performing loans, and the general forecast for economic improvement was pessimistic. On top of this, the government had been hit hard by a number of scandals. In February 2003, it was revealed that the Nagasaki branch of the LDP had been strong-arming local companies to secure political donations, and in March, the Agriculture, Food and Fisheries minister had to resign for allegedly receiving bribes from a construction company. Koizumi himself had to contend with rumours that rivals within the LDP such as Shizuka Kamei, Tarō Asō, and Masahiko Komura were positioning themselves as potential successors, eager to unseat him as LDP president. See International Institute for Strategic Studies, *Strategic Survey 2002/3*, pp. 268–9.

71 Senior Japanese Foreign Ministry official, Japan Institute of International Affairs; personal interview, Tokyo, 9 March 2005.

72 International Institute for Strategic Studies, *Strategic Survey 2004/5* (New York: Routledge, 2005), p. 368.

73 Pritchard, *Failed Diplomacy*, pp. 88–9.

74 Even after the October 2006 and May 2009 North Korean nuclear tests, the likelihood remains strong that Japan will continue to reject the option of becoming a nuclear weapons state. Even though technically such an option remains relatively straightforward, widespread Japanese public antipathy towards nuclear weapons, the fear of the destabilizing consequences of a regional nuclear arms race, and, importantly, the potentially fatal damage to Japan's extensive and critically important civilian nuclear industry are all powerful disincentives pursuing the nuclear option. Japan has a number of bilateral civil nuclear agreements with the United States, the United Kingdom, France, Canada, and Australia. As one analyst notes, these agreements 'stipulate that "everything Japan has imported from these countries, including reactors, related equipment, nuclear fuel (natural and enriched uranium) and nuclear technology, must be used only for the non-military purposes specified in the agreement." If Japan were to renege on these agreements, then it would face stringent sanctions "including the

immediate return of all imported materials and equipment to the original exporting country"... Should that ever happen, nuclear power plants in Japan would come to a grinding halt, crippling economic and industrial activities.' Mike Mochizuki, 'Japan Tests the Nuclear Taboo,' *Nonproliferation Review* 14 (2, 2007): 309.

75 Japanese public concerns about the fate of Japan's abductees, while understandable, arguably should be set against the grievances of Koreans, both North and South, who point to the tens of thousands of Koreans forcibly removed as forced labour to work in Japan or Manchuria during the prewar colonial period. This was brought home to the author in a visit to Pyongyang in May 2004, when a young official from the European Division of the North Korean Foreign Ministry, although acknowledging the legitimacy of the Japanese case, vigorously pointed to discrepancies in the Japanese argument given the far greater numbers of Koreans 'abducted' to Japan.

76 An article in the UK science journal *Nature* subsequently questioned the reliability of the DNA testing methods employed in assessing the remains, in the process casting some doubt on the claim that the remains were definitively not those of Yokota. See International Crisis Group, *Japan and North Korea*, p. 12.

77 Senior official, Northeast Asia Division, Asian and Oceanian Affairs Bureau, Japanese Ministry of Foreign Affairs; personal interview, Tokyo, 23 March 2005.

78 Ibid.

79 Hahm and Kim, 'Remembering Japan and North Korea,' p. 104.

80 Wakamiya, *The Postwar Conservative View of Asia*, p. 340.

81 Ibid., pp. 33, 40–1.

82 Expressing regret and contrition can be especially dangerous and destabilizing to bilateral relations precisely because of the intensity of domestic counterreactions, which can involve denying or even glorifying past excesses. For a useful and detailed examination of the Japanese- South Korean experience in this regard, see Jennifer Lind, 'Sorry States: Apologies in International Politics' (paper prepared for the annual meeting of the American Political Science Association, Washington, DC, 1 September 2005). A more extensive discussion of these themes can also be found in Lind's monograph, *Sorry States: Apologies in International Politics* (Ithaca, NY: Cornell University Press, 2008).

83 Lind, *Sorry States*, pp. 199–200.

84 Won Deog Lee, 'A Normal State without Remorse: The Textbook Controversy and Korea-Japan Relations,' *East Asian Review* 13 (3, 2001): 26; Kim, *The Two Koreas and the Great Powers*, p. 162.

85 Wakamiya, *The Postwar Conservative View of Asia*, p. 257; Kim, *The Two Koreas and the Great Powers*, p. 190.
86 Cited in Lind, 'Sorry States,' p. 25.
87 The full name of the organization is *Atarashii rekishi kyoukashou wo tsukuru kai*.
88 International Crisis Group, *Northeast Asia's Undercurrents of Conflict*, Asia Report 108 (Brussels, 2005), pp. 12–13; Lee, 'A Normal State without Remorse,' p. 39.
89 'Japan-South Korea history group to hold 2nd round of talks in January,' *Kyodo News*, 27 December 2005; available online at http://findarticles.com/p/articles/mi_m0WDQ/is_2005_Dec_27/ai_n15971576, accessed 13 April 2010.
90 William Underwood, 'New Era for Japan-Korea History Issues,' *Oh My News*, 16 March 2008; available online at http://english.ohmynews.com/articleview/article_view.asp?article_class=2&no=382092&rel_no=1, accessed 13 April 2010.
91 International Crisis Group, *Northeast Asia's Undercurrents of Conflict*, p. 21.
92 Seung Ji Woo, Institute for Foreign Affairs and National Security; personal interview, Seoul, 20 January 2005; Chung-in Moon, Yonsei University; personal interview, Seoul, 29 January 2005; Suk Joon Yoon, Secretary to the President for Overseas Communication, Cheongwadae (Blue House); personal interview, Seoul, 25 January 2005.
93 Cited in Kim, *The Two Koreas and the Great Powers*, p. 165.
94 Senior Japanese cabinet office official; personal interview, Tokyo, 17 March 2005.
95 Senior Japanese Foreign Ministry official, Japanese Embassy, London; personal interview, 1 December 2006. It is striking how here, as in other instances, nominally nationalistic actions or declarations are often misread by Japan's neighbours as evidence of a rightward shift in Japan. As Tadokoro points out in his chapter, majority Japanese public opinion remains steadfastly wedded to postwar values of internationalism. The failure of Koizumi's successor as prime minister, Shinzo Abe, during his brief year in office, to realize his political ambition of major constitutional revision demonstrates the moderate nature and 'small c' conservatism of the Japanese public when it comes to polarizing ideological debates over political reform.
96 This was not the first instance in which Roh was criticized for his allegedly undiplomatic language. In a visit to the United States in late 2004, the president gave a public address in Los Angeles arguing for the importance of engagement with the North and seemed to criticize sharply the Bush

administration's more combative approach. While op-ed writers and journalists were quick to attack Roh for his shortcomings, more dispassionate observers within the diplomatic community downplayed the critical aspect to these remarks, interpreting them as shaped by the president's radical background and his combative 'scattergun'-like approach to policy-making. Senior U.S. State Department official, U.S. Embassy, Seoul; personal interview, Seoul, 27 January 2005.

97 Moo Hyun Roh, 'An Open Letter to the Nation Concerning Korea-Japan Relations,' 23 March 2005; available online at http://www.korea.net/news/News/NewsView.asp?serial_no=20050324027&part=101&SearchDay, accessed 13 April 2010.

98 Senior South Korean Ministry of Foreign Affairs and Trade (MOFAT) official, Northeast Asia Division, MOFAT; personal interview, 1 February 2005.

99 Hahm and Kim, 'Remembering Japan and North Korea,' p. 104.

100 Hideki Yamaji, 'Policy Recommendations for Japan: Unification of the Korean Peninsula' (Washington, DC: Brookings Institution, July 2004), p. 13; available online at http://www.brookings.edu/papers/2004/07northeastasia_yamaji.aspx, accessed 13 April 2010.

101 Ibid., p. 7. Of course, no matter how pronounced the tensions between the political elites in the two countries, one should not overlook the engagement that operates at other levels, especially in the fields of cultural exchange and tourism. Even at the high points of bilateral tension, regular flights between Haneda and Kimpo continued, particularly in the wake of the Hanryu 'Korean Wave' boom of the early twenty-first century.

102 Interview with mid-ranking official, Office of Strategy Planning, National Security Council, Seoul, 31 January 2005.

103 Jiyon Shin, 'A New Socio-Political Breeze in South Korea: the New Right and the New Left,' Pacific Forum CSIS, *Issues and Insights* 6 (18, 2006); available online at http://www.csis.org/media/csis/pubs/issuesinsights_v06n18.pdf, accessed 13 April 2010.

104 John Swenson-Wright, 'East Asia: Searching for Consistency,' in *America and a Changed World: A Question of Leadership*, edited by Robin Niblett (Malden, MA: Wiley-Blackwell, 2010), pp. 7–8.

105 John Swenson-Wright, 'Contending with Regional Uncertainty: Japan's Response to Contemporary East Asian Security Challenges,' in *Japan's Politics and Economics*, edited by Marie Söderberg and Patricia A. Nelson (New York: Routledge, 2009), p. 32.

106 Ibid., p. 33.

107 The same is true of cultural rivalry and exclusively defined notions of national identity that have sometimes underpinned the arguments of nationalists in both Korea and Japan when confronting one another. Conceivably, the effect (whether intentional or unintentional) of President Roh's declassification initiatives will be to foster a more open discussion about the colonial period and, in the process, also a more nuanced awareness among Koreans of the nature of historical responsibility. In turn, this may help to challenge existing notions of cultural exclusivity and perhaps reduce bilateral tensions. As Cambridge economist Amartya Sen has recently noted persuasively in commenting about the rivalry between India and Pakistan,

> Paying attention to cultural interrelations, with a broad framework, can be a useful way of advancing our understanding of development and change. It would differ both from neglecting culture altogether (as some narrowly economic models do) and from the privileging of culture as an independent and stationary force, with an immutable presence and irresistible impact (as some cultural theorists seem to prefer). The illusion of cultural destiny is not only misleading, it can also be significantly debilitating, since it can generate a sense of fatalism and resignation among people who are unfavourably placed.

Amartya Sen, *Identity and Violence: The Illusion of Destiny* (London: Allen Lane, 2006), pp. 111–12.

108 Joel Wit, 'Enhancing U.S. Engagement with North Korea,' *Washington Quarterly* 30 (2, 2007): 61.

7 Japan's Relations with Southeast Asia in the Post–Cold War Era: 'Abnormal' No More?

PENG ER LAM

Despite debates within Japan about its transformation into a 'normal country,'[1] from a Southeast Asian perspective its behaviour, as least since the end of the Cold War, has been very much along the lines of a 'normal country.' While domestically the debate persists over the revision of Article 9 – the foundation of Japan's pacifist Constitution – Japan is already accepted within Southeast Asia as one of the region's two great powers, alongside China. Japan's 'normalcy' is thus more readily accepted abroad than it is at home.

Given the history of Japanese aggression and imperialism in the region, intuitively, it might seem more logical if Southeast Asian countries resisted Japanese 'normalcy.' Yet Japanese imperialism was not entirely deleterious in its consequences. Lasting three and a half years, the occupation was relatively brief. In that time, although much of the Southeast Asian population suffered from the privations of war and invasion, with the treatment of overseas Chinese for their support of resistance movements in mainland China particularly harsh, Japanese occupiers also trained indigenous armies in Burma and Indonesia to fight for national independence and defeat the scourge of British and Dutch imperialism. Certainly, Japan's aspirations for building the 'Greater East-Asian Co-Prosperity Sphere' were motivated by self-interest. Through the pursuit of this aim, however, Japan unwittingly paved the way for the independence of the Southeast Asian countries from Western colonialism by shattering the prestige and myth of 'white invincibility.'

Most Southeast Asian states, dependent upon a demilitarized and democratic Japan for investments and aid for economic development, refrain – even if only for pragmatic reasons – from harping on Japan's historical transgressions in the region. In contrast to China and South Korea, who continue to express bitterness toward Japan as a result of their prolonged experience of Japanese imperialism, most Southeast Asian countries are generally unperturbed by the prospect of Japan's 'normalcy' and thus do not promote nationalism and patriotism by fostering anti-Japanese narratives and images in textbooks and the media.

Yet, within Japan, the notion of 'normalcy' remains contested. Disagreements arise due to Japan's historical and contemporary context, mainly defined by its catastrophic defeat in World War Two, the ensuing mass pacifism, persistent domestic political disputes between the left and the right, its pacifist Constitution, and anxieties about resistance from neighbouring countries. Despite U.S. hopes for Japan to play a more active military role in international affairs within the framework of the United States-Japan alliance, becoming a 'normal country' remains a difficult and protracted affair.

Thinking about Japan's status as a 'normal country' without revising Japan's Constitution, particularly Article 9, appears preposterous to many Japanese. Looking beyond constitutional technicalities to Japan's behaviour in the region, however, the possibility seems less remote. In fact, it seems that Japan is very much a 'normal country.' Evidence of this can be found in the growing wariness on the part of Southeast Asian countries about tensions between Japan and China; regardless of the status of Article 9, Japan's actions are perceived to have significant implications for regional security and stability.

In light of perceptions that Japan's search for 'normalcy' is intertwined with an antagonism toward a rising China – particularly over how Japan's historical activities in the region should be interpreted and redressed – the issue of Japan's 'normal' status at times takes on a negative connotation in the context of East Asian stability, even if it is widely accepted by Southeast Asian countries. Yet the prevailing opinion within Japan is that 'normalcy' is objectively a good thing. For Japanese, the question is not whether Japan should become a 'normal country,' but what kind of 'normal country' should it be? Should it maintain a one-dimensional dependence on the United States and adopt a more assertive and confrontational stance toward China? Or should it become the linchpin of East Asian regionalism and a peacemaker in the region?[2]

Certainly, the choices for Japan's identity as a 'normal country' are not necessarily this stark and bifurcated. Regardless of one's definition of 'normalcy,' however, the real challenge is for Japan's 'normalization' to incorporate a balanced approach to competing demands in the international system. Put differently, 'normal country' status will require mediating between Japanese understandings of 'normalcy' and those of its Southeast Asian neighbours. Accordingly, exercising balance will require harmonizing Japan's ties with its U.S. ally, a rising China, the two Koreas, and the ten ASEAN (Association of Southeast Asian Nations) countries. Becoming a 'normal country,' therefore, is not simply about Japan's own power, status, and identity or the gratification of national sentiment; it is a process that must adjust to a dynamic regional environment that includes the emergence of China as a great power and the regional impulse for creating a wider East Asian community.

In this chapter, I undertake an analysis of Japan's potential 'normal' status in the context of both Japanese domestic politics and Southeast Asian regionalism. I examine in depth how Japan's political and strategic activities have led to regional acceptance of its 'normalcy,' despite the absence of any formal designation that Japan has fully 'normalized.' Exploring these activities, I argue that Japanese 'normalcy' is thus indelibly embedded within Southeast Asian (and potentially wider East Asian) regionalism and will subsequently be shaped by growing norms and principles governing the region. I conclude by examining the kind of 'normal country' Southeast Asian states prefer: an economically strong, culturally open, and politically active Japan that extends assistance to its neighbours, balances and harmonizes its ties with a rising China, and acts with China to construct an East Asian community. Japan's 'normalcy' has significant consequences for the stability of Southeast Asia and, despite the aspirations of some right-wing Japanese politicians, the danger is not absent that this process could trigger an arms race with China, engender arrogance toward Japan's smaller and less powerful neighbours, or fail to account for Japan's history of aggression and imperialism in the region.

Despite pressures toward a certain kind of 'normalcy,' uncertainties remain about what kind of Japanese state 'normalization' will produce and how it will relate to the Southeast Asian region. If and when Japan attains 'normalcy' as a state, it remains to be seen whether it can acquire a new identity and carve a constructive role in Southeast Asia that is distinct from other 'normal' states in the world.

The Elasticity of a 'Normal' State

A 'normal' state is both a descriptive and a normative term. Moreover, a variety of behaviours is implied by the notion of 'normalcy.' The concept, therefore, is awkward and complex. Among the behaviours we might consider 'normal' are ones entirely contradictory to each another – it is 'normal' for states to seek hegemony, balance power, appease, or jump on bandwagons; to forge alliances or seek neutrality; to pursue unilateralism, bilateralism, or multilateralism; and to eschew or embrace activities such as peacebuilding or peace enforcement.

Certainly, any measure of 'normalcy' is arbitrary. As the state system has evolved, however, the sovereign right of defence through the use of coercive power has been a defining norm of international politics. In practice, this amounts to the right of a state to have a standing military and to use it defensively if its security is compromised or threatened. Given the existing norms of sovereignty, Japan's forced renunciation of a standing military after its defeat in World War Two and subsequent restrictions on its ability to resort to war as a means to resolve international disputes frustrate many Japanese. Until January 2007, rather than having a Ministry of Defense and a standing army to administer issues of defence and security, Japan's security was conducted by a Defense Agency and euphemistically titled Self-Defense Forces (SDF).[3]

It is also important to note that the definition of normal behaviour varies with a state's status in the international system. What is 'normal' for a small country might not be for a great power or a middle power. At the risk of tautology, a middle power behaves normally when it behaves as a middle power. It would be difficult for a middle power to behave like a great power given the limitations of its resources and the presence of more assertive great powers.

Implicit in the view that Japan is less than 'normal' is the perception that it is a passive and reactive economic superpower punching below its weight in international relations. Accordingly, the question of Japan's status as a 'normal country' arises only because it is considered an emerging superpower. If it were a small state, similar to the majority of states represented at the United Nations, there would be little domestic and international pressure to behave more like a diplomatic giant, engage in collective security efforts, and dispatch troops for UN peacekeeping or peace-enforcement missions. Given that Japan is the world's third-largest economy, however, it must grapple with international and domestic expectations about an appropriate role in international affairs. The key question behind discussions of Japanese 'normal country' status therefore concerns what kind of political role is commensurate with its economic might.

Given the strength of its economic, technological, and demographic resources, some analysts assume that Japan will become a major power again in the geopolitical struggles of the twenty-first century.[4] Japan's status as a non-nuclear state and its reliance on the United States for defence, however, mean that most Japanese do not consider Japan a great power militarily. It is this imbalance, more than anything else, that many see as atypical and renders Japan 'abnormal.' It is important to note that the issue is not merely one of military resources, but also of their use. Japan has a sizable plutonium stockpile, is capable of launching sophisticated rockets, and is ranked fourth in the world in terms of military spending, putting US$42.4 billion of its budget toward defence.[5] Thus, relative to its Southeast Asian neighbours, Japan is significantly more advanced in terms of military technology and spending. The paradox is that, despite this capacity, Article 9 prevents Japan from being able to use or develop military power in a way that coheres with international assumptions regarding the behaviour of economically and militarily advanced countries.

Perhaps much of the debate could be resolved by projecting Japan as a middle power. Apparently, for some Japanese elites, this is an untenable position; for them, only great power status would befit a country of Japan's size, capability, and consequence.[6] Even among its Southeast Asian neighbours, such a depiction would be erroneous, as most consider Japan to be an emerging great power, both regionally and internationally. Both groups accordingly have expectations about Japan's role and responsibilities that differ from middle power roles ascribed regionally to Australia or internationally to Canada and the Scandinavian countries.

The notion of Japan's 'normal country' status as requiring great power capabilities, a position once advocated by political mavericks such as Ichirō Ozawa, now defines the political mainstream. This understanding of 'normalcy' includes a vision of a Japan that supports the United States-Japan alliance, deploys its SDF on UN missions, including peacekeeping, and engages in multilateral diplomacy in the Asia-Pacific.

This vision can be interpreted to entail different requirements. Some hawks argue that nuclear capability is necessary for Japan to assume a position of 'normalcy.' No longer dependent on the United States, Japan would thus be able to defend itself. Alternatively, such hawkish positions ask why Japan should not have nuclear weapons if other great powers, such as China, Russia, France, and the United Kingdom, have acquired them. In contrast, mainstream opinion about Japan's 'normal country' status does not entail a nuclear requirement. An influential opinion asserts that removing Article 9, engaging in collective security, and upgrading the Defense Agency to a Ministry of Defense would suffice to render Japan a normal country.[7]

The absence of a nuclear requirement for Japanese 'normalization' is evidence that discussions of 'normalcy,' both domestically and internationally, are still marked by Japan's defeat in World War Two. Although attaining 'normalcy' is a means to remove the legacy of defeat and forge a new global identity, the constraints of deep-rooted pacifism and the legacy of aggression in the region make the 'nuclear option' unattractive and undesirable domestically and regionally.

Japan as a 'Normal' State in Southeast Asia

Southeast Asia's conception of Japan's 'normalcy' and its associated international behaviour has changed over time. Although at the outset, I referred to Ichirō Ozawa's conception of a 'normal country,' it is important to note that the notion of Japan as a 'normal country' has been differently interpreted at different times.

Despite the rhetoric of the Greater East Asian Co-Prosperity Sphere during World War Two, Southeast Asians viewed Japan as a typical or normal great imperial power interested in conquest and colonization. Beginning in the 1960s, following Japan's stellar economic progress, Southeast Asians saw Japan as a rising economic superpower with little interest in regional or international politics. Given its legacy of aggression and defeat in war, there was neither the expectation nor the desire on the part of Southeast Asian states that Japan match its economic power with political influence. In this period, behaving as a 'merchant state' was the favoured conception of Japanese 'normalcy' among Southeast Asians.

By 1974, the view of Japan's economic progress and its benevolence toward Southeast Asian states shifted, with Japan increasingly being perceived as a regional economic predator. These anxieties were made evident in anti-Japanese riots in Bangkok and Jakarta during visits by Japan's then-prime minister, Kakuei Tanaka. To address this perception, Japan offered more generous aid in the hope that it would cultivate (or, on some interpretations, purchase) more friendly relations with its neighbours. The success of this approach quickly changed the image of Japan into that of a rich, benevolent economic power supporting the growth and development of Southeast Asia through its official development assistance program. Although Japan attempted to create a more active understanding of its political role in the region with the 1977 Fukuda Doctrine, the prevailing consensus among Southeast Asian countries regarding Japan's appropriate 'normal' behaviour continued to eschew the idea of a more politically active Japan.[8]

Following the end of the Cold War, despite contributing US$13 billion to the UN-sanctioned campaign against Iraq's 1990 invasion of Kuwait, Japan was criticized internationally for failing to make a more active contribution.[9] Stung by this rebuke, Japan began a gradual process of instilling an understanding and expectation within Southeast Asia about its resolve and capability to play a larger role in regional political and strategic issues.

To this end, in 1992, Japan dispatched troops for a UN peacekeeping mission in Cambodia, its first deployment of troops since the end of World War Two.[10] This paved the way for Japan to dispatch the SDF for UN peacekeeping missions in other areas, including Mozambique, Zaire, the Golan Heights, and East Timor. Although critics pointed to the limited role that Japan took in these missions, involving SDF troops only in logistical and engineering support and keeping them away from violence and the actual enforcement of peace, such deployments were an important first step in redefining perceptions of the SDF's role and activities, allowing them to be conceived as playing an active security role within the UN framework as advocated by Ozawa.

Japan also signalled that it was seeking a leadership role in regional security matters at the 1991 Post-Ministerial Conference (PMC) in Kuala Lumpur, Malaysia, when then-foreign minister Taro Nakayama startled ASEAN countries by proposing that the Asia-Pacific region should use the ASEAN-PMC as a forum for political dialogue and confidence building. Although ASEAN states were unaccustomed to Japanese initiative and involvement in the security architecture in the region, with hindsight Nakayama's proposal laid the foundation for creation of the ASEAN Regional Forum (ARF) in 1994.[11]

The ARF provided Japan with a venue in which it could promote confidence-building measures, promote greater military transparency by advocating the publication of defence white papers, establish an arms registry, and engage and socialize Chinese leaders into practices of dialogue, consultation, and cooperation. Although the ARF has been criticized as merely a talk-shop unable to engage in preventive diplomacy and address potential flashpoints in the South China Sea, the Taiwan Straits, and the Korean peninsula, it is the only multilateral forum in the Asia-Pacific region that discusses security issues. It therefore offers a useful platform for leaders in the region to hold discussions and build confidence. Japan's contribution to its institutionalization is, accordingly, evidence of an attempt to change regional understandings of its 'normal' behaviour.

Japan's diplomatic track record within the region during the 1990s is a further indication of its desire to reshape perceptions about its 'normal country' identity. Seeking to contribute to international peace and stability, Japan began to mediate disputes between Asian countries. Its most notable involvement came in 1995, when the Philippines approached it to negotiate on that country's behalf to resolve its dispute with China over the Mischief Reef, part of the disputed Spratly Islands in the South China Sea.[12] Although China rejected Japan's efforts on the grounds that it was not a state with a claim on the Spratlys, through this incident Japan made it clear that it was seeking a greater regional political role and had an interest in preventing conflict in the South China Sea.

Japan has also sought to promote dialogue between Myanmar's military junta and Nobel Peace Prize laureate Aung Sang Suu Kyi, leader of the country's democratic movement. Japan has offered generous official development assistance to Myanmar to persuade the regime to soften its hard-line authoritarian rule. Results thus far have been meagre, but there is a growing expectation that Japan will play a key role in the reconstruction of Myanmar if a political compromise is ever forged between Myanmar's junta and the democratic movement.

Japan's position on Myanmar departs considerably from the policy of ostracism adopted by its U.S. and European allies, instead mirroring ASEAN objectives and demonstrating a degree of autonomy and latitude in the formation of its foreign policy goals, an ability often considered constrained by the need to acquiesce to U.S. interests. The ability to develop an independent foreign policy – one that does not necessarily support U.S. objectives – is in fact necessary if Japan is to move toward becoming the kind of 'normal country' promoted by Ozawa.

Arguably, Japan's greatest diplomatic triumph in contemporary Southeast Asia was its brokering of a peace accord in Cambodia in 1997 between Hun Sen and Prince Rannaridh, preventing the outbreak of civil war in that already war-ravaged country. The acceptance by both parties of the political compromise orchestrated by Japan resulted in national elections and relative domestic political stability.[13] This remarkable diplomatic intervention was evidence of changing expectations about Japan's 'normal' behaviour in the region. Far from being a passive political player, Japan was now called upon for political leadership.

Japan forayed further into peacebuilding in the region through efforts to end civil war and consolidate a lasting peace in Aceh, Indonesia.[14] In December 2002, an international conference of donors was organized in Tokyo to offer substantial foreign aid to Aceh if the Indonesian central government in Jakarta and GAM (Gerakan Aceh Merdeka) rebels would honour a cessation of hostilities agreement. Although both parties accepted the agreement, civil war soon threatened to erupt again. In a preventative step, Japan hosted talks between the Indonesian government and GAM in May 2003. Although the talks failed, Japan has remained an active promoter of peace in the region, offering substantial development aid in the hope of encouraging it.

To address the devastation of the tsunami that struck South and Southeast Asia in December 2004, Japan pledged US$500 million to affected countries, with Aceh, one of the hardest-hit areas, receiving a significant portion of these funds. In addition to financial resources, Japan sent roughly a thousand troops to Aceh to provide humanitarian relief – its largest postwar deployment. In April 2005, Prime Minister Junichirō Koizumi visited Banda Aceh, the provincial capital, to assess personally the devastation and reconstruction needed. Following the visit, Japan provided additional funds for humanitarian aid and urged the warring parties to give peace another chance. Yet, while Japan has dedicated significant resources to fostering peace and development in Aceh, it was not involved in the peace settlement reached between the Indonesian government and GAM on 15 August 2005. The silver lining of the tsunami was that it broke the deadlock between the warring parties: faced with demands from the international community that aid for reconstruction would be disbursed only once the conflict had been resolved, both parties found common ground in the Helsinki Peace Agreement. To ensure that the agreement would be honoured, a multinational Aceh Monitoring Mission (AMM) was created that included troops from the European Union, Switzerland, Norway, and five ASEAN members (Thailand, Malaysia, the Philippines, Brunei, and Singapore).[15] Conspicuously absent, despite its previous commitment to the resolution of the conflict, was Japan.

Japan's absence from the final stages of the peace negotiations between the Indonesian government and GAM was likely the result of both domestic and international issues. The domestic issue was the postal savings reform debate, which led to Koizumi's dissolution of the lower house of the Diet and a subsequent election. Internationally, the Japanese leadership became preoccupied with the campaign for a permanent seat on the UN Security Council, the Six-Party Talks regarding North Korea's nuclear program, and emerging disputes with China over the East China Sea. In the final analysis, however, Japan's absence from the AMM was a missed opportunity to further 'normalize' itself in the eyes of its Southeast Asian neighbours. Moreover, it would have proved more popular domestically than the deployment of troops to the U.S.-led occupation of Iraq.

Despite Japan's failure to maintain a significant leadership role in the resolution of the Aceh dispute, its activities in other areas have added weight to its status as a 'normal country.'[16] In 2000, then-prime minister Keizo Obuchi began an initiative to secure the Strait of Malacca. With nearly 60,000 ships, including oil tankers, passing through the Strait annually, it is an economic lifeline for Japan, but one that is often threatened by pirate attacks. Obuchi therefore convened a conference inviting the ten ASEAN members, China, and South Korea to address the issue. Although Japan had hoped to use its Coast Guard to secure the Strait, Malaysia and Indonesia resisted this proposal, fearing the infringement of their sovereignty by extra-regional powers. In light of this, and the abduction of three crewmen from a Japanese tugboat by pirates in March 2005, Japan urged Malaysia and Indonesia to establish a 'cooperative framework' that would stem piracy. According to the Japanese media, 'Koizumi's comments came after Indonesia and Malaysia both rejected a Japanese proposal to send Japan Coast Guard ships and aircraft to patrol the Malacca Strait to combat piracy.'[17] In January 2007, the Japan Coast Guard dispatched five officials to an information-sharing centre established in Singapore under a cooperation treaty forged by 14 Asian nations to deal with pirates in the region.[18]

No other activity better exemplifies Japan's 'normalcy' than the SDF's participation in the multilateral Proliferation Security Initiative (PSI), intended to halt the spread of weapons of mass destruction, held in Singapore in August 2005.[19] In addition to the PSI, Japan engaged for the first time in May 2005 in joint exercises in the South China Sea with 13 other naval forces from Pacific Rim countries. The exercises included tactical sharing of electronic information, coordination of mine-clearing and search-and-rescue operations, and identifying best practices for tasks such as anti-piracy sweeps.[20] This use of military resources for regional security is indicative of Japan's capability and willingness to involve itself in matters of high politics in Southeast Asia.

Japan's ability to garner the support of ASEAN countries in its bid for a permanent seat on the Security Council is further evidence of its increasing 'normalization.' To date, Japan has had verbal support from Cambodia, Laos, Malaysia, the Philippines, Singapore, Vietnam, and Indonesia.[21] This support for Japan's bid can be interpreted as growing recognition and acknowledgment of Japan's power and stature within the Southeast Asian community.

Although Japan's postwar activities increasingly are seen as a concerted attempt to exercise autonomy in its foreign policy and demonstrate leadership in Southeast Asia, its acquiescence to U.S. policies has called into question Japan's ascendancy in the region.[22] Three episodes are noteworthy. In 1990, Malaysian prime minister Mohammed Mahathir proposed an East Asian Economic Caucus to act as a counterweight to the European Community and the North American Free Trade Agreement. Despite initial interest from Japanese diplomats and the business community, Japan retracted its support in the face of U.S. opposition. Japan further yielded to U.S. interests when the United States opposed its suggestion to establish an Asian Monetary Fund to assist East Asian countries recovering from the 1997–98 Asian financial crisis. It is important to note that despite submitting to U.S. pressure, Japan offered US$63 billion to assist severely affected East Asian countries. Moreover, Japan was involved in the Chiangmai Initiative to establish a regional financial architecture to prevent another regional financial crisis. The initiative paved the way for the ASEAN Plus Three (Japan, China, and South Korea) process and ideas about a larger East Asian region. Perhaps the most controversial support of U.S. foreign policy was Japan's deployment of troops to aid the U.S.-led occupation of Iraq in 2003. Many claimed that Japan's 'normalcy' in the region hinged on its ability to disagree with the United States, as did Germany and France.[23]

Conclusion

In the post–Cold War era, Japan's diplomatic track record – especially in the area of peacemaking and the consolidation of peace in Southeast Asia – is second to none. Southeast Asia is the testing ground on which Ozawa's Japan as a 'normal country' thesis has come closest to fruition. Japan's diplomatic activism in Southeast Asia since the end of the Cold War, particularly in Cambodia, has been impressive. Certainly the influence of the United States remains, through both diplomatic pressure and its military presence in the region. Japan's economic power and influence is further threatened as China offers free trade agreements, as Japan has, to other Southeast Asian countries. Despite these impediments, Japan has carved out an active diplomatic niche in peacemaking and peacebuilding in Southeast Asia, one that has not been emulated by the United States or China. Yet Japan's growing 'normalization,' along the lines suggested by Ozawa, is not widely acknowledged or appreciated by the forces that shape Japanese public opinion.

Arguably, Japan has fulfilled Ozawa's criteria of being a 'normal' state in Southeast Asia. Japan dispatched troops for UN peacekeeping missions in Cambodia and East Timor; it has demonstrated diplomatic initiative in promoting peace and stability in the region, as evidenced by its involvement in Cambodia, Myanmar, Aceh, and Mindanao; it has promoted multilateralism in the region by establishing the groundwork for the ARF, ASEAN Plus Three, and the construction of a larger East Asian Community; and it has offered assistance to secure the Strait of Malacca.

In August 2009, the Democratic Party of Japan won the lower house election, ending 54 years of nearly continuous LDP rule. The peaceful transfer of power from the LDP to the DPJ means, at last, that Japan can be regarded as a 'normal' liberal democracy in which the rotation of parties in power is standard. Prime Minister Yukio Hatoyama promised to make Japan's relations with the United States more 'equal' and to promote an East Asian Community. Ichirō Ozawa, the DPJ's secretary general and the man most associated with the idea that Japan should become a 'normal country,' is the power behind the DPJ throne. Presumably, the new DPJ government's desire for greater autonomy from the United States and for the development of an East Asian Community will be viewed by many Southeast Asians as further evidence of Japan's becoming a 'normal country.'

NOTES

1 My discussion of a 'normal country' is based on the definition adopted by Ichirō Ozawa: 'First, it is a nation that willingly shoulders those responsibilities regarded as natural in the international community. It does not refuse such burdens on account of domestic political difficulties. Nor does it take action unwillingly as a result of "international pressure" ... A sec-

ond requirement of a "normal nation" is that it cooperates fully with other nations in their efforts to build prosperous stable lives for their people … Japan must satisfy these two conditions if it is to go beyond simply creating and distributing domestic wealth and become what the world community recognizes as a "normal nation."' Ichirō Ozawa, *Blueprint for a New Japan* (Tokyo: Kodansha, 1994), pp. 94–5.

Christopher Hughes notes that 'Ozawa's concept of a "normal" Japanese security role and his radical, UN-centred collective security option was rejected at the time of the Gulf War, and his presence on the Japanese political scene has ebbed and flowed. Nonetheless, since the early 1990s, the idea of the "normal" state has been explicitly and implicitly appropriated by other sectors of the policy-making community and is now the central reference point for the debate on the future of Japan's security policy.' Christopher W. Hughes, 'Japan's Re-emergence as a "Normal" Military Power,' *Adelphi Paper 368-9* (Oxford: Oxford University Press, 2004), p. 50.

2 In 2002, the Koizumi administration committed Japan to peacebuilding in various Asian regions suffering from domestic conflict and violence: East Timor, Sri Lanka, Aceh in Indonesia, and Mindanao in the Philippines.

3 The official interpretation by the Japanese government is that Article 9 does not constrain the country from exercising self-defence in the event of a foreign invasion.

4 According to Kenneth Pyle, 'What does seem clear is that after more than half a century of withdrawal from international politics, Japan is revising its domestic institutions and preparing to become a major player in the strategic struggles of the twenty-first century.' Kenneth B. Pyle, *Japan Rising: The Resurgence of Japanese Power and Purpose* (New York: PublicAffairs, 2007), p. 17.

5 According to the Stockholm International Peace Research Institute (SIPRI), the top five military spenders in 2004 were the United States (US$455.3 billion), the United Kingdom (US$47.4 billion), France (US$46.2 billion), Japan (US$42.4 billion), and China (US$35.4 billion). Japan spends more on armaments than does Russia, a former superpower, now ranked eighth in military expenditure at US$19.4 billion. The results of the SIPRI ranking were taken from the *Straits Times* (Singapore), 9 June 2005.

6 Yoshihide Soeya has prescribed 'middle power' diplomacy for Japan; see *Nihon no 'Midoru Pawa' Gaiko* [Japan's 'middle power' diplomacy] (Tokyo: Chikuma Shinsho, 2005). However, Takashi Inoguchi told me that Japan is simply too big economically and politically to be a middle power. Nevertheless, few Japanese thinkers would advocate their country's becoming a

nuclear-armed great military power given the enduring pacifism among the Japanese public. In this regard, they envisage Japan as a big power only in the economic and political rather than the military dimension.

7 Shintaro Ishihara, one of the most popular politicians in the nation, is a Japanese Gaullist. He wrote: 'Regarding nuclear weapons, Charles De Gaulle said that a great country like France could not entrust its fate to other nations. Although the atomic arms had no strategic significance, France acquired them, successive governments modernized the *force de frappe*, and NATO members accepted France's possession of an independent nuclear deterrent.' Shintaro Ishihara, *The Japan That Can Say No* (New York: Simon & Schuster, 1991), p. 70. Against the backdrop of North Korea's detonation of a small nuclear device in October 2006, right-wing politicians including former prime minister Yasuhiro Nakasone, Foreign Minister Tarō Asō, and LDP policy chief Shoichi Nakagawa argued the need for a debate on the nuclear option. However, then-prime minister Shinzo Abe declared that Japan would adhere to its non-nuclear principle and would not debate this within his government. Despite his reputation as a hawk, Abe rejected the nuclear option. There is, therefore, a spectrum of views concerning the nuclear option even within the mainstream right-wing groups within the LDP. At the time, 78 per cent of Japanese citizens opposed the acquisition of nuclear weapons, 14 per cent supported the option, an 8 per cent had no opinion; *Mainichi Shimbun*, 26 November 2006.

8 On postwar Japan's codification of a foreign policy toward Southeast Asia, see Sueo Sudo, *The Fukuda Doctrine and ASEAN: New Dimensions in Japanese Foreign Policy* (Singapore: Institute of Southeast Asian Studies, 1992). The Fukuda Doctrine has three principles: Japan will not become a great military power; will establish a 'heart to heart' relationship with Southeast Asia; and will play an active political role as a bridge between the non-communist ASEAN states and communist Indochinese states to promote regional stability.

9 The Japanese Ministry of Foreign Affairs noted, 'At the time of the Gulf Crisis, the limited presence of Japan in international cooperative actions was a subject of international criticism.' Ministry of Foreign Affairs, *Diplomatic Bluebook, 1990* (Tokyo, 1990); available online at http://www.mofa.go.jp/policy/other/bluebook/1990/1990-contents.htm, accessed 14 April 2010. According to Okamoto, Japan had to endure intense pressure and criticism, particularly from the U.S. Congress, for its passivity during the Gulf War.; see Yukio Okamoto, 'Japan and the United States: The Essential Alliance,' *Washington Quarterly* 25 (2, 2002): 59–72.

10 Tokyo dispatched 600 personnel from its engineering units to Cambodia

between September 1992 and September 1993. It also dispatched 75 civilian police between October 1992 and July 1993.

11 Tsutomu Kikuchi, *APEC: Ajia taiheyo shin jitsujo no mosaku* [APEC: Searching for a new order in the Asia Pacific] (Tokyo: Nihon Kokusai Mondai Kenkyujo, 1995), pp. 264–73.

12 Lam Peng Er, 'Japan and the Spratlys Dispute,' *Asian Survey* 36 (10, 1996): 995–1010.

13 According to the Japanese-brokered peace plan, 'Prince Ranariddh would stand trial for weapon smuggling and collusion with the Khmer Rouge and, upon conviction by Hun Sen's kangaroo court, would receive a royal pardon from his father, King Sihanouk. Ranariddh also agreed to give up further dealings with the Khmer Rouge and his remaining … troops were to merge with the national army. In turn, the Prince would be permitted to compete "freely" in the proposed July national elections.' Lam Peng Er, 'Japan's Diplomatic Initiatives in Southeast Asia,' in *Japan and East Asian Regionalism*, edited by S. Javed Maswood (New York: Routledge, 2001), p. 125.

14 Lam Peng Er, 'Japan's Peace-building Diplomacy in Aceh,' *Asian Ethnicity* 5 (3, 2004): 353–66. To attain peace in Aceh, Tokyo worked with the Henri Dunant Center, the Swiss-based non-governmental organization.

15 On the AMM, see Aceh Monitoring Mission, 'First phase of re-location and decommissioning completed,' press release, 27 September 2005; and AMM Fact Sheet, 27 September 2005.

16 In October 2006, Japan became the first non-Muslim country to join Malaysia, Brunei, and Libya on an international monitoring team to observe the ceasefire between the government of the Philippines and the Moro Islamic Liberation Front in Mindanao. See Peng Er Lam, 'Daiippo o fumidashita nihon no heiwa kochiku he no torikumi: Mindanao wahei jitsugen he' [Japan's peace-building as a milestone: Forging peace in Mindanao], *Gaiko Forum* 222 (January 2007).

17 'Koizumi seeks anti-piracy cooperation with Asian countries,' *Kyodo News*, 22 March 2005.

18 See 'Coast Guard to expand anti-piracy cooperation,' *Japan Times*, 5 January 2007. The ISC is part of a Japanese-initiated ReCAAP (Regional Cooperation Agreement on Combating Piracy and Armed Robbery against Ships in Asia) to address the scourge of piracy. The members of ReCAAP are Japan, China, India, Sri Lanka, South Korea, Bangladesh, Thailand, Singapore, Cambodia, the Philippines, Laos, Brunei, Vietnam, and Burma. Malaysia and Indonesia have yet to join. The ReCAAP Agreement was concluded in Tokyo in November 2004 and came into force in September

2006. This is the first agreement among Asian governments on anti-piracy matters.

19 'Ono: SDF plans to join WMD drill,' *Asahi Shimbun*, 2 May 2005. The training drill involved the use of force to halt ships and confiscate 'suspicious' cargo.

20 The participating countries belong to an 18-member group called the Western Pacific Naval Symposium. See 'Singapore navy to host 14-nation sea exercise,' *Straits Times*, 19 May 2005.

21 Southeast Asian support for Japan's bid for a permanent seat on the Security Council has been neither automatic nor guaranteed. Offering verbal support is relatively easy, but if asked on principle, for most Southeast Asian states the issue is complicated by the fact that a vote for a Japanese seat entails supporting Brazil, India, and Germany as well.

22 To Shintaro Ishihara, Japan's inability to say 'no' to the United States is indicative of a country that is not 'normal.'

23 The countervailing argument is that Japan had to earn the goodwill of the United States (for example, by dispatching Japanese troops to Iraq) to win U.S. support for Japan's preferred approach to dealing with North Korea; see Seo Hyan Park, 'Domestic-International Issue Linkage in Alliance Politics: A Comparison of Post-Iraq War Japanese and Korean Relations with the United States' (paper presented at the International Studies Association 48th annual convention, Chicago, 28 February 2007).

Contributors

Peng Er Lam is a Senior Research Fellow at the East Asian Institute, National University of Singapore. He received his PhD from Columbia University in 1994. His publications have appeared in international journals such as *Pacific Affairs*, *Asian Survey*, *Asian Affairs*, *Japan Forum*, and *Government and Opposition: An International Journal of Comparative Politics*. His most recent book is *Japan's Peace-Building in Asia: Seeking a More Active Political Role* (Routledge, 2009). His other books include *Japan's Relations with China: Facing a Rising Power* (edited, Routledge, 2006) and *Green Politics in Japan* (Routledge, 1999). His research interests include Japanese peace-building in Asia and Africa, and Japanese local politics.

Cheol Hee Park is Associate Professor in the Department of International Studies, Graduate School of International Studies, Seoul National University, where he also serves as International Area Studies Program Chair. He received his PhD from Columbia University in 1998. His research interests include contemporary Japanese politics, comparative analysis of South Korean and Japanese politics, South Korea-Japan relations, and international relations in East Asia.

Yoshihide Soeya is Professor of Political Science in the Faculty of Law and Director of the Institute of East Asian Studies, Keio University. He received his PhD from the University of Michigan in 1987, and is the author of *Japan's Economic Diplomacy with China, 1945–1978* (Clarendon Press, 1989), and *Japan's Middle Power Diplomacy* (Chikuma-shobo, 2005).

John Swenson-Wright is the Fuji Bank Senior University Lecturer in Modern Japanese Studies and a fellow of Darwin College, Cambridge. He is a graduate of Christ Church, Oxford University, and the Paul H. Nitze School of Advanced International Studies (SAIS), Johns Hopkins University, in Washington, DC, and has a DPhil in International Relations from St Antony's College, Oxford. His early research focused on early Cold War United States-Japan foreign and security relations and was published as *Unequal Allies? United States Security and Alliance Policy towards Japan, 1945–1960* (Stanford University Press, 2005). He has also published an edited translation of the memoir of Wakaizumi Kei entitled *The Best Course Available: A Personal Account of the Secret U.S.-Japan Okinawa Reversion Negotiations* (University of Hawaii Press, 2002). He writes and comments regularly on the international relations of East Asia. His current research focuses on contemporary political and security interests in Northeast Asia, with particular reference to Japan and the Korean peninsula. In addition to his work at Cambridge, he is an Associate Fellow at Chatham House, where he convenes a research and discussion group on contemporary Korea.

Masayuki Tadokoro is Professor of International Relations at Keio University and studied at Kyoto University and the London School of Economics. His main field of study is international political economy, and he also works on Japanese foreign and security policy and international organizations. His publications include *The Dollar Goes beyond 'America'* (Chuokoron Shinsha, 2001) and *International Political Economy* (Nagoya University Press, 2008). His recent publications in English include 'Why Did Japan Fail to Become the "Britain" of Asia?' in *The Russo-Japanese War in Global Perspective*, edited by David Wolff et al. (Brill, 2007), and 'After the Dollar?' *International Relations of Asia Pacific* 10 (3, 2010).

Jianwei Wang received his BA and MA in International Politics from Fudan University in Shanghai and his PhD in Political Science from the University of Michigan. He is currently Professor and Head of the Department of Government and Public Administration, University of Macau. His teaching and research interests focus on East Asian politics and security affairs, Chinese politics and foreign policy, Sino-American relations, Sino-Japanese relations, UN peacekeeping operations, and U.S. politics and foreign policy. He has published extensively in these areas.

David A. Welch is CIGI Chair of Global Security, Interim Director of the Balsillie School of International Affairs, and Professor of Political Science at the University of Waterloo. His 2005 book, *Painful Choices: A Theory of Foreign Policy Change* (Princeton University Press), is the inaugural winner of the International Studies Association ISSS Book Award for the best book published in 2005 or 2006, and his 1993 book, *Justice and the Genesis of War* (Cambridge University Press), is the winner of the 1994 Edgar S. Furniss Award for an Outstanding Contribution to National Security Studies. He has written extensively on international relations theory, foreign policy decision-making, and ethics and international affairs. He received his PhD from Harvard University in 1990.